The Media
in Question

Robert Ferguson

ARNOLD

First published in Great Britain in 2004 by
Arnold, a member of the Hodder Headline Group,
338 Euston Road, London NW1 3BH

http://www.arnoldpublishers.com

Distributed in the United States of America by
Oxford University Press Inc.
198 Madison Avenue, New York, NY10016

British Library Cataloguing in Publication Data
A catalogue record for this book is available from the British Library

Library of Congress Cataloging-in-Publication Data
A catalog record for this book is available from the Library of Congress

ISBN 0 340 74078 7

1 2 3 4 5 6 7 8 9 10

Typeset in 10/13pt Garamond by Servis Filmsetting Ltd
Printed and bound in the UK by CPI, Bath

What do you think about this book? Or any other Arnold title?
Please send your comments to feedback.arnold@hodder.co.uk

Contents

Acknowledgements

Many people have contributed directly or indirectly to this book over the years. My colleagues at the Institute of Education, David Buckingham, Andrew Burn, Gunther Kress and Jagdish Gundara, have had a considerable impact upon my thinking on a wide range of issues. My students at the Institute have provided intellectual sustenance and challenge over the years. Many of these students are now established figures in the fields of media and cultural studies and though I do not name individuals, I owe them much. I wish to acknowledge above all the debate, understanding and, more recently, editorial counsel that have been generated over the years by Dan, Galit and Shlomit. Needless to say, none of the above is responsible for any errors or weaknesses in the book. These are mine alone.

The author and publishers would like to thank Mike Jensen for allowing the use of Figure 11.1 on p. 160.

chapter one

What's it all about?

Only dead fish swim with the current.

— Anon.

What's it all about?

This book is the result of many years of teaching media and cultural studies in the Institute of Education. It is written in the hope that its arguments and approach may be relevant to students of media and cultural studies at all levels, as well as to interested general readers. This is a somewhat ambitious aim, but it is based upon a belief that it is possible to study or engage with a subject at many levels without any of those levels becoming either patronizing, simplistic or over-complex. The text has been kept as simple and clear as possible. Sometimes this has been easy and other times, when dealing with complex ideas, it has become a little more difficult. I hope that you will not be put off by the simplicity of some parts or the complexity of others, even when they occur in the same chapter. The references in the text are to a wide range of books and other materials which you are going to need if you decide or are required to pursue matters a little further. I hope that you follow up some of those that interest you. This book is often polemical. That is because I believe that without debate and argument about the media, asking questions is likely to become soporific and sanitized.

We are not short of books about the media. So what makes this one any different from the others? Perhaps the first thing about it is that it puts some faith in you, the reader, as both interpreter and questioner of the media. It is also a book which attempts to build upon a foundation of asking questions about the media. There will be occasions when the book will be concerned with addressing those questions in a manner which comes quite close to offering answers. It may seem strange to suggest that answers are not our immediate priority, but that formulating relevant and sharp questions comes first. I hope that in reading this book you may discover that the formulation of questions is sometimes just as revealing as the formulation of answers. The formulation of questions also requires, eventually, the formulation of strategies through which we might arrive at some kind of meaningful and even useful 'answers'. Along the way we are likely to encounter a variety of existing methodologies, debates, thinkers and ideas. It is important, when relevant, that we acquaint ourselves thoroughly with relevant ideas and methodologies. This will enable us to develop skills of analysis and diagnosis (Kellner, 1995). We have to remember that questioning the media requires us to accumulate a certain amount of information, but it is not merely an exercise in absorbing facts. It is an activity and a process.

There has been a long history, in media research particularly, of investigating questions based upon pre-formulated or pre-judged answers. These pre-formulated answers do not necessarily have the sophistication to warrant the name 'hypothesis'. They are more of the 'find me a question which when answered will prove that watching violence on television makes young people violent' type (Philo and Miller, 2001; Gauntlett, 2003). Millions of dollars have been spent on this thankless task – thankless, at least, for the media studies student. Someone must have thought one group or another would benefit from such research. Who could that have been and why would they have thought that? Research may be conducted and the 'results' used to provide just about any answer to any question about the media (Lowery and de Fleur, 1994; Barker and Petley, 1997). So where does that leave us? Well, if we are studying the media, it leaves us with several interesting and important challenges, which I will now enumerate. The rest of the book will then consider some of these questions in more detail.

Which media do we study and question?

We live in an era of rapid and often fundamental changes in the world of communication. The coming of the computer, the Internet, digital media and satellite broadcasting are four of the most significant factors contributing to such changes. In historical terms they can be seen to have developed at breakneck speed. But these developments have not occurred in a vacuum. Changes in technology are related in important ways to changes in societies. This has always been the case (Winston, 2000). When television arrived in the UK, for instance, it became the new fireplace in many homes. All the chairs in the room had to be realigned to face a tiny screen rather than the flames of the fire. We found a new point of interest and a new source for our pleasures, dreams and meditations, and eventually for frustrations and occasional rage. In the last half century there have been many more changes in society which are related to the operations of the media; they sometimes remind me of moving chairs around on the deck of the *Titanic* rather than in the living room.

So we are faced with an array of media which include the now conventional television and radio, along with DVDs, CD-ROMs and digital music players, operating in the same world as traditional newspapers. And even those traditional newspapers are often available on the World Wide Web. The latter is a facility which allows us access to more information than could have been dreamed of only a generation ago (Slevin, 2000). It places a researcher in a much more powerful position than was previously the case – just as long as that information remains accessible through the multitude of search engines now available. The more traditional media of television, radio, movies and newspapers are, however, still some of the most influential in our day-to-day living. This is apparent, above all, in their presence in our lives. Meanwhile subcultures associated with the newer media are springing up like mushrooms (Gauntlett, 2000). If we are going to question the media, we need to attempt to situate these media in relation to each other and to the societies in which they operate. One answer to the question about which media we should be studying is that it does depend upon our context, interest and the nature of our investigations. What might that mean?

If we want to study the media, do we have to study anything else?

The social context of media production and utilization is something which is inextricably linked with any study of the media. What this means is that studying the media involves studying much more than the media. It is not always a welcome thought for those who are wishing to enter 'the media' as a professional, or to those who consider themselves to be on a vocational course where their main concern is to acquire necessary skills for their putative future employment. To those who are on such courses, I would only say that questioning the media is not supposed to replace their skill acquisition, but to complement and sometimes facilitate it. I will return to this issue in the final chapter. For the moment it has to be noted that the media which we study need to be studied in relation to a range of cultures, capitalist economies, political struggles and increasingly global issues. The enthusiast for any specific medium cannot study that medium with any success or productive outcome unless such study is situated. It is an illusion to think that we can involve ourselves with the media from a position of neutrality. Any research methodology adopts an explicit or implicit epistemological position. This means that it is informed by one or more theories of knowledge about the world. Theories of knowledge are, in turn, linked with the realities of power (Gordon, 1980). Those who try to hang on to an attempted neutrality in relation to media research are often reduced to saying something like, 'I simply did the research. I cannot be held responsible for the way in which it was used.'

For those of us who are either students of the media or interested citizens, the issue of how we position or situate ourselves is equally significant. There are those who study the media because they think that the media represent all that is base and wicked in the world. There are others who regard the media as a force for liberation, pleasure or excitement, or as a site upon which a career can be erected. Any of these positions may provide an interesting starting point for the student of media, but following a particular line of enquiry also has consequences. In the end, all students of the media have to choose the approach they feel best able to sustain when challenged. The study of the media, as with the study of history if it is done with integrity, often breeds insecurity and discontent. Part of the argument of this book is that this discontent, or what I have called 'productive unease', is the lifeblood of the discipline. One answer to the question about whether we need to study something else if we are studying the media is: if you are not studying something else as well, you are not really studying the media.

Which is most important, the medium or the message?

There is a case for considering in some detail the debates about the relationship between media and messages. This book starts from the position that the two are inseparable. In other words, you can't have a message without a medium. We may become more interested in the medium than the message or vice versa. Either way, it is a question of proportional rather than exclusive interest. Communication is also social and always involves more than one person. Because of this there is always some kind of mediation going on. The mediation is, not surprisingly, identifiable in relation to particular media. In this context, mediation does not have the connotation of bringing about agreement, such as the work of United Nations mediators, for instance. In relation to the study of media, the term mediation implies a forming or re-forming of a message in a specific way in order to signify a particular meaning. There are, then, specific signifying practices which can be identified, described and analysed in specific contexts. A great deal of what we do when we question the media requires us to engage with specific signifying practices. There will be more on this as the book develops.

If messages and media are inseparable, then which messages and which media should we study?

This is an important issue because it has implications for the kinds of theory and method we may wish to study and the way we approach the media of our choice. The choice of media to study may be established in advance though a syllabus, or we may have the freedom to pursue our own interests. There is a serious debate to be had about whether we should first choose our medium and then look for a way of studying it, or whether we need to learn about ways of studying and then apply them to a chosen medium. The position offered here is that the first thing to do is to find out what the possibilities are. In other words, we need to be willing to spend time reading, thinking about and engaging with the media (through watching, reading, listening, playing). Then we need to formulate our questions about the media according to a range of theoretical positions. We may wish to engage with theories of pleasure, or theories of identity, or theories of signification. We may wish to consider the economic structures upon which the media are built, and ask questions about ownership and control of the media. At some time or another we should do all these things. But we need to keep a productive tension between our specific analyses of specific media and our theoretical and methodological predilections. We have to test out our ideas in relation to our perception and understanding of the world. The two may not always be the same.

What's the point of questioning the media if we want/don't want to make the media our profession?

People who wish to make a career in the media are likely to formulate different questions for study than those who see themselves primarily as consumers. There is also a third category of people who see themselves as above the ordinary people and so study the media in order to advise their lesser fellow humans. There are more of these people around than one might think. They are very protective, often believing in censorship and often more concerned with violence on the screen than with violence, deprivation and injustice in the real world. Some of them argue that everything that is bad in the real world has been created by the media. There are yet others who are motivated to study the media by a liberal concern with ensuring that the media are accountable and responsible in all that they do, though they do not always say to whom.

If we wish to make a career in the media we will still need to address certain questions about the role and purpose of the media in the society. But we are also likely to spend a great deal of time thinking about what makes something 'good' in the media. It does not matter whether we are concerned with advertising, documentaries, multimedia presentations or any number of other media forms. It is the issue of quality that will exercise us. The understanding of what we mean by 'quality television', for instance, is something which needs ongoing attention. There are two main debates in relation to the media and quality. One is a debate about concepts of 'high' and 'low' culture and which is better. The other is about how we identify quality in different spheres of culture and representation (Frow, 1995; Dyson and Homolka, 1996). We may ask, for instance, what makes a 'quality' coverage of a football match on the radio, and how we recognize the charactcristics of such quality. We may also ask how we recognize 'quality' in the presentation of news and what that might mean. It goes without saying that these debates are also of significance to those who see themselves simply as consumers.

Whether we are media professionals or just ordinary citizens, we may have other reasons for studying the media besides our preoccupation with quality. We may also think that there should be some kind of meaningful relationship between our lives and the representations we find in the press, on TV and in other media. In other words, we may want to know if the media provide an accurate, distorted, reassuring, romantic or other view of the world as we understand it. This will bring us up against a whole range of problems in the formulation of questions. On many (or is it most?) occasions, the media represent issues of which we have no direct experience. It does not matter whether we are dealing with wars, singing competitions, cup finals or royal weddings. Most of us have only ever experienced these things through the media. So how do we test their accuracy and reliability? The reason we study the media is to try to provide appropriate and viable answers to some of these questions.

What do we mean by 'answers' and 'strategies for action'?

Rather than answers, perhaps we should be thinking about ways of addressing questions. So we formulate questions and then devise a way of addressing them (some kind of research). After this we have an important decision to make. On the basis of our analysis, should we then do anything? If we are professional researchers, our task is somewhat clearer. We have to submit our research findings to our funders, usually in the form of a report, and following the protocols of professional research. We may then publish our findings in a professional or scholarly journal. Then we are free of further obligation. If we are citizens, our study of the media may lead us to keep our opinions to ourselves, or we may become involved in a group which is concerned with the ways in which the media operate. If we do this, it is usually because we are concerned about the kind of community, society or even world in which we live. This kind of concern can move us from formulating questions to participating in providing answers. If we are registered students of the media we are in a somewhat privileged position, because we may have access to equipment which will allow us more easily to become producers as well as consumers of media messages. This book aims to encourage a range of possible activities in relation to the questioning of the media, from writing to or ringing broadcasters to make our views (positive as well as negative) known, to making material for local (or Web) exhibition.

Is questioning the media concerned with what is new all the time?

This question is aimed at those who would argue that it is important, in studying the media, to be up to date with the latest trends or fashions. Part of what we do when we study the media is to consider trends, tendencies and developments. But the best way to understand the new is to have something to compare it with. It is here that study of the media blends productively with study of culture and history. Newness in itself is a notoriously poor guide to what is happening in the media. We may extend this wariness in the face of all that is new to the theories by which we study the media. Wariness does not mean having a closed mind or inbuilt conservative tendencies – quite the reverse. Simply, we need to keep in mind the wise counsel that fashion can mean change without change. The patterns of representation which have evolved in various media require us to develop a longer-term view of what we are studying. This will also provide us with a basis for comparative study when we come to new technologies and the media they have engendered. We know, for instance, that the earliest cars, or horseless carriages as they were called, had a holder by the driver's seat in which to place the whip (McLuhan, 1964). With new technologies, there is a tendency to imitate digitally that which is old and reliable in order to win over potential customers or consumers. So, for instance, advertisements for computer software or desktop publishing may contain images of leather writing desks and fountain pens bathed in golden light (Bolter and Grusin,

2000). This book will address some new issues and some that are not so new, both in relation to theory and to specific media examples. I argue that questioning the media of the future should always be done with an eye on the past as well as the present.

What about 9/11?

This question is both valid and frustrating for any contemporary writer of a book on the media. The events of September 11 2001 in New York have certainly resulted in a change in the political and military landscapes of the globe. They may have a long-term effect on the future of the world, but have they had a long-term effect on the media? Have the media responded to the tragic events of September 11 and its aftermath in a way which has changed their specific signifying practices or their patterns of ownership and control? Is it not the case that, for many, the events of September 11 were a disaster movie come to life and were represented as such? Is it not the case that some of the comics in the United States have incorporated their superheroes in their responses to September 11 as though they were real (or divine) personages? Is it not the case that these events have been appropriated, enveloped, swallowed up by popular culture and then sold back to us as commodities? In American culture at least, everything from toilet paper printed with the head of Osama bin Laden to a sexually stylized, leather-clad, Judith-like figure carrying his severed head and a bloodied carving knife has been available for purchase. It may be that the events of September 11 have changed the political terrain of the world. There is little evidence at the moment that it has changed either the terrain or the practices of the media and popular culture. A mixture of chauvinism and downright tasteless arrogance is sometimes the outcome of what was supposed to have been a sobering 'wake-up call', in the words of so many prominent Americans (see, for instance, http://www.authentichistory.com/images/attackonamerica/artifacts/911artifacts_01.html).

How is the book structured?

The chapters in the book range across a variety of theories, approaches and media examples. Chapter two considers theories of ideology and the ideological dimensions of media messages. In the spirit of this book, such ideas are out of fashion (Corner, 2001). Media analysis in this chapter includes press re-presentations of another September 11 – that of Chile on 11 September 1973 – and the contemporary fate of the dictator Pinochet. Chapter three considers the importance of the concept of discourse to the study and questioning of the media. Particular emphasis is given to the earlier work of Gunther Kress and the discipline of social semiotics. There is then a detailed analysis of a programme from the English version of *Blind Date*. In chapter four, I consider some aspects of the debates about postmodernism and postmodernity. These have been most influential in relation to the study of the media. I offer an analysis of Woody Allen's movie *Crimes and Misdemeanors*, followed by a consideration of the now defunct United Colors of Benetton campaign, managed by O. Toscani.

Chapter five discusses the question of realism, arguing that it is still a field ripe for investigation and debate, in an era when 'virtual reality' is often given more attention in debates about the media. In chapter six, I consider aspects of 'race' and the media, drawing upon media examples from the press, from Mills & Boon romantic novels and from the movie *True Lies* – an example which has a certain tragic and ironic poignancy after September 11, compounded ideologically by the recent election of Arnold Schwarzenegger as Governor of California. In chapter seven, I address issues of gender and class in the media, with particular reference to the popular and successful movie *An Officer and a Gentleman*. In chapter eight, I discuss the ways in which history is represented on television. I consider programmes made for schools and documentaries made for the adult viewing public, including a series about the history of Ireland. I also make reference to the phenomenal success of contemporary 'television historians'.

Chapter nine takes up the debates about identity and otherness, and considers how these issues have impacted upon our understanding of the media. Chapter ten moves on to a consideration of debates about the audience for the media and reviews some of the main issues which bear upon our understanding of what we mean by an audience. In chapter eleven, I turn to the new technologies and their impact upon the forms, consumption patterns and messages which are available to increasing but unevenly distributed numbers of people around the world. Chapter twelve investigates the potential and significance of practical work and the ways in which we consumers of the media can become producers with the help of the new digital technologies. The final chapter is, simply, a defence of media study. This is offered in the light of the hostile treatment which such study receives from politicians, some educators and, most significantly, the media.

There are many absences in this book. I have not tried to give an encyclopaedic overview of the field. However, I do provide a suggested list of further reading at the end of each chapter (except this one). I have chosen the further reading because it is, I believe, both challenging and relevant. You, the reader, can decide whether you agree. The process of acquiring understanding in relation to the media takes time. I have concentrated on approaches which I consider to be both productive and necessary. I am interested in where the study of the media leads, why we bother and who benefits from it. If this book encourages any readers to pursue these questions, it will have fulfilled its main aim.

A note on how this book might be of use

Most of the chapters in the book can be read independently, although the overall structure is designed to develop an argument if read in sequence. There are often quotations at the beginning of chapters or the beginning or end of specific sections. These quotations are designed to stimulate discussion and debate. They are never offered as definitive summaries. Sometimes they contradict one another or represent views from which I would wish to distance myself. It is my hope, however, that they may stimulate private thought or public debate.

chapter two

The question of ideology

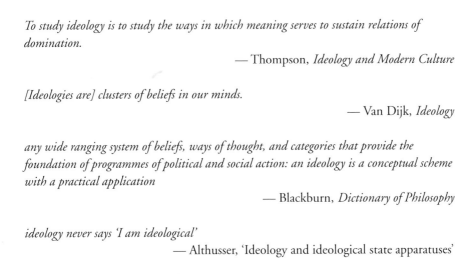

To study ideology is to study the ways in which meaning serves to sustain relations of domination.

— Thompson, *Ideology and Modern Culture*

[Ideologies are] clusters of beliefs in our minds.

— Van Dijk, *Ideology*

any wide ranging system of beliefs, ways of thought, and categories that provide the foundation of programmes of political and social action: an ideology is a conceptual scheme with a practical application

— Blackburn, *Dictionary of Philosophy*

ideology never says 'I am ideological'

— Althusser, 'Ideology and ideological state apparatuses'

What is ideology?

In the previous chapter I tried to suggest some of the reasons why the study of the media is both important and potentially productive. I want to spend this chapter considering the issue of ideology, with particular reference to the study of the media. It will be necessary first to clarify what I mean by ideology, in the face of numerous competing definitions. I will then argue my case for considering an evolving definition of ideology and the ideological to be a central activity for any student of the media. This is not the most popular idea in the late twentieth century, because the term ideology has been associated with a whole host of failures. Apart from the failure of media analysts of the radical left to inspire the generations of the 1980s and 1990s, there has been the failure of those who tried to demonstrate that the world was populated by dim-witted media audiences who were the hapless victims of anything ideological. The term ideology seems to have been at the centre of these failures, and it is a term that has been associated with moribund media projects and doctrinaire media analysts. On some occasions such criticism has been justified. But those who mount such attacks can usually dismiss the term ideology because it has been reduced, often by those same attackers, to a mechanistic belief system, or a mode of deception that could be decoded only by those 'in the know'. So what do we mean by ideology in relation to the media and why am I arguing that it should be central to our media studies work?

Is ideology a system of beliefs?

The rich man in his castle
The poor man at his gate
God made them, high or lowly
And ordered their estate

— Cecil F. Alexander, 'All things bright and beautiful'

There are those who would argue that ideology is a system of beliefs, much in the way that Blackburn defines the term in the *Dictionary of Philosophy* (Blackburn, 1994). This usage is the most common sense (and hence the most ideologically suspect) and was particularly popular during the cold war. It allowed one to describe those with whom one did not agree as 'ideological', though the term was reserved for very specific strata of groups and individuals. Communists and socialists tended to be ideological, whilst conservatives and various fundamentalists tended to 'hold very strong views'.

A much more sophisticated account of ideology and the ideological as 'clusters of beliefs' has been put forward by Van Dijk (1998). Van Dijk's model of ideology sees it as primarily cognitive. Despite it sophistication, Van Dijk's approach is one which has to insist that people have attitudes which are likely to have a determining effect upon their ideological behaviour. The problem with any model of ideology that is concerned with systems and clusters of beliefs is that it is likely to become somewhat mechanical in use. I am not arguing that ideology is not about systems of belief. It is, however, about much more than this. The concept of a 'system' tends to invoke relative certainty that there are (preordained) rules by which the system operates. Translated into the language of media analysis, it can mean that one only has to crack the representational code and the operations of ideology will be laid bare. I am arguing that there are recurrent patterns in the signification of ideological relations in media messages. This does not mean, however, that these patterns yield up unproblematic meanings to the readers of the message.

I prefer to argue for something which I have called a 'discursive reserve', which is drawn upon by individuals or groups according to a complex and changing set of possibilities in any meaning-making situation (Ferguson, 1998). In other words, I do not walk around with a ready-made attitude to one or another topic which I then apply if I am provided with a suitable stimulus. It is more likely that I have acquired an evolving and hence changeable repertoire of meaning-making potential. This may be combined, recombined or creatively juxtaposed in response to a whole range of possible situations and contexts. The ways in which I 'make meaning' in specific situations are not always comfortable. I may have to negotiate, on my own or in the company of others, certain dilemmas which the ideological process throws up at me as I make sense of (or meaning from) my environment, my social situation or my identity. In terms of ideology, it is important to recognize that there is a social dimension to individual meaning making. The values, judgements and opinions upon which we draw are always negotiated in relation to a discursive reserve, which in turn is socially acquired and sustained. A similar process sometimes occurs, as we shall see, with the way the media re-present the world and the people in it.

Ideology and conceptual maps

It may be possible, in the face of the previous difficulties, to plot tentatively a conceptual map of the general operations of ideology. The most successful attempt at this has been undertaken by John Thompson in *Ideology and Modern Culture* (1990). He has offered the following table (p. 60) to outline conceptually the modes of operation of ideology.

Table 2.1

General modes	Some typical strategies of symbolic construction
Legitimation	Rationalization Universalization Narrativization
Dissimulation	Displacement Euphemization Trope (e.g. synecdoche, metonymy, metaphor)
Unification	Standardization Symbolization of unity
Fragmentation	Differentiation Expurgation of the other
Reification	Naturalization Eternalization Nominalization/passivization

If we do this, we may discover that, in relation to the media, ideology operates through recognizable modes of symbolic construction. Thompson has identified five such modes, but I am going to mention only one here in relation to a specific example. It is concerned with the concept of legitimation (Thompson, 1990: 60). Legitimation is the process by which an audience is 'won' to the content and/or form of a media message. In the realms of ideology, legitimizing images and messages is of crucial importance, though the process is seldom one of overt proselytizing. Instead there is a sense in which the media may work to naturalize the way the world is presented. There will then be no need to question the message because it is 'only natural'. In relation to the news, for instance, we may ask whether or not there exists a natural ordering of newsworthy stories. If this question does not produce a satisfactory explanation, we may want to know whether there may sometimes be an ideological purpose in the ranking of news stories. Another way of conceptualizing our interest might be to ask in whose interests a particular ordering of representation works.

I will offer one brief example here, though many others will appear in relation to specific contexts throughout the book. On the day that I wrote this text, the Central American countries of Honduras and Nicaragua had been devastated by hurricanes and floods, leaving several thousand people dead (not discursive dead, but material dead). The television news on one channel relegated this story to second in the headlines, in favour of one about the singer from the group Oasis, Liam Gallagher. He had been arrested outside a pub in North London for allegedly damaging the camera of a photographer who was trying to take his picture. The story then included a studio interview with the photographer which lasted several minutes – an eternity in television airtime. The photographer was asked whether he felt bad about calling the police as a result of the incident. He said no. He was asked whether he had sought Gallagher's permission before he took the picture and he prevaricated, making some kind of comment about Gallagher knowing the rules of the game. After the interview, the news about Nicaragua and Honduras was shown. There were images of people struggling for their lives in torrents of mud-laden water. There were shots of children in shock as they gazed helplessly at the mayhem around them, and other such harrowing scenes.

What was being legitimized here? At one level, it could have been a set of news values which suggested that a 'late-breaking' story about a mildly controversial pop singer is a useful way to grab the audience. It would be, in this sense, an ideological hook. At another level, it could be read as a way of legitimizing the need for a little light relief from the woes of the world in an up-to-the-minute revelation about the lifestyle of someone rich and famous. The story about Gallagher, it might be argued, was just breaking, whilst the deaths in Central America were already old news. What this means, as part of the ideological process, is that the death of a few thousand inhabitants of Latin America simply cannot compete with the 'legitimate' news values which prioritize popular culture over human tragedy in certain situations. And what are these situations? The answer to this has to be related to perceptions of the relative significance of different kinds of human tragedy. Take a hypothetical example. Imagine that there had been a mining disaster in Wales and several hundred children had been killed. A television news broadcast that evening then began with a story about whether or not the singer Tom Jones had had cosmetic surgery, followed by shots of the mining community and the grieving parents. Such a programme is, in broadcasting terms, unthinkable, possibly obscene. But that is because there is, in the operations of ideology and the media, a largely unwritten code of priorities.

One of the most successful attempts to formalize the ways in which 'foreign' news is prioritized is still to be found in Galtung and Ruge's research (Galtung and Ruge, 1965). Legitimation, in this context, is the process by which such priorities are accepted by media audiences and media producers. But legitimation is not limited to representations in the news. The history of media representation is brimming over with examples of the ways in which non-fictional media narratives have won and continue to attempt to win legitimacy for specific positions. This may include the ways in which femininity and masculinity are constructed as incidental aspects of a feature film. It may also include the ways in which narratives remind audiences, even after the growth of the women's movement, either literally or ironically, that 'a man's gotta do what a man's gotta do'. In another register, the media also legitimized for more than a generation the concept that a person without a cigarette was likely to be deficient in some way, unable to make the appropriately dramatic gesture without the exhalation of smoke or the click of the lighter. Legitimation works across a wide range of representations and it is just one of the central currents in the ideological stream. It should be noted, however, that total legitimation is a rare occurrence. There will usually be an audience, or part of an audience, who do not accept the way in which specific issues are represented in the media. The opposition of various groups to the processes of legitimation makes for tensions in what we may call the interpretative communities. These tensions remind us that the process of hegemony is neither mechanical nor necessarily smooth. If the media suggest that we should all wave flags, there will always be some that decline the offer.

Ideology and dilemmas

Neither conceptual maps nor systems of belief are sufficient to explain the operations of ideology. Whether in daily life, or the relatively secure boundaries of media representation, ideology is a process that is fraught with dilemmas. If a media text is a realist version of a literary 'classic' on film or television, for instance, the heroine may be seen to experience dilemmas as part of the plot which are, in turn, mediated via that text. The audience or viewer is then required to experience or make meaning from the represented dilemmas. If the media representation is one which purports to be objective, as some documentaries attempt to be, it may be that the audience, collectively or individually, experiences different dilemmas. Here they may be about coming to terms with the text's (rather than the fictional character's) relationship with the material world beyond the screen. Ideological dilemmas are part of the discourses of our everyday life and a structured part of the discourses of a whole range of media representations. In practice, of course, they are interwoven as part of everyday living. The most extreme examples of this phenomenon can be found when audiences debate in the media (as real people) the fate of fictional stars in their favourite soap operas. So what is a dilemma and what is 'dilemmatic thinking'?

The following section is indebted to the work of Michael Billig and his colleagues (see particularly Billig *et al.*, 1988). I have also allowed myself to bring a more media-oriented interpretation to their work. In a common-sense way, having a dilemma means that we don't know how to make up our minds about something. As part of a media audience, our dilemmas are seldom based around simple binary decisions. When we watch a programme or read a newspaper, we may find that there are three or four different ways of making sense of a text. Indeed, we may interpret the same media message differently according to the context of its reception. A man or woman in a pub with friends may react differently to a documentary about male strippers than they would if they saw it at home with their two young children. But ideological dilemmas in relation to the reading of media messages are usually more diffuse and confusing. They may come about because of a complex intersection of variables. These could include whether one is in a public or private domain at the time of reading; whether or not one thinks it is likely that anyone will ask a direct question about one's reading of a programme or text; whether or not one is ignorant about the subject matter of the representation; whether one is viewing or reading in the company of friends, acquaintances or strangers; whether or not one is already committed or hostile to the cause which the media text propounds. The list could go on. Dilemmas, however, are seldom about only one of the above categories. They are more likely to involve the overlapping of several, which can be combined in a multitude of ways. Negotiating dilemmas requires the making of choices, and these choices are in turn affected by the complex patterns of variables that intersect at a given moment. I have not included other possibilities, such as the fact that one may be hungry at the time of reading, or that one might owe a great deal on one's mortgage and have been made redundant. There is a purpose in identifying this intellectual and emotional turmoil which so often constitutes the 'normal' pattern of media consumption: it is to guard against any simplistic or reductive approach to either the construction or the reading of media messages.

Within the media text we may also detect dilemmas as the producers struggle with, manipulate, construct and re-form their subject matter. This is just as true for the writer of a feature film as it is for the writer of a newspaper editorial. There is likely to be evidence of dilemmas in the ideological structuration of all media messages except those of the fanatic or bigot. The only way in which dilemmatic thinking (and, one might add, dilemmatic representation) can be eradicated is through dogma. This may be religious or political, personal or social. It is by retracing the paths and practices of signification that we may identify dilemmas and their ideological import. We will see, as we explore various aspects of the media, how these dilemmas manifest themselves in our understanding of both media texts and media audiences.

It should also be noted that dilemmas are not phenomena that somehow stand outside history. The dilemmas of today are not necessarily those of yesterday or tomorrow. In terms of media representations and media audiences, it is clear that the nature, quality and impact of dilemmas move and shift with the changing social and economic climate. If there is a constant in the process, it is the ideological nature of those dilemmas.

Ideology and deception

WYSIWYG

— Acronym in computer jargon for 'what you see is what you get'

A word needs to be said about the concept of ideology as deception. It is one of the most attractive concepts for some critics of the media. It is even more attractive to those who have made up their minds about the nature of the media in advance of any analysis. If the media are there to deceive, it is surely the duty of all those who can see the deception to tell the rest of us what is happening. And they do. It is only a short distance from claiming that the media are great deceivers to developing a disdain or contempt for the media audience. This may be justifiable for the morally superior, the proselytizer or the cultural elitist. It is not, however, to be confused with media studies.

Media studies may recognize that there are occasions when all of us are likely to be deceived by what we see, read or hear. The media student will also recognize, however, that there are times when the very structure of a media message may carry with it an implicit or explicit frame of reference, and that this frame of reference may be ideological. We have only to think of the mediation of the public and private lives of Prince Charles and Princess Diana to see how powerful such frames of reference can be. We will return to this in a moment when we consider ideology and questions of determination.

There is little evidence to suggest, however, that there is a conspiracy by the media to deceive the audience in democracies. There may be occasions when this does happen, but most of the time the media are involved in the construction of a world which they take to be a fair representation. Stuart Hall has summed this up with clarity and cogency when he says that the media work to produce a kind of underlying unity in their understanding of the world. This means that they construct their messages in ways which are not so much partisan, but 'fundamentally oriented within the mode of reality of the state' (Hall, 1977: 346). What this means is that, despite disagreement about individual media representations, there are certain social, political, aesthetic and discursive ground rules which apply across all media. It is true that different media, or different media producers, may construct a rather different version of this world for the audience's consideration. Jerry Springer may show us an aspect of contemporary North American life that sits uneasily alongside the reruns of *Lassie* on the same cable station. The tabloid press in the United Kingdom may offer us a range of opinionated representations of everything from the behaviour of politicians to the latest in female breast formation. All of this is done, however, within a mode of reality for which there are unifying characteristics. It is these unifying characteristics that provide the bedrock upon which the delicately poised notion of normality is maintained or contested. In order to understand how these characteristics operate, we may learn much from a close study of the work of Thompson and Hall on ideology and the media.

We have to remember that an approach to ideology and the media that is based on the notion of deception requires a workable theory of 'truth'. This is not a bad thing, but it is often implied that the undeceived media analyst is closer to that truth than those who are somehow subject to the ideology that s/he manages to stand outside. This does not help in the development of analytical methodologies, tending instead to produce formulae for 'reading off' the ideological in any media message. It also leads to explanations of the relationship of the mass media with their audiences, of more or less complexity, which suggest that the uninitiated are living in a state of false consciousness. (For a useful discussion of the concept of false consciousness, see Eagleton, 1991.) This concept has been wrongly attributed to Marx, who never actually used the phrase. Because of a whole range of science-fiction novels and films, false consciousness has come to be linked, in popular discourse at least, with brainwashing and audiences as dupes. Such simplistic interpretations have done two things. First, they have allowed critics of theories of ideology an easy ride as they (rightly) ridiculed ideas that would cast the audiences of the mass media as semi-lobotomized victims of the media moguls. Second, it has meant that crucially important issues about the relationship between the codes of the media and structures of meaning have been overlooked or ignored. Arguments about the relationship of (media) language to consciousness and the possibility that it may have ideological significance have likewise been sidelined in much contemporary media research.

Ideology and determination

Where the concept of ideology has been linked with determination, it has usually been suggested that ideology had the capacity to make people do things, or to make them see things in a particular way. This has very often been linked with false consciousness and it turns ideology, once again, into an 'it', which is applied to the unsuspecting like liniment to an athlete's limbs. A much more subtle and productive account of the process of determination has been put forward by Raymond Williams (1980). Rather than suggest that determination is an act of manipulation, he has argued that determination may be about setting limits or exerting pressures. This argument has much more potential for the media analyst, as we can see if we consider media representations of the royal family in the United Kingdom, particularly the relationship of Charles and Diana.

Debates about whether or not the media have determined the public response to the life and death of Princess Diana are likely to run for many decades. In terms of setting limits and exerting pressures, however, there can be little doubt of the ideological power which the media have exerted. On the day after the royal wedding in July 1981, the headlines in the British press were unambiguous. They were usually linked with a caption that served as an anchor for the meaning they hoped the reader would take from the page (Barthes, 1977). Here are some examples:

Daily Mirror:	Headline – MY PRINCESS
	Caption – The remembered kiss of a Princess in love on a palace's balcony of kings.
Daily Record:	Headline – MY PERFECT PRINCESS
	Caption – The Royal couple leave St. Paul's together after the magnificent wedding . . . the beginning of their life together symbolising the nation's hope for a brighter new future.
Sun:	Headline – AND THEN HE KISSED HER
	Caption – For all the world to see . . . Charles and Diana proclaim their love with a tender kiss on the Palace balcony.
Daily Express:	Headline – SEALED WITH A LOVING KISS
	Caption – The kiss that delighted the world. Charles and his new Princess share their joy with millions after their fairytale wedding.
Daily Mail:	Headline – PERFECT!
	Caption – Balcony scene at Buckingham Palace: to huge cheers from the crowd, Prince Charles kisses his beautiful bride.

There is reference, we may note, to the 'fairytale wedding' and the 'kiss that delighted the world'. It might be argued that the newspapers on this occasion were allowing themselves more than the usual amount of hyperbole or euphemization (Thompson, 1990: 62). To suggest that anything can 'delight the world' is a somewhat gross claim, unless it is interpreted as an ideologically charged statement. One might have to add that not to have been delighted by that kiss was to act in a manner that was socially and emotionally deficient. To have interpreted such a kiss as a gesture by the ruling class to assert its ideological (and material) supremacy would have been beyond contemplation for most observers and analysts. Ardent republicans may have found all this rather repugnant, but for the 'normal' English person, it was hard to resist the pull of the royal romance. The media may not have determined exactly what everyone thought about the wedding, but it was almost impossible not to think something. The messages as they were constructed did several things. They appealed to apparently timeless concepts of romantic love. They offered to those who wanted it the chance to take vicarious pleasure in watching and perhaps fantasizing about their ideal wedding. They also offered the possibility of endless colour supplements and special magazine feature articles, plus a booming trade in wedding souvenirs. Believing in the royal wedding was certainly good for business.

The appeal to romantic love also carried with it a heavy charge of patriarchy and male chauvinism, albeit clothed in fairytale terms. There is much here about possession: 'his beautiful bride', 'his new Princess' and the headline 'MY PERFECT PRINCESS'. The concept of a woman belonging to a man is certainly a core value in this romantic wedding ceremony.

Limits were certainly set and pressures were certainly exercised. To that extent, the ideological dimensions of media messages about the royal wedding exerted a range of determining influences. For the media studies student, there are difficult issues to be addressed in relation to these phenomena. One has to ask whether the interest in royalty and the royal family is something that is an integral part of being British. One also has to ask whether weddings, especially 'fairytale' weddings, touch on a fundamental human need: to find (if you are a male) a beautiful mate in order to procreate. One has to ask whether the media are merely making publicly available sentiments and representations that are part of collective consciousness (or maybe the collective unconscious). One has to investigate the possibility that the people, or perhaps one should say the media audiences, are using the royal wedding to establish their own sense of worth and their own respective roles as part of the social formation. And, of course, one has to ask whether the representational package which constituted the royal wedding is nothing more or less than ideological construction at its most persuasive and insidious. It is also important to note the ideological significance of the royal wedding in the light of the royal divorce and the tragic death of Diana and her companions. Instead of suggesting that the ending of Diana's life undermined the security of the fairytale existence which had been mapped out for her, the main thrust of media coverage of her death was towards the construction of a new fairytale to replace the previous one.

Ideology, the media and identity

Whatever you may be sure of, be sure of this – that you are dreadfully like other people.
— James Russell Lowell

Since self-identity refers to the constellation of meanings an individual attributes to herself or himself, the 'search' for identity is essentially a search for meaning.
— Lodziak, *Manipulating Needs*

No identity is fixed, each one needs to be construed – and, moreover, without any guarantee that the construction will ever be finished and the roof will be laid over the completed edifice.

— Bauman, *Life in Fragments*

The study of the media in the twenty-first century will have to be concerned with issues of identity, if for no other reason than the fact that they have been placed firmly on the agenda by the media themselves. From talk shows to dramas, from news broadcasts to feature films, from newspaper editorials to Internet sites, questions of identity seem to be paramount. Identity is also linked with concepts of ethnicity, gender, sexual orientation, nationality and, very rarely, class.

As with so many concepts, that of identity has, in the past, been essentialized – that is, made to seem eternal, natural, normal. That same concept is now recognized by analysts as both changeable and related to a process. The process is that of identity formation and it is less secure than was once the case. The media can and do explore and exploit the concept of identity in relation to commercial interests, fictional narrative structures and documentary commentaries. Identity is at the core of most advertisements when read as texts, and many studies of advertising. It is also central to the burgeoning programmes on radio and television that purport to tell and/or ask viewers how they or their fellow human beings should live. I will be exploring this issue in more detail later. For the moment, it is important to ask how questions of identity might be related to ideological issues in the media. The answers to this question will depend upon a number of factors, including whether or not we argue for an essential human identity, which can then be represented with more or less accuracy in the media. It also depends upon whether we consider that identities are created by the media, or merely reflect already existing identities, or whether there is some kind of dynamic interaction or circular process in operation. Finally, for the moment, it depends upon whether or not we consider the possibility that questions about and representations of identity are a way of turning all politics into the politics of the personal. This and all the previous suggestions require the development of theoretical positions and modes of analysis. They are all, without exception, heavily implicated in questions of ideology and the ideological.

Ideology and lived relationships

Ideology is about the way people relate to each other in specific societies, from the most personal to the most abstract levels. It is, in part, about what we believe. It is also about the ways in which what we believe manifests itself in our behaviours, as individuals (both gendered and of ethnic origin), as communities, as nations.

Ideology is, then, a lived relationship in which power is always exercised. Power relationships, in the ideological process, are never equal. They are always asymmetrical. In other words, power is not equally distributed in society, and it is through the process of ideology that the unequal distribution of power is re-presented to us as citizens in societies. The great bulk of that process of re-presentation takes place through the mass media. We then come to know it simply as representation, and for many people a representation is a faithful rendering of an original. Debates about ideology and the media constantly circle and re-circle what is meant by the original and its re-presentation. In philosophy such debates about what I have just referred to as the original have been concerned with whether there is actually a world out there beyond my perceptions (or in media terms, beyond the television, the computer screen or the newspaper page). We will be considering some of these issues later when we look at debates about realism and postmodernity and the media. For the moment, it is important to register that, for those people who doubt whether there is a world beyond media representations, this book will not be of much use. It is also important to note that the relationship between what goes on in the world beyond the media and specific media representations will be of central interest. A theory of ideology is not much use to the media studies student if it is exclusively concerned with comparing one media representation with another. Intertextuality is important, but only if it is seen as a prismatic reference to something beyond the (media) text. That something is material existence. It is empirically verifiable, although such verification is, paradoxically, usually dependent upon some form of media representation.

Ideology is, then, a lived relationship of power and subordination in which we all take part simply by virtue of being born, but not as social, political or economic equals. It is also a relationship which is unlikely to declare itself without the development of critical thinking. Critical thinking involves the capacity to doubt, and possibly the development of a sense of humour.

Ideology and power

The issue of power is central to the broad definition of ideology within which I am suggesting that the media studies researcher or student should work. In order for a relationship to involve power, it must be, by definition, an asymmetrical relationship. Someone or some group will always have more power than another in any ideological relationship. It has also been pointed out, most notably by Michel Foucault, that power relations permeate societies from top to bottom, from the macro- to the micro-levels (Gordon, 1980). While this is, I believe, the case, one has to be careful of stressing the omnipresence of power so much that it is somehow devalued. We have to be able to argue that the media have particular powers, and that, in turn, they are able to represent a wide range of power relations in the world beyond the media text. The media also have the power to prioritize and to define issues for debate and representation. We will encounter other examples of this process in the chapter on discourse and social semiotics. Power relations, particularly as they manifest themselves in media texts, are of course susceptible to detailed study. They can, in turn, be related to a study of the societies and contexts within which such power relations are signified. There is, then, a historical dimension to ideological representations, as well as a need to recognize that the media may, on many occasions, be an instrumental part of power relations. I will try to illustrate some of these points through an example that is concerned with power and politics. I have chosen an example here that relates directly to the world of national and international politics. In doing so, I am not denying the significance of the ideological dimensions of media messages concerned with the mundane and the everyday, with pleasure and with entertainment. These will be addressed elsewhere in the book.

In November 1998, Senator for Life Augusto Pinochet of Chile learned that the Law Lords in Britain had rejected the appeal against his detention in Britain and possible extradition to Spain. He stood accused of torture and genocide, among other crimes, while he was a dictator in Chile, having seized power in a military coup in September 1973. The coup involved the bombing of La Moneda, the presidential palace in Santiago, and the murder of the democratically elected president, Salvador Allende. What Pinochet had done as chief of staff under Allende would be the equivalent of seeing the Houses of Parliament or the White House bombed by the armed services, and the British prime minister or the American president murdered as they defended themselves and their democratically elected governments. At least, it would be the equivalent if, on the ideological scales of media representation, issues were assessed using the same weights. They are not. This is not to say that there was little sustained condemnation of Pinochet in the British media in the 1970s. The British government, however, took just one day to recognize the new order in Chile. The condemnation of what had happened not only did not last, but eventually Pinochet became a valued ally of Britain, particularly when he allowed British warplanes to use Chilean runways when involved in the Falklands/Malvinas conflict. This brief background is necessary to provide a minimum contextualization for the media representations I wish to consider.

Visual representations of Pinochet in the 1970s showed him unsmiling, always in military uniform and wearing dark glasses. In the late 1990s, however, he was more often represented as a charming if somewhat befuddled old gentleman. His family were all shown as a respectable and concerned group, in a way that the family of Frederick West or Myra Hindley could never hope to be seen. The level of ignorance among contemporary media audiences about the coup in Chile and just who Pinochet is also needs to be taken into account. In popular discourse, there is the possibility that he is perceived as just another of those Latin American dictators ('they have them all the time'). For those who are younger than about 45, it is not likely that knowledge of the situation in Chile will be a significant part of their discursive reserve. Non-specific knowledge about Latin American dictators in general (whether real or fictional) is more likely to be part of such a reserve. The ideological battle over the future of Pinochet was being played out as this text was written. The editorials in the press are an important indicator of the ideological power struggle that is involved. The contemporary questioner of the media would need to appraise that power struggle over the fate of Pinochet and consider which way the balance of ideological power has tipped as he approaches his demise.

I will consider three editorials from November 1998 in order to highlight the ways in which power, politics and signification are interwoven in ideological struggle. They have been selected from three newspapers that represent identifiable ideological positions. The *Sun* and the *Mirror* are the two largest circulation tabloid papers in the United Kingdom. They both supported the government/Labour Party in 1998. The third paper is the *Daily Mail*, which gives voice to the views of conservative Britain. The analyses which I will offer will avoid, at this stage, any jargon and will seek to highlight the ways in which what is written or left unwritten identifies the political and ideological positions of the respective papers. I will not attempt to prove a single thesis from the analysis, but rather to show that the ideological force of newspaper editorials is not dependent upon the rigour with which their arguments are structured. I will also show that the structure of editorials concerned with politically sensitive issues is likely to be fragile and potentially fraught with contradictions. I will be paraphrasing each of the editorials with brief quotations included where necessary.

The first is from the Labour-supporting tabloid newspaper, the *Sun*. The *Sun* is renowned for the brevity and simplicity of its prose style. The message is clear. Jack Straw, the Home Secretary, should send Pinochet back to Chile. There are four key points to the structure of the argument:

1. Pinochet is not a Serb or Nazi war criminal
2. he is old
3. his arrest threatens democracy in Chile
4. Chile is a good friend to Britain.

I will return to a more detailed consideration of the use of language after I have discussed the structure of the editorial in the *Daily Mail* and the *Mirror*. The *Mirror*, it should be noted, has been a long-term supporter of the Labour Party, while the *Sun* began to support the Labour Party in the 1996 general election. The language and argument of the *Mirror* are uncharacteristically militant. There is a call for British justice to shine like a beacon across the world. The language is uncompromising: 'Pinochet's crimes included having tiny children whipped in front of their parents. Women had rats and mice put inside them. Others were repeatedly raped.'

The argument in the *Mirror* is hortatory, outraged and proud:

1. Britain can be proud of its sense of justice
2. Britain will no longer be a hiding place for dictators or ex-dictators
3. Jack Straw must send Pinochet to Spain and we are sure he will (he better had!)
4. Pinochet is not too old to face justice
5. Pinochet is responsible for unspeakable torture
6. Pinochet's lawyers tried to suggest that even Hitler could not have been held responsible for genocide because he was a head of state
7. that absurd argument was defeated by a narrow margin.

The editorial in the *Mail*, apart from being longer than the editorial in the *Sun*, uses a similarly straightforward argument:

1. the Law Lords were wrong
2. disastrous consequences will follow from their decision
3. Pinochet is old; the procedure for his extradition will be lengthy; democracy in Chile will be under threat
4. our excellent relations with Chile could be damaged
5. double standards are involved in the arrest of Pinochet

6. it is deliberate that a right-wing person has been chosen for possible prosecution; left-wing leaders will not be touched

7. Pinochet is a brute, but . . .

8. the government has a prime duty to uphold British interests.

I will now review these three pieces of argument and discuss their ideological implications. The *Sun* asserts that Pinochet is not a proper war criminal. With the emphasis of italic type, it reminds us that he is old and that he came here *in good faith*. With equal surety, the editorial tells us that the arrest threatens democracy in Chile. The distinction is made between war crimes in Europe and unidentified activities in Chile. The emphasis instead is on the suggestion that Pinochet is an *ailing ex-head of state*. There is much sympathy in this judgement and a complete disregard for the *manner* in which Pinochet became head of state. Yet part of the argument of the editorial is that democracy is unstable in Chile. The ideological dimensions of this argument are directly concerned with power relations, but they are mainly implicit rather than explicit. The implicit judgement of the editorial is that democracy needs to be preserved in Chile. Another dimension of the implied argument is that you don't rub ex-dictators and their friends the wrong way, or they may seize power once again. And it might also be suggested that Pinochet was *only* a Latin American dictator, and hence not to be taken as seriously as European war criminals. The brevity of the editorial does not allow the paper to comment on Pinochet's behaviour whilst head of state. Avoidance of the political and indeed the moral dimensions of the case is accomplished by reducing the whole affair to a 'farce'.

The *Daily Mail,* on the other hand, offers a more complex ideological overview. The judgements it makes are somewhat more bile-laden than those of the other two papers. The first emotional and ideological point is the implication that the decision of the Law Lords will have 'disastrous consequences', though these are not specifically identified. It seems that they include the alleged precariousness of the democracy that has been established in Chile. This is not as important for the *Mail*, however, as our 'excellent diplomatic and trading relations with Chile'. This is implicit in the comment that Pinochet came here 'in good faith'. If this piece of discourse is completed, it would need to explain that Pinochet came here in good faith to buy arms and the arms trade is a very lucrative business.

The *Mail* brings in the names of Sinn Fein leaders who have been invited to Downing Street for tea, in order to suggest that there are double standards in play. The argument is dependent upon a kind of linear addition of points. We are asked to equate the military overthrow of a democratically elected government by the chief of staff of the armed forces with the taking of tea in Downing Street during an internationally recognized peace process, and with accepting that Fidel Castro is a bloodstained dictator of the left. The *Mail's* editorial is in part an ideological complaint, railing against the prosecution/persecution of right-wing dictators before tackling anyone on the left. The choice of the phrase 'international "human rights" lynch mob' needs some unravelling. It is a way of identifying that, for the *Daily Mail*, many of those who say they are interested in human rights are actually interested in 'human rights', with scare quotes around them. The implication that a lynch mob is after Pinochet also demonstrates considerable empathy with the predicament of an ex-dictator of the right, whilst passing implicit judgement on those who want to see Pinochet brought to justice. It is also a warning that this kind of justice could lead to a great deal of activity in the courts of the civilized world – a rhetorical triumph of quantity over quality. The *Mail* is willing to concede, finally, that Pinochet is 'a brute'. This oddly forgiving noun is reminiscent of the *Boys' Own* version of villainy, and it is followed by an ideologically imperative 'but'. And here the ideological position of Britain in world politics is championed over any naïve judgements about international justice. British interests come first. That is the harsh reality of political life. It could be argued that the ideological honesty of the *Mail* is refreshing, though the same cannot be said for the rigour of its logic. The *Mail*'s own naïvety when Adolf Hitler was elected Chancellor of Germany bears serious study in relation to its contemporary position. It was full of praise for 'Mr Hitler'. The editorial relating to Pinochet finishes with a journalistic piece of world-weariness which is the ideological equivalent of Hardy speaking to Laurel as they insist that Labour ministers have 'landed themselves, their country and Chile in one almighty mess'.

The *Daily Mirror* takes a much more stringent line, deliberately confronting its readers with details of the kinds of torture that took place in Chile. The main thrust of the piece, apart from demonstrating moral outrage, is to remind the Home Secretary of his duties. The claim for British justice to shine like a beacon is perhaps a little misplaced and premature. There is a clear ideological appeal to national pride here that has been denied to the other papers as they make their ideological case. It is embarrassing to be proud of putting British interests first over the prosecution of an ex-dictator. It is hard to be proud of describing an ex-dictator as an 'ailing head of state'. Yet one can also wonder at the ideological hubris which claims a victory for British justice in a case which takes its main power from the force of international law.

The above examples from 1998 are intended to demonstrate that questions of ideology are central in the reportage of international politics. This is hardly surprising, but it is in the detail that we often find the contradictions, the unexpected nuance, the implied judgements which fracture or undermine the apparent argument in the newspaper. It is also in the more detailed analysis that we can note that any individual ideological position is seldom articulated without the inclusion of contradiction. I think that it is these contradictions and tensions in the ways which texts concerned with politics signify their meaning which distinguish them from texts that are simply propaganda.

Ideology and the media

I want to conclude this chapter by offering a series of statements which need investigating by every media studies student and researcher. They are questions around which issues of ideology and the ideological revolve, and I wish to argue that media studies cannot be undertaken productively unless they are addressed. An engagement with ideology and the ideological is centrally important to the media studies student because it recognizes:

1. that there is a material world beyond media representations
2. that the material world is constantly 'structured for meaning' or re-presented to us through the media

3. that the material world certainly has an impact upon media representation, but that the reverse is also the case. Media representations can have an effect upon material reality; whether in the form of advertising becoming a part of our urban environments, or in terms of news broadcasts on radio or television becoming temporal markers of a normal day, or the fact that the sports page is on the back of my tabloid newspaper

4. that the paradoxical situation of twenty-first-century life involves a recognition that media representations have also become a part of material reality and need to be studied as such

5. that this should not be confused with the serious and perverse error of those who would insist that reality has been dissolved somehow into media representation

6. that questions of identity, power, contradiction and complexity have to form an integral part of any theorizing or methodological development in relation to media studies.

The almost daily occurrences in the contemporary world, whether concerned with outrages, elections, economic matters or questions of ecology, need our serious attention as students of the ideological dimensions of media messages. All such issues are mediated and they are mediated through media discourses. Questioning the media inevitably involves the investigation of media discourses; this is important as we engage with the numbered points that I have put forward here. In order to do this I will turn to a different set of media examples in the next chapter, as we consider the importance of discourse and social semiotics.

FURTHER READING

Corner, J., 2001, ' "Ideology": a note on conceptual salvage'.
This is a recent meditation by Corner and one which I believe to be seriously flawed. It is also a piece which all questioners of the media should read.

Eagleton, T., 1991, *Ideology: an introduction*.
This is a combative, witty and sometimes outrageous text. For the open-minded, it is also a great challenge to engage with the issues which debates about ideology and the ideological put before us.

Ferguson, R., 1998, *Representing 'Race': ideology, identity and the media*.
Contains a potentially useful chapter on theories of ideology, with an emphasis on representations of 'race', but concerned with the implications of theories of ideology for the questioner of the media.

Thompson, J., 1990, *Ideology and Modern Culture*.
A formal and conceptual approach to the question of ideology. It is based upon a wide-ranging and demanding engagement with relevant theorists, and a central interest in questions relating to the media.

chapter three◀

Discourse and
social semiotics

*A discourse organises and gives structure to the manner in which a topic, object or process is
to be talked about.*

— Kress, *Linguistic Processes in Sociocultural Practice*

This is a book about studying and questioning the media. The activity of study is essential
and requires the development of a range of analytical and conceptual approaches. This, in
turn, means that we have to introduce some of the different arguments and debates which
the study of the media can generate, wherever possible without too heavy a reliance on the
use of jargon. In this chapter, however, it will be necessary to offer a few basic definitions in
order to demonstrate the nature of the debates under consideration. I have spent some time
arguing for the importance of the concept of ideology in relation to the study of the media. I
want to move on now to the ways in which media discourses are of central importance to the
media student or researcher, and why an engagement with social semiotics is part of this
process.

What is discourse and why should we analyse it?

The word discourse is not often used in everyday speech. In popular understanding it has
come to be associated with a near Dickensian use of language (learned people discourse upon
matters of mutual concern). Yet discourse and the discursive have become key concepts in a
range of sociological, historical and other academic and research contexts. For the media
student or researcher, it is important to consider how discourse, and media discourse, have
become central analytical and theoretical concepts. As with the concept of ideology, questions
of defining terms immediately arise. Linguists have often referred to discourse as a unit of text
that is longer than a sentence. Discourse analysts specialize in taking chunks of discourse from
a variety of sources and, using recognized techniques, demonstrating how these discourses
operate. We will be considering some of these. It might be most productive, however, if we
treat discourse as a process of signification, not confined to any one medium or mode of
communication. This leads us to explore what it is that discourses do and how they do it.

Gunther Kress's definition at the beginning of this chapter is helpful here, and it merits a fuller quotation:

> Following the work particularly of the French philosopher Michel Foucault, I refer to these systematically-organised modes of talking as *discourse*. Discourses are systematically-organised sets of statements which give expression to the meanings and values of an institution. Beyond that, they define, describe and delimit what it is possible to say and not possible to say (and by extension – what it is possible to do and not to do) with respect to the area of concern of that institution, whether marginally or centrally. A discourse provides a set of possible statements about a given area, and organises and gives structure to the manner in which a particular topic, object, process is to be talked about. In that it provides descriptions, rules, permissions and prohibitions of social and individual actions.
>
> (Kress, 1989: 6–7)

I want to try to develop this statement without distorting it beyond recognition, so that it may be of more direct relevance to our discussion of the media. Some of what I will now write will offer a commentary on what I take Kress to mean. Gunther Kress has given generously of his time in the formulation of this chapter. He cannot, of course, be held responsible for my interpretation of the significance of his work.

I want first to extend the concept of an 'institution' to include more than such recognizable entities as the educational system, the media or the legal profession. It is the case, I believe, that discourses do determine the ways in which institutions such as these may be addressed or may address us. But institutions may also be construed as the material manifestations of ideological phenomena. We may recognize in this context the institution of the family, marriage or national identity, as well as a host of others. Discourses, especially media discourses, may be said to constrain, to formulate, to sustain and rarely to challenge their own construction. Media discourses are seldom self-reflexive. What this means is that the media seldom interrogate themselves, except in a somewhat congratulatory manner. For instance, a television channel may decide to demonstrate to the viewers *how* it produces a programme in a given way. It would almost never publicly question *why* it does things the way it does, or demonstrate that it has tried other ways. This is particularly true of news and current affairs discussion programmes.

It is interesting to note that television news broadcasting in the United Kingdom sometimes appears to be changing, because it is becoming less formal. On Five (formerly Channel 5), the presenter may sit *on* the desk rather than *at* the desk. This is then taken up by Channel 4, which gives its main presenter a more informal chair from which to present. What this demonstrates, however, is that the systematically organized ways of speaking which constitute media discourse actually can transcend any surface modifications. We can ascertain this because the programmes may first look different (and then more like each other), but their discourses offer no perceptible change. It could be argued, alternatively, that the minimal changes in the relation with the audience which the placing and poise of the presenter offer, might bring about some minimal change in the institution. It is very difficult, without prolonged historical study, to identify the nature and potential which such minimal changes may offer. It is certainly possible that changes in modes of address may have some kind of impact upon discourse, but one has to be very careful about making excessive claims on behalf of specific changes. One of the best introductions to the analysis of television discourse is that of Robert C. Allen (1992).

Euphemization is a process by which discourses can be softened, whether through the use of spoken language or body language (Thompson, 1990: 62). It is, for instance, possible to present unpleasant news in a way which makes it seem of little significance, just as it is possible to dramatize the mundane and banal. The dynamic between changes in modes of presentation and changes in ideological significance is a research issue requiring constant attention. The suggestion that a media discourse may delimit what it is possible for its producers to say is, however, of crucial importance to the development of media studies. This does not imply that the media are (constantly) involved in a process of deception. It is much more persuasive to suggest that the media structure what they say or what others can say within their own 'universe of discourse'. It also raises an important question about whether a specific universe of discourse limits what it is possible for the audience to understand.

I take the phrase 'universe of discourse' from the philosopher Herbert Marcuse, whose work on questions of discourse has been hugely influential and largely unacknowledged. Marcuse suggested that patterns of thought could be linked with patterns of behaviour. He was not concerned specifically or even predominantly with the mass media. For him, it was important to note the striking contrast between 'critical radicalism in scientific and philosophic method on the one hand, and an uncritical quietism in the attitude toward established and functioning social institutions' (Marcuse, 1972: 26). This, in turn, led to the establishment of a universe of discourse and action (note that Marcuse linked the two), and this was a universe that was not easily challengeable. The reason for this was that, unsurprisingly, any discourse tends to work most smoothly when it is operating by its own rules or systematic organization! It is more usual for such discourses to attract little attention because they will be unrecognized as discourses in the first place. The process of naturalization is pervasive and often very persuasive. We have to find ways of recognizing and identifying naturalizing discourses before they can be analysed or challenged. If anyone tries to challenge a specific way of describing the world, particularly as represented in a specific medium, the response is generally to reject it or to modify the challenge until it can be described and then analysed in terms of the medium's existing discourse. The alternative is simply that the challenge will be thrown out. Anyone who has ever tried to challenge a particular media discourse will know very well how difficult it can be. Republicans who may be unhappy with the discourses of royalism which they perceive in the media, or anti-capitalists who consider the system of capitalism fundamentally flawed will find it almost impossible to shift the ground upon which key discourses are situated. The key point to note, for the moment, is that media discourses are systematically organized ways of describing or re-presenting the world. The extent to which they are accepted or challenged is, unsurprisingly, a significant indicator of their influence.

What is semiotics and what does it do?

It is difficult to discuss questions of discourse and the media without an engagement with the subject of semiotics. In the final chapter I will argue that semiotics is a favourite target for critics of media studies. But what is it about this field of study which induces so much splenetic fervour? Semiotics is about the ways in which meaning is made. For meaning to be 'made', a producer and a receiver of any message are necessary. There is nothing particularly radical in this suggestion, but semiotics goes a little farther than this. First we need to recognize that the word 'message' is taken to include a whole range of communicative possibilities, from advertisements to feature films, from semaphore to fashion. Some messages, such as orders, are short and apparently simple. Others, such as stories or operas, are longer and apparently complex. All messages signify something to others. The processes of signification are very important for the semiotician. These processes are developed and structured because people make signs in order to signify. When people make signs, some form of agency is involved. Signs do not come from nowhere, and they are used for a purpose. Things (objects etc.) also signify, and they do so because they become part of a system or an element in a system of signification. The semiotician wants to know how signification occurs, and indeed what a sign is. Consider the following example.

A red flag can mean danger, or something to do with revolution, or the letter 'b' in the international flag alphabet. How it is interpreted will depend upon the context in which it is used, who sends it and who receives it. In all three cases, what can be agreed is that we are looking at is a flag, a piece of cloth which can be attached to a cord and hung on a pole. For the flag to communicate to us, it is important first that we recognize it as an intended medium of transmission (rather than someone's washing, for example). It is one of the ironies of the semiotic activity that it can also be concerned with understanding the potential significance of that which was not intended to send a message (not an intended signifier). In this case, the hanging out of washing can indeed become a form of signification!

To return to our example, we need to recognize that it is a piece of red cloth on a cord attached to a pole (acting as a signifier). Next, we associate the redness of the flag with danger (in this case, the signified). The relationship between the red flag and danger constitutes the sign. This is pretty basic, but like most things in the communication process, it is only basic because it is offered as an example. In practice, the meaning on offer is usually much more complex. What I have just outlined is a way of recognizing a flag as a piece of fabric held on a pole, usually with a rope (denotation). But flags almost always mean more than 'here is a flag'. They may mean, for instance, 'here is a festival', 'here is your political party', 'here is your enemy' or 'here is a message from the admiral'. We call this extra dimension of meaning 'connotation'. All messages connote something, and they do so through the use of signs.

Semiotics has been described as the science of signs and it is certainly a productive way of analysing media messages. But there are a few more basic variables that we need to consider in order to acquaint ourselves with this important analytical and philosophical tool. I said a moment ago that a sign is a relationship. It is a relationship between a signifier and a signified.

In order for that relationship to be established, there has to be someone to perceive the sign. That may be me, if I am a member of a media audience, or if I am addressing a media audience. In the latter case, I may be putting signs together with my audience in mind. I may be trying to consider what sense my intended audience will make of my signs and I may be trying to ensure that they will make the same sense of them that I want them to make.

In practice, there is always the possibility that my audience (or perhaps I should say audiences) may take different meanings from my signs. This is because signs have the potential to convey several meanings, or be polysemic. I have deliberately used the suggestion that signs have the potential to be polysemic. This is because, for some, multiple meanings are an inherent property of the sign. This would mean that any sign is saying to any observer, 'Look at me. I can mean a whole range of things.' In practice, what usually happens is that the observer of the sign actively makes sense of that sign. For the reader, it is seldom polysemic, but rather becomes the reader's new (non-polysemic) sign. For Kress, this is a crucial point in relation to the development of social semiotics. Once again, the polysemic nature of the sign is dependent upon the audience and their relationship to both the sign and the sender of the message. Consider the red flag. If I hoist a red flag in my garden, my neighbours may read this in a number of ways. It may connote different things to them. One neighbour may think that my gas boiler is finally about to explode. Another may think that I have decided to ally myself with a revolutionary group. Yet another may think that I am feeling festive because it is my birthday. Each of these readings could be sustained and my neighbours would have to negotiate with each other over which meaning was the correct one should they happen to come together for a debate on the issue. If, on the other hand, I was standing next to a large notice in the countryside which said ARTILLERY FIRING RANGE. DANGER WHEN RED FLAG IS FLYING, and I hoisted the flag, there would be little confusion over its meaning to those who could read English.

But, to pursue this example just a little further, the fact that there is no confusion over what a sign means at the denotative level does not mean that there will be no problems at the connotative level. If you are a rambler out for a walk in the countryside, you may be enraged to see the red flag flying. If, on the other hand, you are an enthusiast for all things military, you may decide to wait around and listen for the sounds of the guns, hoping to see a puff of smoke or an explosion.

Before considering the importance of the field of social semiotics, it is important to offer a word of warning. I have posed the question about what semiotics might do. My immediate response to this is to suggest that semiotics allows one to develop systematic ways of studying the media. This is important, but not at all unique to semiotics. Nevertheless, through the judicious use of semiotic analysis, one is likely to discover the richness of meaning in some texts, the banality of others and the ideological significance of others. When I say that one has to make judicious use of semiotics, I mean that one has to avoid simplistic analyses, which 'read off' meanings from media messages in unproblematic or even dogmatic ways. There have been enthusiasts for the realms of semiosis who have read off racism, sexism, ageism and any number of other isms until the superficiality of their analyses simply undermined the often worthy motivations which led them to undertake their work. There has to be some sensitivity linked to the reading of signs, as well as the desire to extend one's knowledge of the world. To read a sign only from one's existing knowledge of the world is to veer towards uncritical semiotics. This, in turn, is to render semiotics a mechanical decoding exercise which is ideologically suspect. Daniel Chandler has provided a first-class introduction to semiotics, which is available on the Internet and as a book (Chandler, 2001).

I have argued here that signs are powerful, context specific and audience related.

What is social semiotics and how is it different?

For the social semiotician, the basic semiotic form is the message. Messages have directionality. For Hodge and Kress, this means that messages have a source, a goal, a social context and a purpose (Hodge and Kress, 1988). Messages refer to a world outside themselves. The suggestion that a message refers to something outside itself may seem mundane, but it is in fact crucially important, and in relation to the study of the media it has become of critical significance. Some analysts of the media have privileged the media text to such an extent that they either discount or relegate in significance the referent. Referent usually means some thing, process or state of affairs in the world outside language. Semiotics was often quite happy to speak of signifier and signified without any undue worry about anything outside the system of signification. Social semiotics, on the other hand, recognizes that messages relate to lived existence and this means that they have material bases and material consequences in the social world. Of course, nothing that exists can be debated or identified outside language and discourse. Even when we speak of the sublime – that which is beyond description – we have to use language to describe it. But the emphasis on the material conditions of existence is what gives a critical edge to social semiotics and stops it from becoming either complacent or smug in its analytical functions.

The use of the term 'text' is also important for the social semiotician. Hodge and Kress describe the significance of the text as follows:

> 'Text' is also opposed to another important concept, 'system'. Mainstream semiotics has developed the notion of a system of signs as an abstract structure which is realised or instantiated in text. It tends to treat such systems as static, as a social fact which is not, however, implicated in a social process of development or change. [. . .] Texts in a system have value by virtue of their place in that system. At the same time, a system is constantly being reproduced and reconstituted in texts. Otherwise it would cease to exist. So texts are both the material realisation of systems of signs, and also the site where change continually takes place.
>
> (Hodge and Kress, 1988: 6)

This abstract language should not deter us from attempting to grasp the crucial dynamics of signification which are being identified. For these authors, meaning is something which is negotiated socially. Of course, that meaning can only be made because at any one time an agreed system of signification is in play. But meaning is not a purely mechanical attribute of a text.

If we think this is all very theoretical, we have only to remember the various struggles over meaning that have taken place in recent times. The word 'bad' in the English language, for instance, has come to mean precisely its opposite in some discourses (as in, 'That was a *bad* solo', meaning, 'I thought your solo was extremely accomplished'). A more long-term struggle has taken place over the meaning of the flag of the United Kingdom. The Union Flag has constantly shifted in significance, from being the unproblematic (to most of the British population, at least) signifier of Britain as a world power and the centre of a great empire, to being a signifier of Britain in the 'swinging' 1960s, to being a reviled signifier of the political parties of the far right. Here we are discussing the same signifier in the same signifying system. The changes in its meaning depended upon different social and historical contexts and different discourses which situated that very particular signifier in very particular ways. But these discourses were not mere language games. They were related to hard realities in a very material world. When those who were opponents of Britain's colonial aspirations called the Union Flag the 'butcher's apron of the British Empire', they were not merely playing language games. They based their judgement upon a hostility to the destructive actions of colonialists in a world which existed parallel with and sometimes outside discourse, but which could only be re-presented through discourse.

Social semiotics is important because it can identify the ways in which meanings are either confirmed or contested in the discourses we find in texts. There are different kinds of texts in circulation and they are related to their particular contexts and purposes. In relation to the press, for instance, we find different kinds of texts produced for different purposes. The editorial is different from the sports column. Cookery columns are different from problem pages. They each follow specific rules of language use, layout or other media-specific practices which enable us to recognize the kind of column they are, almost irrespective of their content. In the cinema we find films which are produced for different purposes within the general context of public entertainment. They may be structured as comedies, adventures, musicals or romances, or they may be varying combinations of these. On television and radio, we find chat shows, magazine programmes, sports programmes, news programmes and a host of others. The different kinds of media texts which are in circulation, some of which I have just mentioned, can be identified through what we call their genre. Within genre we may find various generic subcategories which help us to clarify their type and purpose. For instance, an adventure may be a crime story, a western, or even a musical. We can also identify genres because of their production bases. This means, for instance, that we may expect different things from editorials in different newspapers, according to their political sympathies, audiences, circulation figures and ownership. The key point about genre is that it can play a formative role in relation to the meaning of a given media text. Particular genres can be said to build up particular expectations in their audiences. Their processes of signification can be so seamless that an audience can have their expectations established by two or three bars of music, or by the sight of a particular typographic layout or audio-visual montage. These expectations can be so well established that they pass by almost unnoticed under 'normal' conditions of media consumption. It is only if these expectations are not fulfilled, because specific forms of signification are absent or changed beyond recognition, that audiences will become suspicious or insecure. If CNN evening news began with Stevie Wonder singing 'I

Just Called to say I Love You', it would not pass by unnoticed, any more than if *Blue Peter* began with a stirring rendition of 'The Red Flag'. Genre and generic expectations are significant factors for the media analyst.

Drawing upon the ideas of Kress, we can say that media texts are determined in at least two ways: 'by means of the discourses which appear in the text, and by the forms, meanings and constraints of a particular genre' (Kress, 1989: 20). Discourse and genre are certainly not the only two issues which are significant for the media analyst or researcher, but they are sufficiently important to warrant further exploration. I will do this by referring to a specific media example, the popular television show, *Blind Date*. In doing so I will be drawing selectively upon aspects of the work of social semioticians and those concerned with the power of discourse.

The discourses of *Blind Date*

I have chosen *Blind Date* as my example for analysis because of its popularity. It is also a programme which has taken different manifestations in different countries over the last decade. The programme I will analyse belongs to the penultimate manifestation in the UK. There were some modifications made for the last series which Cilla Black hosted. *Blind Date* began in its UK version, hosted by Cilla Black, in 1985. Black first made her name in the 1960s as a singer who was a contemporary of The Beatles and Gerry and the Pacemakers, and who, like them, comes from Liverpool. By the late 1990s, she had adopted a persona of a kind of mother figure who watched over, encouraged and disciplined those who would seek the kind of romance or sexual liaison which *Blind Date* offered. Participants in the show may have been young (in their early twenties) or more mature (sometimes in their eighties), but were seldom in the same age group as Cilla. In the United Kingdom, the show went out on a Saturday evening at around seven o'clock, presumably to attract the younger viewers who may have been on their way out for the night.

The generic structure of the show was important, partly because it encouraged viewer identification, and partly because it facilitated certain judgements about relationships and 'romance'. It was important that any implicit or explicit values in the programme were lightweight and amusing. It was structured in what I will call four acts and followed an almost identical pattern each week.

ACT I: We meet Cilla, and she reminds us of the two couples who went on holiday together as a result of last week's show. We are then introduced to the first three contestants. They enter to much applause and loud music. Each contestant is asked their name, where they come from and what they do. There is opportunity for a limited amount of simple banter and pre-arranged displays of unusual talents like being able to touch one's nose with the tip of one's tongue.

The 'chooser' of the opposite sex to the first three is then introduced. This person is also interviewed briefly and allowed to make one or two comments about their interests or habits. The chooser then asks three questions, each of which is addressed to the three contestants. They give carefully prepared and often innuendo-laden responses to each question, followed by carefully orchestrated gasps or whines from the audience.

The attributes and personalities of the three contestants are then summed up by a voice-over associated with a man called 'our Graham'. The chooser then makes their choice, and the unsuccessful contestants leave, after ritually kissing the chooser and Cilla. The couple then see each other for the first time, and they usually embrace or take in each other's looks, dress, shape etc.

Act I finishes with one or both of the winners choosing a card on which is outlined the promise of a date together almost anywhere in the tourist-inhabited world. They are asked if they will come back the following week and say how they got on. They agree. Cilla then tells us who we will be seeing next, and we are shown the moment when they met the previous week. This is followed by a commercial break.

ACT II: The second act begins with the entry of the couple who went on a date together the previous week. They ritually kiss Cilla and sit down on a sofa facing her and the audience. What follows is a series of short videos of the holiday/date, interspersed with comments by each individual about the other. Whilst the video is playing, there is an insert at the corner of the screen where we see the person being talked about 'live' as they respond to their companion's comments. After both contestants have had their say, Cilla interviews them about their comments and the date as a whole. She also asks them whether they intend to meet again after the programme. We are then given a preview of the next three contestants.

ACT III: The next three contestants are introduced and the rest of the act is structurally the same as Act I, with the gender of the contestants and the chooser swapped round.

ACT IV: In the final act the second of the previous week's dates is shown, following the same pattern as in Act II. Cilla then comes over to the camera position in front of the audience, standing and facing the camera. From here she says her brief but cheery farewell.

This structural outline is designed to demonstrate those aspects of the show which provided us with generic points of reference and identification. Part of the pleasure to be gained from the programme was derived from having our generic expectations fulfilled or, occasionally, jolted a little. I will now move to the consideration of a *Blind Date* programme which was first broadcast on 12 December 1998. The ideological and discursive force of the show is only fully apparent when the structure is fleshed out with dialogue, body language, fashion sense and, above all, a chance for the viewers to watch, unobserved, as the drama is played out before them.

The performance

Act I begins with Cilla promising us that we will be seeing how Sam and Terry got on in Mauritius and, later, how Scott and Rachel managed in Hamburg. First, however, we are introduced to the three female contestants. They are Nicola, a hotel supervisor from the Republic of Ireland, Melanie, a sales consultant from Leicester, and Rachel, a restaurant receptionist from Manchester.

Each of the contestants is given a chance to say something of interest to the viewers. Amongst other things, we learn that Melanie does a lot of dancing. She immediately re-pronounces 'lot of' as 'lorra' in imitation of Cilla's Liverpool accent. Cilla and the audience reciprocate with sounds of appreciation. Nicola has a little more to say, including the fact that she enjoys eating Indian food. Sometimes, it seems, she has as many as 'five Indians a week'. Cilla immediately picks up on this with 'well, you are a greedy little Nicola', followed by, 'Have you ever thought, let's go out and have an English?' Rachel also offers one or two brief comments. These comments are partly ice-breakers, designed to warm up the audience and the participants to their tasks. They also offer regular reference points to eating, dancing or courting habits, and seldom miss a chance to make use of the double entendre. The latter is an essential discursive and ideological feature of the show.

The chooser is then introduced. This week it is Freddie, who is tall and broad-shouldered with very short, cropped hair which has been dyed blonde. The entry of the chooser is now a significant feature of each show, as they are expected to make some kind of poised or posed entrance. Freddie pauses at the top of the stairs and blows a double-handed kiss to the audience. Cilla greets Freddie with a kiss on the cheek and sits him on his stool behind the screen. She then says to him, 'Sit yourself down there, Freddie. Freddie, Freddie, Freddie, Freddie! Are you ready, Freddie?' The tone of her voice is that of maternal yet sexually aware appreciation. He tells Cilla that he is a chef and works in a famous London restaurant. Cilla asks him how he would describe his ideal girl 'foodwise'. He suggests that she would be like ravioli, 'because it's gonna be beautiful and hard on the outside and succulent and soft on the inside'. This comment is greeted by Cilla and the audience with a concerted, 'Whoo!' Freddie then proceeds to ask his questions, and I will give just one example of how this part of the ritual is played out.

'I am a chef and I can't resist a top-class greengrocer, where I find I can get plenty of ideas for new dishes. What would you suggest I buy, and what could I create with it?' The contestants offer responses which allow them to advertise their potential as a companion on a date. Nicola suggests he should buy a jacket potato because she is Irish. The reference to the Irish and potatoes is presumably linked somewhere in Nicola's discursive reserve to the potato famine, but we cannot know. Her comment suggests, otherwise, that the Irish are likely to be potato eaters and nothing else, except perhaps that Nicola's suggestion (if it is her suggestion) is deemed by her (or someone who wrote her lines) to be amusing. Melanie suggests a mixed salad, because 'like me it's crisp, fresh, delicious, dressed or undressed'. Freddie responds with interest to what Melanie says and moves briefly from his seat, levered up by his arms. Cilla interjects, 'Oh, you got out of your seat for that one, Freddie!' Each action or comment by Cilla is accompanied by a ritualistic response. Finally, Rachel suggests that Freddie should buy a mushroom because he sounds like a 'fun guy' to be with.

Freddie's next question begins, 'The first thing that people notice about me is my slightly blonde hair'. Cilla and the audience have a good-natured laugh at this and Freddie then says, 'though I have to admit it's not real'. Both Cilla and the audience, now and throughout the show, studiously avoid mentioning the fact that Freddie is black. This is to be welcomed, it could be argued, in a show which is clearly against racism or prejudice based upon ethnic origin. There is also, in this particular case, a sense of strenuous over-compensation in evidence. Cilla mentions Freddie's sexy voice on more than one occasion and is more than usually physical with him. Freddie's skin colour is a public secret. We know it and we do not know it. We affirm it as we deny it.

After two more questions have been asked of each contestant, Cilla suggests to Freddie and the audience at home and in the studio that we go to 'our Graham with a quick recap'. Graham's disembodied voice provides a witty summary of each contestant as we look at them on the screen, with their biographical details as part of the image. Freddie chooses Melanie, and the other two have to leave, preceded by the familiar, 'You also turned down – oh, how could you?' from Cilla. She finally refers to 'our Melanie from Leicester'.

The meeting of the chooser and the winning contestant is another nodal point in the show. It is their chance to hug, kiss if they wish, and above all to appraise each other. This is one of the most ambiguous (or better, potentially polysemic) moments in the show. How are we supposed to appraise the appraisal that is taking place before us? Do we watch the facial expressions, the movement from foot to foot, the placing of the arms against the body or any other cues? Whatever the choice, the ideological 'work' of the show has been successful just as long as the audience is involved in the process. This is a boy-meets-girl scenario with the narrative pared to a minimum. It has a quality which in animals is associated with bottom sniffing. And the viewer is invited to take vicarious pleasure in the process. If the couple become too enthusiastic, we may giggle as Cilla comes between them with her bunch of envelopes and the promise of a holiday. There may also be occasions when Cilla has to bring the couple closer together because their body language suggests that they are not, on first sight, thrilled at the prospect of a holiday together. The holidays are then described by Cilla as she reads from the cards, ending with 'and it says here' when some reference is made to love blossoming or the like. The apparent contradiction between possible romantic love and animal attraction is one of the keys to the show's success. It is also one the show's most ideologically interesting dimensions.

The above outline is no more than a brief account of part of one show, from a series which attracted several million viewers each week. From an extended engagement with both the generic form and the specific signifying practices used in each show, we can begin to assemble its explicit and implicit discourses. These include those discourses associated with generic form:

- the ritual question-and-answer sections
- the ritual introduction of the contestants
- the emphasis on the banal and the bizarre in the behaviour of contestants
- the 'staged' videos made on the date
- the bad jokes and sexual innuendo
- the couples recalling their experiences with increasing licence to insult their companion
- the session on the sofa with Cilla after the date.

The other discourses are those associated more directly with the ideological. They include references to romance, romantic love and possible marriage. These discourses, brief and seldom given more than cursory acknowledgement, nevertheless constitute a reworking of what these very terms might mean. Romance, romantic love and marriage become signifiers in a discourse which attempts to exclude contradiction. On such occasions we might argue that the programme was providing signification which could only be socially decoded. It became now a generic convention of this version of the programme to ask if Cilla would be buying a new hat – a coded reference to possible marriage in the future and her attendance at the ceremony (with the cameras, of course). There was also a careful dialectic in play between the discourses of motherliness and those of unbridled lust. In both, Cilla had a key role to play. In relation to the former, Cilla sat on the sofa with the winning couples after their dates and solicited romantic or sentimental responses. The body language of both Cilla and the couples was important here. There was seldom, on the sofa, much direct talk of sex. That was reserved for the chats on the stools in the earlier parts of the game, mainly through heavy innuendo. It was there that Cilla could act as a catalyst or provocateur in encouraging some lusty responses. At the same time, Cilla acted as a kind of moral referee if things looked as though they were going to get out of hand. She had to reconcile the possibility of casual sex (implicitly unacceptable conduct in this series) with a move towards romantic love and family values. It was a delicate and demanding role.

In the show I have considered we were offered more drama as two of the previous winners, Samantha and Terry, recounted their unpleasant date and their complete dislike for each other. The pattern repeats like a tartan on a roller. The mix is one of occasional 'love-at-first-sight' insinuations, to more frequent comedic mismatches and the occasional bout of open hostility. It produces apparently endless pleasures for the audience. There is an implicit invitation to decode the show from a position relevant to your own interests. Hence younger audiences are inclined to jeer at the sentimentality which can be so appealing to some of the older viewers, whilst younger viewers enjoy the bawdiness and brazen arrogance of some of the contestants. These are, of course, no more than tendencies, because younger viewers may allow themselves a private engagement with the discourses of romantic love if they wish, just as other viewers may indulge in some vicarious lustfulness as part of early evening family viewing. It is a happy commercial mix.

What can the media student or researcher learn from all of this talk of semiosis (the social process by which meaning is constructed and exchanged) and discourse? First, that even asking the question is enough to have some journalists diving for their metaphorical notepads with a view to another exposé of media studies. But more seriously, one can discover the ways in which ideological positions and societal values are embedded in popular entertainment. One can also note the contradictions which are at the core of the pleasures which the programme offers its audiences, particularly those between amorality and traditional family values. There is also an inherent and sometimes profound conservatism in the way the show ignores anything but a particularly restricted notion of heterosexuality.

Another issue which is important is that the readings of this programme are unlikely to produce unanimity amongst interpreters. There will be disagreement, particularly over whether or not one is reading too much into a sequence or a shot, which is another way of saying that one may be making the wrong meaning from the message. There will also be disagreement depending upon whether the readers are young, old, mixed in terms of gender or ethnicity, hold religious convictions of one or another kind, and many other issues. The key questions however, remain, related to the identification of various discourses and the ways in which they operate in the show. It is my contention that through textual analysis they can be recognised irrespective of one's ideological position. They are characteristics of the programme as text. The importance of the discourses identified (and remember that discourses are systematically organized ways of speaking or signifying) is that they may be encouraging a particular reading or possibilities for reading from a particular reader. However, the Italian semiotician Umberto Eco has pointed out that we should not imagine that just because there is more than one way of reading a text, that the possibilities are infinite. They are not (Eco, 1990). How we structure and make use of our analyses will depend very considerably upon our own ideological positioning. The important point for media studies is that the act of analysis and the clarification of ideological positions should be recognized, identified and articulated. Ideological positions are embedded in discourses.

Multimodality

In this chapter I have tried to explore just some of the ways in which discourse and social semiotics are important for the media researcher. *Blind Date* can be read, if we wish, as a text within a system. It would have to be understood, also, as a text belonging to a genre. The interesting question for the analyst is to ask in what ways that text can be seen to be offering confirmation of a semiotic system, and in what ways it could be seen to offer any challenge to that system. The system to which I am referring here is one which structures possible meanings in the general field of popular televisual discourse. This, in turn, may be narrowed to a system concerned with popular discourses about the nature of romance and heterosexual relations. Within this system, there would seem to be a variety of messages on offer and they may be read in different ways. The structures of signification through which popular television operates are not at all simple. They are complex, overlaid and interwoven. I have, in my discussion, given priority to the spoken word. This is a choice from which certain advantages follow. I am able to transcribe the words and isolate them for any analysis. They are, however, only a small part of that which signifies in the text. There are other sounds, of course, most notably the sound of the audience and, above all, the use of the music. There are also occasions when the written word is displayed on the screen, as in 'The Decision is Yours' just before the chooser completes their task.

The other mode of signification, from which a great deal of unspoken meaning is derived, is the image. Any television show is made up of a succession of (usually moving) images, linked together by a language of cutting from image to image. These cuts are sometimes emphasized by the use of various wipes, dissolves and other electronic effects. In a show such as *Blind Date*, however, the main passages are very conventional in the ways in which cameras cover the main speakers and the facial expression and body language of those to whom or about whom they speak (reaction shots). The title sequence for the series in question centred on the image of a sofa, on which two animated cushions cavort, finally forming the shape of a heart, over which the title *Blind Date* appears. There are also other electronic effects which may be used to invigorate the videotapes of the couples on their respective dates. But when the serious drama of the programme is designed to unfold, it is done with the most conservative techniques of cutting and reaction shots. We know that all shots can be identified using a relatively simple language of description which involves the recognition of close-ups, big close-ups, mid-shots, camera angles etc. But the identification of these shots provides limited information unless linked with the other simultaneous moments of signification. These might include a cough off screen, a movement of an eyebrow by one participant, the clothes someone is wearing and a whole host of other possibilities. Because all these factors always work together to offer up meanings to the viewers, we have to recognize that this form of communication is multimodal. The media researcher may decide, for reasons which would have to be argued, that a particular analysis of a media discourse would concentrate on a single mode of communication. Such analysis would then, of necessity, be based upon only a part of the processes of signification. It is important that we recognize that all media analysis, however sophisticated or formally complex, is bound to be based upon such partiality.

I have made my emphasis here the spoken word, but I want to demonstrate now how the decoding of the spoken word in context is actually a multimodal activity for the media researcher. I will do so by referring back to a particular moment in the show. It is the moment when Freddie discusses the fact that his hair is dyed: 'The first thing that people notice about me is my slightly blonde hair.' The number of ways in which this statement can be interpreted depends upon whether or not one is watching the screen at the time. Freddie is looking down at his questions and smiling, while Cilla is moved to run her hand over Freddie's shoulder as she laughs in a good-natured but embarrassed way. These relatively small moments of signification combine with the overall context to offer up meaning which is not based upon what has been said, but what we, as viewers, must know. Freddie is black and it is being ignored. This, as previously mentioned, may be seen as a marker of multi-ethnic or possibly anti-racist participation by all concerned. Or we could read the body language of both Cilla and Freddie, plus the undue mirth about his dyed hair (on a show where this is quite common), as signs of embarrassed recognition of 'otherness' by all concerned. It could be argued that Freddie is being both embraced and recognized in these moments. The recognition is a cause of laughter because the knowledge of Freddie's skin colour is being withheld from the three contestants. Regular viewers of the show will know that contestants are not shy to brag about those features which they possess which are likely to be winning or impressive. They often refer to the length of their legs, their long hair or their fine physique. Freddie is black, but this remains unacknowledged. Possible readings of this sequence have to extend beyond the immediate context of the show to the society of which it is a part. Freddie is going to choose a woman who is white. In a society at home with such a possibility, the sequence might have been seriously addressing Freddie's hair. I wish to suggest, however, that it is an example of how implicit discourse can tend to dominate explicit discourse. It is also likely to have a considerably different impact upon readers of the text if they happen to be black or white. One of my own students who is black explained to me how the people with whom she shared a flat (all white) also managed to ignore Freddie's skin colour until she pointed it out to them – or so they said. One can see from this tiny example, I hope, that even relatively everyday media representations are complex and multilayered in the meanings which they offer.

The 'social' in social semiotics

If meaning in the media is related to the potential for polysemy, this is largely a result of the social contexts in and through which the message is received and then decoded or interpreted, and who is doing the interpreting. Texts stubbornly remain the same, whilst their meanings may slide or change over time. The problem for the media studies researcher is to decide how much of the meaning of a text resides or is weighted in the text and how much of it is negotiated socially. The frustrating answer to that question has to be, 'Well, it all depends . . .'. The social dimensions of meaning making can and do vary over time. If we are to study the ways in which meaning is negotiated, both in contemporary media and in communicative forms from previous generations, we have to develop a sense of their historical context. This may seem at first an odd thing to say about media studies, which is so often vilified for its implied mindless contemporaneity. But we soon discover that the meaning of a media text from only a decade ago requires serious contextualization if it is to be analysed rather than merely observed. Even then, we also notice that contemporary readings of media texts may differ according to the social, political, gender and other positionings of the readers of that text.

There is, and indeed I would argue that there has to be, a dynamic in all social semiotic and discourse analysis. It is a dynamic which has to encompass contradiction in meanings and contradictory meanings sometimes in the same text. This dynamic is precisely what facilitates an involvement by the reader or analyst beyond mere formal identification of a text's characteristics. Meaning is something which was, is and should be a contested field. But this is not to imply that all meaning making is nothing more than my opinion versus your opinion. Some meanings are agreed upon, such as a red light meaning that I should stop my car. Other meanings may be contested, such as that of a national flag or a portrait of a man in military uniform. Both contested and uncontested meanings are context specific and historically positioned. What this suggests is that there is a necessary and intimate relationship between messages and readers. You can't have one without the other. A new set of problems then occurs as we try to identify just what we mean by readers in the context of media studies. This will be addressed in the chapter which is concerned with media audiences.

I want to end this chapter with a warning and a challenge. The warning is one which I have hinted at already. It is neither possible nor desirable to envisage social semiotics or a mode of analysing discourse which is mechanical and certain in its methodologies. 'The most scrupulous reading of signs must always be complemented by a scepticism based on an awareness of the inherent slipperiness of meaning in use' (Hodge and Kress, 1988: 110). The dynamic of social semiotics is sustained by an endless negotiation of the relationship between a series of messages and discourses, and the material consequences or correlates of those discourses. We have to move, in media studies, between the specific signifying practices of the media, the meaning of specific messages, and the consequences and correlates of those messages in specific contexts. In doing so we will not be denying the centrality of analysing how meaning is made. We will, however, be asking about the material implications of those messages in specific material contexts. This act of contextualization will require more rather than less analysis of media texts, but always in relation to the social and material world from which they emanate and in which they are being interpreted. It is a controversial and delicate activity. I am not arguing for another bout of effects analysis. I am arguing for a careful and sustained engagement with the ways in which meaning in the media is historically negotiated or contested and how such meaning is related to the material conditions of those represented and those who receive the messages. It means entering the realms of semiosis, and it is no small task (Hodge and Kress, 1988: 240).

I have spent a considerable amount of time in my discussion of discourse with an analysis of *Blind Date*. I chose this example because it is everyday, contemporary and, at the same time, historical. The study of the mundane and the ordinary is at the heart of some of the most perceptive, politicized and aesthetically aware media research. There will be more to say about this in relation to questions of identity. For the moment, let me only note that the critical study of everyday pleasures is not a glib or superficial activity. It is a way of identifying the key ideological elements in a given society, and a way of identifying the formation and sustenance of the social and political world as it is structured and re-presented to us in discourse.

FURTHER READING

Hodge, R. and Kress, G., 1988, *Social Semiotics*.
This remains one of the founding texts in the field. It can be taken whole or in parts, and is both readable and illuminating.

Kress, G., 1989, *Linguistic Processes in Sociocultural Practice*.
Despite its arid title, this is one of the best introductions to approaches to and analysis of discourse and the concerns of social semiotics. It is also readable and relatively short.

Kress, G. and Van Leeuwen, T., 2001, *Multimodal Discourse*.
The move from social semiotics to multimodal discourse is one which all students of the media need to follow with interest. Kress and Van Leeuwen make the case well for the former, though they do perhaps turn away a little from some of its cutting-edge qualities. Another important work, the shortness of which belies its significance for analysts of the media.

chapter four

Postmodernism and media studies

Modern Art at postmodern prices

— Sign outside a London store

What is postmodernism?

I have tried, in the previous chapter, to indicate the importance and some of the potential which is offered to the media studies student or researcher by an engagement with approaches to discourse and social semiotics. I have also suggested that to engage with social semiotics means that we have to be aware of the significance of a historical dimension to the ways in which meanings are made and discourses constructed and sustained. How we respond to this suggestion will have a significant impact upon the kind of media studies in which we are involved. I have, so far, turned to the media text as a means of anchoring my arguments. The media student or researcher must also recognize, however, that media analysis and media studies are closely linked to intellectual debates and developments in a given era. This has become even more significant in an era which has been associated so much with the phenomenon known as postmodernism.

In this chapter, I intend to explore the significance of postmodernism for the media student or researcher, and to consider examples of what some would call postmodern media texts. As the quotation at the beginning of this chapter suggests, postmodernism has entered popular discourse in a way which is uncommon for a term which sprang from philosophy and sociology. The first question we need to ask is exactly what the term might mean. I will attempt to answer this question somewhat obliquely. The reason for this is that there is no single definition, and to begin with definitions results in the production of nothing more than an intellectual shopping list. It is also important to realize that many contemporary forms of study involve the student or researcher in the main paradoxes and contradictions of our time. Postmodernism has become of significance, both as a fashionable term and as a core debate in the social sciences. Because there is, simply, too much to find out and too little time in which to do it, there is a danger that we may be tempted (or even required) to make pronouncements upon complex issues having read no more than a paragraph here or there on the matter in hand. This is wrong. At the same time it is unproductive and unwise to suggest, as do some critics, that we should not pronounce upon issues relating to philosophy and the media at all until we are experts in the field. We have to live with our relative levels of ignorance and understanding, and perhaps learn a little of the humility which should accompany the development of scholarship. It is in the spirit of opening an investigation that this chapter is offered. It is not a summary of the thoughts of all the key thinkers in the field. For those who wish to study a useful summary of these thinkers, excellent texts are available such as Bauman (1992), Harvey (1989), Callinicos (1989) and Eagleton (1996 and 2003), as well as Anderson's superb but demanding engagement with the work of Frederic Jameson and approaches to postmodernity (1998).

At the heart of postmodernism is a whole host of paradoxes and contradictions. Postmodernism is apparently concerned with the superficial, the glossy, the trite and the humorous. It is also deadly serious. Postmodernism is about rejecting big explanations or stories that tell us about the ways things are, whether these involve political, psychoanalytical or other means of 'summing up' aspects of our lives. Postmodernism is so insistent upon the impossibility (and undesirability) of big explanations or metanarratives, that it becomes dogmatic and totalitarian. The new 'big' explanation (metanarrative) is that there are no big explanations (metanarratives). Postmodernism is also, sometimes, about the celebration of difference. The assertion of difference has, however, been the cause of much conflict and aggression, as well as allowing for a blossoming of many different ways of expressing identity. The concept of identity will be explored in more detail in chapter nine. All the above issues and ideas have had considerable impact upon the mass media, and the ways in which the media represent the world. Whether this impact means that postmodernism is a term which can be used with any accuracy of meaning, however, is open to debate. Before we come to this, we should first consider what it is that is meant by the modernism which preceded the 'post'. I suggest that it is more productive to begin such a consideration by speaking of modernity as a precursor of postmodernity. The 'isms' come later.

Modernity was here first

Modernity is associated with the development of industrial societies and the advance of the secular state and the world capitalist economy. It is also associated with a belief that 'man' [*sic*] could be 'the measure of all things'. In other words, modernity had been (and perhaps still is) a period in which there was a belief that human beings could control their destiny and shape the world according to their needs. For the champions of modernity, all this seemed like a good idea. Superstition could be replaced by science, irrationality by rationality. This optimistic outlook was also linked with the possibility that knowledge achieved through rational research was likely to be objective knowledge with universal implications. The problem with such confidence about the ways in which human beings might develop is that it can result in the invention of political programmes and strategies which are drastic in their implications. The two most often quoted are those of fascism on the right and communism on the left. It is all too easy to fall into the trap of equating fascism with communism because both had global plans and both committed acts of unimaginable horror. It should be remembered, however, that the horrors of fascism were the fulfilment of a plan, whilst the horrors committed in the name of communism were nothing more or less than an aberration based upon lies and hypocrisy. It could be argued that equating fascism and communism has helped to lay the ground for postmodern rejection of grand explanations, big stories and metanarratives. It has also facilitated the portrayal of capitalism as (like it or not, the least worst option) the only workable solution to the major problems of the world.

The most subtle and scholarly of the negative appraisals of the period of modernity have come from the sociologist Zygmunt Bauman. Bauman has argued that it is a myth to consider than humanity is embarked on a journey from barbarity towards civilization. He takes, as his central example, the Holocaust. He suggests that the attempted genocide of the Jews was 'a rare, yet significant and reliable, test of the hidden possibilities of modern society' (Bauman, 1989: 12). The planning, the rationalism and the bureaucracy of the period of modernity have provided the necessary structure on which mass murder can be accomplished with an almost desperate emphasis placed by its perpetrators on the normality of the process. There are also similarities between Bauman's analysis and that of Marcuse, mentioned in chapter three:

> Dehumanisation is inextricably related to the most essential, rationalising tendency of modern bureaucracy. All bureaucracies affect in some measure some human objects, the adverse impact of dehumanisation is much more common than the habit to identify it almost totally with its genocidal effects would suggest. Soldiers are told to shoot *targets*, which *fall* when they are *hit*. Employees of big companies are encouraged to destroy *competition*. Officers of welfare agencies operate *discretionary awards* at one time, *personal credits* at another. Their objects are *supplementary benefit recipients*. It is difficult to perceive and remember the humans behind all such technical terms. The point is that as far as bureaucratic goals go, they are better not perceived and not remembered.
>
> (Bauman, 1989: 103)

The extent to which Bauman's analysis stands up when applied to detailed empirical analysis of media texts is an interesting focus for investigation. Of course, Bauman suggests that we now live in a period of postmodernity, so whatever media texts we now have may need to be examined with that in mind. Yet one cannot help feeling that much of what he argues about bureaucracy applies very well to the present, whether we name the period modernity or postmodernity. At the same time, his warnings about the dangers of planning and the normalization of persecution or murder as a process of cleansing society provide a chilling reminder of the necessity of keeping a critical social base in any of our semiotic or media studies activities. The modernity of which Bauman writes has not disappeared, despite his insistence that we live in an era of postmodernity. But that is only part of the story.

The same period, which produced the conditions for the bureaucratic normalization of genocide, also saw several revolutions in the arts and in communications technology. In the late nineteenth and early twentieth centuries, in the face of the unspeakable suffering and inhumanity of two world wars and the Holocaust, various generic forms in the arts underwent radical reappraisals. Realism in the novel and in paintings and films was challenged. It did not disappear, but there were alternative media messages produced which sought to involve the reader or viewer in a process of understanding requiring effort and commitment. For critics, the realist, whether through the use of writing or imagery, had lulled the audience into a sense of uncritical security. The modernist (and now it seems appropriate to introduce the term) wanted to challenge readers with the ways in which a given text was put together, and often to leave the audience with much on which to reflect. Hence the well-known suggestion from Jean-Luc Godard that films should have a beginning, a middle and an end, but not necessarily in that order. This challenge was also made in the other arts, particularly in music, painting and sculpture. Perspectival space was challenged as an insufficient and ideologically suspect way of representing the world. Multiple viewpoints were introduced through cubism. Celebrations of energy, the machine age and even war were also the central tenets of other schools of painting, from the Fauves to the Futurists and Vorticists. In all this work there was a mixture of rebellion, celebration, optimism and sometimes a will to power. Bauman is right to remind us that modernity provided the organizational context and political hubris from which mass murder and philosophies of cruelty could spring. But modernity and modernism were also the springboards for as yet unfulfilled ambitions. To understand these it is important to consider the work of Marshall Berman.

Berman's major work is entitled *All that Is Solid Melts into Air: the experience of modernity.* The first part of the title is in fact a quotation from *The Communist Manifesto* by Karl Marx and Friedrich Engels. That work, according to Berman, was the first great modernist work of art. For Berman, as for Marx, the modern world is a place where contradictions and tensions abound. Modernity is a period in which we can find positive aspirations for change and growth alongside philosophies of despair, negativity and nihilism. In Berman's words:

> In the course of time, modernists will produce a great array of cosmic and apocalyptic visions, visions of the most radiant joy and the bleakest despair. Many of the most creative modernist artists will be simultaneously possessed by both and driven endlessly from pole to pole; their inner dynamism will reproduce and express the inward rhythms by which modern capitalism moves and lives.
>
> (Berman, 1993: 102)

From this dynamic environment have sprung the ideas of Darwin and Freud as well as those of Marx. And at the negative poles of this environment we find the different aberrations of Nazism and Stalinism. The modernism for which Berman argues is one which constantly attempts a renewal of all that is liberating, positive, creative. There is, however, no false sentimentalizing in his work. The best he offers is what he calls a dialectic of hope (Berman, 1992).

What is postmodernism?

By 'postmodern', I mean, roughly speaking, the contemporary movement of thought which rejects totalities, universal values, grand historical narratives, solid foundations to human existence and the possibility of objective knowledge. Postmodernism is sceptical of truth, unity and progress, opposes what it sees as elitism in culture, tends towards cultural relativism, and celebrates pluralism, discontinuity and heterogeneity.

— Eagleton, *After Theory*

Debates about the alleged differences between modernism and postmodernism depend upon shifting criteria and shifting interpretations of events and cultural productions. These debates are unlikely to be resolved. My own position is that analysis of the postmodern has to be undertaken as an analysis of the response to failure. The failure (or I should say alleged failure?) is that of modernity because so much which is wrong, counterproductive and reactionary has been done (or allegedly done) in its name. This rejection of totalizing theories because they have been harmful leads to a new form of totalizing called fragmentation. It is one of the paradoxes of our time and its consequences will be significant for the media, the arts and politics. It is one of the supreme ironies of our age that as fragmentation is the order of the day for some, totalizing theories are gaining ground in religion and politics, with capitalism as the system laying claim to universal validity.

This does not mean, however, that debates about issues related to postmodernity and postmodernism are not productive. The brief overview I have given of some trends in thinking about modernity and modernism can provide enough of a context for us to re-approach postmodernity and postmodernism. I will do this by first returning to the (postmodern) suggestion that we can no longer trust metanarratives which attempt to explain the way the world has developed or will develop. They key figure in putting forward this argument was Jean-Francois Lyotard, in his work *The Postmodern Condition*, first published in French in 1979 and in English in 1984. This work, the subtitle of which was *a report on knowledge*, gave careful consideration to what it was that constituted teaching and research. Lyotard refers to 'the game of producing scientific knowledge', which is part of what he called 'the dialectics of knowledge' (Lyotard, 1984: 25). Perhaps we should ask to what extent the production of knowledge in the field of media study is treated as a game. Many of the debates engendered by Lyotard derive from his readings of a host of other philosophers, from Kant to Wittgenstein. The point to note here is that postmodernity (if it exists) has arrived as the result of historical processes and did not just drop out of the sky as an idea for the end of the millennium. The insecurities (or, for some, liberation) which the attack on metanarratives has brought in its wake are much more apparent in identifiable characteristics associated with the arts and the media. It is to the qualities associated with postmodern media texts that I will now turn.

It cannot be much of a surprise to find out that writings on postmodernism offer just as wide a variety of definitions of its meaning as do those on modernism. This need not lead, however, to cynicism or despair. The plain fact is that postmodernism is a slippery issue and the lack of agreement about what it is ensures that debates in the field are unlikely to ossify for some time. Postmodern social theory also has a radical conceptualization of language, semiotics and theories of representation. Silenced and minority voices are more likely to be heard, according to the postmodern argument, as forms of essentialism are eroded. Various forms of feminism have been able, through cultural and media studies, to assert their presence, as have discourses about questions of identity in relation to ethnicities, sexual orientation and nationalisms. With one or two notable exceptions, however, the postmodern rejection of totalizing theory has meant that questions of class have somehow been relegated in importance or simply ignored.

Stefan Morawski has offered a persuasive set of characteristics associated with artistic postmodernism. They are as follows:

1. rejection of all emancipatory and Utopian aspirations;
2. palpable, even if not declared, conformity;
3. the denial of avant-garde faith in the development of art through the activity of the future-oriented elite;
4. the ostentatious turn towards mass culture with its laws of the market;
5. the return to figuration, narration and melody and in general to those components of the work of art that support close contact with the broadest public;
6. the eclecticism, quotation of old styles of art or masterpieces in order to indicate that the world of culture abounds with used signs and any presence of authentic novelty or originality will be a mystification;
7. hedonism consisting in the unpretentious pleasure of producing something which, according to the institutional rules, is still treated as a work of art and at the same time affording short-term joy and relaxation on the part of the recipient.

(Morawski, 1996: 5)

Here, for the first time, we can see some specific claims about the characteristics which could relate to media texts, and the values and principles upon which such texts are said to be built. With reference to social semiotics and discourse analysis, it is not too difficult to begin to translate these assertions into analytical procedures which can be tested in use. I am aware that what I have just quoted from Morawski is one of those interminable lists to which I referred earlier. I will, however, suggest that by exploring this particular list, many of the characteristics of the postmodern can be identified and utilized or rejected. Morawski is writing about what he calls artistic postmodernism, but it applies just as well to postmodernism and the media.

The claim that we live in an era when all emancipatory and utopian aspirations have been rejected follows on from the thinking of Lyotard. It is also provides the basis for an interpretation of the media which refuses to recognize any totalizing tendencies, whether they be ideological or economic. So Coca-Cola can be the 'real' thing from Singapore to Southend and Phoenix, though we cannot draw too many conclusions from its ubiquitous presence, because that might involve an act of totalization. Media monopolies may be interpreted with a postmodern hat on as the result of individual ambitions rather than any structural or political tendencies. At the same time, attempts to change the world may be deemed futile, leading to a proliferation of media texts concerned with cynical rejection of any aspirations (called plans by their opponents) for building a better world. From the absence of utopian aims, it is a short step towards artistic and political exhaustion. Morawski refers to a particular form of exhaustion as *the* constitutive feature of the artistic version of postmodernism:

Exhaustion is expressed in the stress on pastiche and parody, the collage of quotations, travesties, the idolatry of comic strips, the main strategy of satisfying the public's 'hunger for pictures', the absence of confrontative and rebel attitudes, the perverse mix of values, the collapse of the humanistic heritage, vibrant anti-elitism and an all-embracing eclecticism.

(Morawski, 1996: 12)

This rich sentence provides a set of assertions which could usefully be adapted to become research hypotheses. It is an interesting exercise to try to cite examples from the media to prove or disprove the various assertions made here. Even a cursory examination of media trends and aspects of representation suggests that Morawski's assertions are relevant to media students and researchers. A more sustained engagement with his ideas would reveal the potential profundity in the suggestion that postmodernity and philosophical, creative and political exhaustion are all closely related. Whether you as media student or researcher agree or disagree with this suggestion is not the main concern of this argument. What is important is that we recognize that debates about postmodernism have serious consequences for the way we interpret the world and the place of the media in that world. An alternative conceptual framework might suggest that postmodernism is hegemony dressed in very new and glamorous clothes. This is a matter for (your) argument.

Another important stylistic point about the postmodern text has been noted by the writer Charles Jencks in his discussion of architecture. He argues that there is, in postmodern architecture, a tendency to adopt multiple or double codings.

> To this day I would define Post-Modernism as I did in 1978 as double-coding: the combination of Modern techniques with something else (usually traditional building) in order for architecture to communicate with the public and a concerned minority, usually the architects. The point of this double coding was itself double. [. . .] an architecture that was professionally based and popular as well as one that was based on new techniques and old patterns. Double coding to simplify means both elite and popular and new/old and there are compelling reasons for these opposite pairings.
>
> (Jencks, 1986: 14)

Jencks is suggesting here that postmodernism provides an opportunity for popular and elite aspects of culture (or high and low, if you prefer) to come together in specific works of architecture. This can certainly be observed in many contemporary architectural examples. Whether that tells us anything of value depends upon our interpretation of the postmodern. We should remember that many modernists, whether in literature, the visual arts or music, drew upon the arts of the 'people' in their work. So how is postmodernism different? Is it because it refuses any tendency to totalize? Or is it, intentionally or not, a way of ensuring that elitism retains its power by allowing popular elements into the postmodern as a kind of gloss on conservative values which are still lurking in the discourses of media texts? This would be very much a postmodern irony, given the declared interest from many postmodern thinkers in the omnipresence of power in our societies. What Jencks does do is to provide a more formalized account of the ways in which postmodern eclecticism operates, through his concept of double coding. It can be argued that some postmodernist texts have made a move towards contact with a broader public. The controversial question is whether or not that move has retained a hierarchy of values and statuses associated with traditional elitist texts in the arts. When it comes to the popular arts, particularly film and television, these questions can be tested by making a variety of readings of specific media texts. We are also likely to generate more productive readings if we cease trying to prove that a specific text is either modern or postmodern, but concentrate first upon identifying its characteristics. The rest of this chapter will consider two examples of media texts which have been associated with the postmodern period or called postmodernist. In doing so I will be highlighting possible characteristic features of the postmodern which you might test out against a range of other texts and contexts.

Problems with the rule book

There is but one truly serious philosophical problem and that is suicide. Judging whether life is or is not worth living amounts to answering fundamental questions of philosophy.
— Albert Camus, *The Myth of Sisyphus*

The guy was not sick at all. And he left a note. He left a simple note that said, 'I've gone out the window.' And this is a major intellectual, and he leaves this note. 'I've gone out the window.' I mean, what the hell does that mean? This guy was a role model. You'd think he'd leave a decent note.
— Clifford Stern (Woody Allen) on the suicide of Professor Louis Levy in
Crimes and Misdemeanors

Woody Allen has been described by Norman K. Denzin as postmodern America's cinematic moralist (Denzin, 1991). Postmodern morality is either a pathetic oxymoron, or a way of describing the necessary contradictions which modernist thought leaves us to deal with. I want to consider here Allen's 1989 film, *Crimes and Misdemeanors*, and attempt to identify some of its narrative and other modes of signification. In order to do so, a brief reminder of the plot of this multilayered text is necessary.

Crimes and Misdemeanors is a film with two main storylines which cross each other and eventually combine as the film reaches its bleak, ironic and bittersweet conclusion. The first and lesser storyline is that of Clifford Stern (Woody Allen), an unsuccessful documentary film-maker, whose marriage is about to disintegrate and who falls in love with Halley (Mia Farrow), while reluctantly shooting a film about his brother-in-law, Lester. Lester is very successful and the mirror image of Clifford as an 'artist'. Clifford makes movies about toxic waste and leukaemia, though his dream is to complete his documentary about his philosophical mentor, Professor Louis Levy. Instead he has to shoot Lester as he pontificates about the quality of comedy ('If it bends, it's funny. If it breaks, it's not'). Clifford's feelings for Halley are not reciprocated, though she does appreciate his sincerity and hopes to help him complete his film about Professor Levy. Throughout *Crimes and Misdemeanors*, Clifford is in competition with Lester, particularly when Lester takes an interest in Halley. Professor Levy unexpectedly commits suicide, thus depriving Clifford of his mentor and the completion of his film. Halley then leaves to work in London for some months. Clifford does complete the film about Lester, for which Lester fires him. The film likens Lester to Mussolini and Francis the Talking Mule without any pretence at subtlety of montage. When Halley returns from London she meets Clifford (and the rest of the main characters in the film) at a wedding and announces that she has married Lester. By this time, Clifford's marriage has finally disintegrated. He is out of work and deeply disillusioned and perplexed by the behaviour of Halley. He sits in a quiet corner and has a significant conversation with the film's main protagonist, Judah (Martin Landau).

Judah Rosenthal is an ophthalmologist and the film makes much of metaphors around eyes (Is), seeing and blindness. Judah is very successful, married with grown-up children and a recalcitrant mistress, Dolores (Anjelica Houston). When the film begins, we first encounter Judah as the grateful, narcissistic recipient of a reward for his services to ophthalmology. We also encounter Dolores who has decided the time has come to confront Judah's wife with the fact that she has had a long-term affair with Judah. The situation quickly deteriorates, particularly when Dolores mentions, after a row with him, that Judah has illegally mismanaged or embezzled funds. She implies that she might make this public if he tries to rid himself of her. Judah first seeks counsel from his friend Ben, a rabbi who is steadily going blind. He then turns to his brother Jack, who is more pragmatic and less law-abiding. Jack says he knows people who can solve his problem for a fee. Judah is appalled at the idea that he might pay to have his mistress murdered, but it only takes one more crisis, when Dolores threatens to come to the house, for him to change his mind. The murder is arranged and carried out professionally with Jack's help, and Judah immediately enters a period of remorse, first visiting Dolores's flat, where he sees her dead, staring with wide-open eyes. Judah's remorse then takes him back to the house where he grew up. Here he imagines a family conversation about right and wrong, good and evil, as they sit around the meal table. Time passes. Judah begins to come to terms with his 'crime'. By the time he meets with Clifford at the end of the movie, it has become no more or less than a misdemeanour.

Judah and Clifford sit together at the wedding feast. Ben's daughter is marrying as Clifford's marriage is breaking up. Judah talks with Clifford about his profession as a film-maker. He offers him a possible plot for a 'perfect murder' film. It is, of course, a summary of Judah's journey from murder towards self-redemption. Clifford is not convinced by the plot and is left looking more isolated than ever. Judah goes happily with his wife and the rabbi, now completely blind, dances with his daughter as the orchestra plays 'I'll be Seeing You', over which we hear the voice of Professor Levy as he comments upon the importance of choice in the way we live.

This brief summary cannot do justice to the delicacy with which Allen manages to move from the comic to the serious to the tragicomic in the film. It has been described as a comedy of tragedies and this is not inaccurate. Allen is not a postmodernist film-maker, if such a creature exists. He is, however, one of the most significant narrators of the postmodern condition, and it is no joke. Yet the French writer Albert Camus seemed to be very much aware of many of these issues long before postmodernism came on the scene. The condition of postmodernity has always been one half of the Janus face of modernism. Without it, modernity would degenerate, as has sometimes occurred, into unquestioning dogma.

Part of the business of the media studies student would be to consider the ways in which Allen uses the language of film and the structures of narrative, and there is much to discuss. I will highlight, however, two moments in the film in order to illustrate the ways in which Allen demonstrates some central problems of philosophy, ethics and morality within the realms of popular culture and without patronization. The first example is from the imagined discussion which takes place in Judah's home. It is the time of the weekly Seder, and there is prayer, eating and talking. Judah, plagued by remorse over the murder of his mistress, watches this imagined conversation standing in the doorway. The argument around the table is very much rooted in debates about good and evil which relate to the Holocaust and the need for a moral and spiritual order in the world. The conversation is between Aunt May, Saul (Judah's father) and other guests.

Aunt May: You're afraid that if you don't obey the rules, God is going to punish you.

Saul: He won't punish me, May. He punishes the wicked.

Aunt May: Oh, who? Like Hitler?

Saul: How can you say that?

Aunt May: Six million Jews burned to death and he got away with it.

Saul: How did he get away with it? How?

Aunt May: Oh, come on, Saul. Open your eyes. Six million Jews and millions of others, and they got off with nothing.

Guest 1: How could human beings do such a thing?

Aunt May: Because might makes right. [. . .]

Guest 2: So what are you saying, May? You're saying that you challenge the whole moral structure of everything?

Aunt May: What moral structure? Is that the kind of nonsense you give your pupils?

Guest 2: Do you not find human impulses basically decent?

Aunt May: Basically nothing.

Saul: She's such a cynic my sister. A nihilist. Back to Russia!

[. . .]

Judah: And if a man commits a crime, if he kills?

Saul: Then one way or another he will be punished.

Guest 3: If he's caught, Saul.

Saul: If he's not caught, that which originates from a black deed will blossom in a foul manner.

[. . .]

Aunt May: And I say if he can do it and get away with it, and he's not bothered by the ethics, then he's home free. Remember, history is written by the winners.

This dramatic encapsulation of much philosophical discourse is handled with bleak humour and somehow balances mass murder with Judah's individual torment. The answer in both cases is that if you keep a cool head and don't get caught, the whole thing is of no further concern. Such a debate goes to the core of the dilemma of living in a period of postmodernity. Can one have rules of conduct if there is no bigger justification for such rules in the form of a metanarrative? The answer in the film's main narrative is a clear no, or a clear what does it matter? But there is still a thread of hope in the film in the form of the increasingly bathetic Clifford. It is about him that his sister says at the wedding reception: 'he's got this fantasy about changing the world. This is a man who makes films that come to nothing. They're nothing.' There is, however, a splendid irony in the fact that it is Woody Allen, not Clifford Stern, whose films have had a significant impact. It is an impact which is, however, fraught with contradiction. The main words of wisdom come from a fictional professor who takes his own life, leaving the message, 'I've gone out the window.' Allen insists that he did not model Professor Levy on Primo Levi, but the similarities are striking. The main point which comes from the film is that love does not always transcend all. Sometimes it simply grinds to a halt. Allen is caught in this postmodern trough. If Sisyphus had a stone to roll up a hill through eternity, Allen drags around New York the metaphorical weight of nostalgia for pleasures that were probably not that good even when he experienced them. He offers us an example of Morawski's postmodern exhausted artist. And yet there is the nagging sense that Allen has not reneged on the modernist project. He still does believe that the world can be changed, but not without a lot of complaining.

At the end of the film, we hear the voice of Professor Levy once again. Levy reminds us that we define ourselves by the choices we make. He speaks gently and with authority:

> Human happiness does not seem to have been included in the design of creation. It is only we with our capacity to love that give meaning to the indifferent universe. And yet most human beings seem to find joy from simple things like their family, their work, and from their hope that future generations might understand more.

Allen's profound construction of the era of postmodernity is insecure and sustained by a kind of dialectic between the forces of comedy, romance, beauty, despair and love. He gives little concern to any kind of socio-economic framework in his aesthetics, and is apparently blind to the social realities experienced by African-Americans. In relation to the former he adopts a silence which is characteristic of the era of postmodernity. It is another of the profound ironies of the period of postmodernity, that it celebrates superficiality, parody and rampant consumerism whilst turning its back on the structural organization and economic and social consequences of capitalism.

The postmodern mode of dress

horses f…ing

— Title on one of Benetton's web pages

My second example is of a corporate media text which relates to the postmodern: that of the Italian clothes manufacturer, Benetton. The advertising which has become associated with Benetton has been described by some as 'socially concerned'. John Hartley has gone so far as describing Benetton as 'the most passionate and public advocate of the philosophy of world integration, and not just at the commercial-sexual level' (Hartley, 1999: 10). It was certainly difficult to ignore the Benetton campaign over the last five years of the twentieth century, because it caused such controversy through its use of images. These included photographs of a newborn child, still attached to its umbilical cord; a pair of jeans and a blood-soaked T-shirt, which belonged to a victim of contemporary warfare; and the deathbed of an AIDS victim, with his family around him. These images were seen on enormous hoardings as well as in countless magazines. They became part of the media landscape of the late 1990s, and they are associated with the small green rectangle with the words 'United Colors of Benetton' written on it in white sans serif capitals. If the little green rectangle were removed from these images they would be utterly devoid of anchorage. We had to learn to become Benetton readers. A Benetton image speaks of a world which includes suffering and the potential for harmony. In this it could be seen to be aligned with the spirit of modernism. It is, of course, a world where both harmony and suffering only take on their full potential if that little green rectangle is to be seen in one corner of the image. Benetton speaks of the 'real' world in the same way that Coca-Cola is the real thing. Reality, in this case, is only recognizable in relation to a product.

What could be argued to be postmodern about the Benetton advertisements is that they evade the social, historical and economic specificity of the conditions from which they spring. They appear to be concerned, but at a level of generality which is politically anodyne. Sometimes they offer the potential for reactionary readings. The image of a black military figure standing with his back to us shows this unnamed and location-free individual with an automatic rifle on his shoulder and a bone (yes, it is human bone) held behind his back. A range of readings may be made of this image, but unless one is informed about world politics (or reads Benetton publicity about its publicity), one is unlikely to know where this person comes from, what he is doing or why he is carrying a human bone in his hands. The blood-soaked T-shirt belonged to someone called Marinko Gagro. From the Benetton website we could learn that this young man's father sent the jeans and T-shirt to Benetton. Mr Toscani, who had been mainly responsible for the image campaign associated with Benetton, wrote a letter to *Oslobodenje*, the independent daily in Sarajevo. In it he said:

> United Colors of Benetton is sending this message out to the world. Through the power of its advertising it doesn't wish to give answers but to provoke questions: about civilians, about children but also about dead soldiers. Because behind every soldier there is always a man with a story and feelings. Behind every broken life lies the responsability [*sic*] of the world which stands by, watching.

There is something potentially honourable in wanting people to ask questions about world politics. This is, indeed, an educational aim. But what do the manufacturers of Benetton products want to provoke questions about? Mr Toscani's letter reduces that vast complexity of human interaction at the level of the economic, the political and the social to a single phenomenon called simply 'the world'. The world, it seems, stands by and watches as it destroys itself. Put another way, it might imply that the world of which Mr Toscani speaks is, in fact, suicidal. Those who are killed and the killers are all part of the same visual display. And a visual display is what Benetton offered. Its communication policy was based around producing 'images of global concern'. It said it did not show us 'a fictitious reality in which you will be irresistible if you make use of our products'. It said that it is important for companies to take a stance in the real world, 'instead of using the advertising myth that they can make purchasers happy through the mere purchase of their product'. What it ignores is that images can only make discursive and political sense if and when they are structured into frameworks of meaning. Unanchored signification means everything and nothing. Blood-soaked T-shirts and newborn babies signify in the realms of myth in the Barthesian sense (Barthes, 1972). They have been deprived of their history, of the ideological dimensions of their existence. Instead, the world stands accused through a tautologous and emotive lament. I am referring here to the letter sent by Mr Toscani. The casual or everyday observer of Benetton advertisements, however, has only the little green rectangle as a semiotic stabilizing factor.

The seriousness of the Benetton advertising campaign was unfocused and inarticulate. For Benetton, social issues were important, but mainly through reference to their universal implications. 'Universal' in this context allowed mushy thinking to stand in for serious analysis. While celebrating 'difference' in their localized, multicultural campaigns, that difference was actually a difference in the colours of Benetton garments. Beyond that rainbow coalition of sartorial elegance, there was little to be said until we reached the lofty heights of the Declaration of Human Rights which topped Benetton's web page over the generic title: 'What We Say'. In that enormous discursive and representational chasm we would find, if we looked, the world of politics and power, of economics and technological change. In relation to these, Benetton (and the rest of us) do have to come up with some answers. The postmodern dimension of Benetton was identifiable through its tendency to sentimentalize solidarity and to ogle (seriously) at conflict. In its controversial web opinion pages, it mentioned the divided opinion over its posters of two horses copulating, or may we dare to complete Benetton's tacky modesty and say fucking. Two opinions were quoted. The first was from someone outraged at what they saw as animal pornography. The second was from someone who wanted to know where it might be possible to get hold of a copy of the picture. The second comment appears under the title 'horses f…ing'. This simple title encapsulates the politics of Benetton. It is lurid where it is safe and prudish where it should speak out plainly. In short, it is the discourse of p…modernism. Since the departure of Mr Toscani, the website and the advertising campaigns of Benetton have changed. The question is, precisely, how?

Postmodernism and media studies

Many other examples of alleged or putative postmodern media texts could be cited. Some may find my choice of examples to highlight characteristics of the postmodern to be quirky. They are, of course. Postmodernism has become the means by which a certain insecurity can be recognized through the identification of recurrent traits in the processes of signification. These traits are multiple and can be intellectually productive. At the same time they can also facilitate a form of analysis which denies or evades material political conditions. In a sense, the main purpose which postmodernism has served has been to require those with a mind to do so to question what they mean by modern and modernity. For some this has meant that they have been able to identify what they see as the partial or total failure of the project of modernity. For others it has led to a reappraisal of a project which they do not see as moribund, but in need of a drastic overhaul. For the media studies student who wishes to engage critically with the concept of the postmodern, there is a different problem. It requires the development of modes of analysis which try to make some kind of sense of the frenetic and omnipresent simulacra which apparently constitute the postmodern moment. A simulacrum is an image which, in turn refers to another image, and so on. Simulacra remove the possibility of a referent for those who embrace the term uncritically. So images offer meaning in relation to other images. John Frow has noted:

> If I think postmodernism means Olson and Heissenbuttel and Pynchon and catastrophe theory, and you think it means MTV, fashion advertisements, political sound-bites, and the excremental vision, and someone else thinks it's hypertext, *trompe-l'oeil* facades, 'Oprah', and *Blue Velvet*, then we're probably talking right past each other, since the definition of the concept shifts with the concepts taken to exemplify it. This is to say that the concept cannot be thought as the representation of a given field of cultural production, or of a tendency within this field; it is rather the embattled attempt to *construct* the unity of such a field or tendency.
>
> (Frow, 1997: 27)

The main challenge offered by the concept of postmodernism for the media studies student and researcher is that it invites a debate for which there will be no easy or final conclusion. Postmodern media texts open the door to the celebration of consumerism and liberation from the constraints of various forms of totalitarianism. At the same time, postmodernity is a period of intense insecurity. In its denial of totalizing theory, it is prone to a new totalitarianism which is insistent upon fragmentation and difference. Political solidarity does not sit happily beside the postmodern.

Postmodernism also invites the media student to celebrate the everyday and the mundane. The pleasures of postmodern nostalgia are, however, only a melody away from the terrors of *Blue Velvet* and the recognition of the underworld of normality. Here, postmodernism means the absence of fixed points of reference, whether in relation to the aesthetic or the ethical. In the postmodern everyday underworld, the unthinkable is thought and articulated in the form of sadomasochistic narcissism. The audiences for this facet of postmodernism are allowed to wallow in the pleasure of pain, sexual humiliation, easy death. These phenomena are detectable in the popular work of Quentin Tarantino, as well as the work of David Lynch. They are also not far from the core considerations of the late Foucault (Miller, 1993). Postmodernism is, considered in this way, a potential indicator of a crisis in modernity. It also offers revealing insights into the human condition which have a lineage which goes back to the mean-minded pessimism of Schopenhauer, the hideous intensity of Nietzsche and the Spartan austerity of Albert Camus. Before the term postmodernism is used with impunity, it is wise to consider some of these thinkers in more depth.

I have not attempted, in this chapter, consideration of the extraordinary number of publications which have, in one way or another, included reference to postmodernism and the media. I have presumed to suggest, however, that there are some underlying issues which need to be addressed in relation to postmodernism, postmodernity and media studies. I am painfully aware that what I have suggested is no more than a beginning. My choice of Woody Allen and Benetton as examples was deliberate and serves to locate my interest in postmodernism and the media in particular ways. I will end with a final quotation from Morawski. Here he summarizes his relationship with postmodernism, and it might usefully offer a direction for any student of the media:

. . . I am far from maintaining that postmodernism has no merits; it does because it reinforces and deepens self-critical awareness of the shortcomings and mistakes of modernism. It gives new vigour to metaphilosophy; refreshes the knowledge that art is animated by archetypes and *topoi*; turns attention to mass culture (the strata of which have to be examined without prejudice and preconception); adds new incentives to reflections on the status of science; denounces intellectual pundits who thought they were the only signposts of wisdom. But on the whole I appreciate it as a negative adventure because of its obedience to the status quo. I am mentally goaded by its challenge. I disapprove of the intellectual dance around the New Idols, the dance which throws aside all foundations and worships victorious consumerism, and hence I cannot be a silent observer of the new cultural mutation.

(Morawski, 1996: 120)

How a media studies student or researcher relates to matters concerned with modernity and postmodernity will have a considerable impact upon their intellectual work. It will also bring to the fore questions about relations between the media and the real world. Such questions will then lead to another set of debates about the nature of realism. It is to these that I will now turn.

FURTHER READING

Anderson, P., 1998, *The Origins of Postmodernity*.
This is an intellectually sparkling account of the origins of postmodernity, centring on the work of Frederic Jameson. It is best read after Kellner and Eagleton.

Best, S. and Kellner, D., 2001, *The Postmodern Adventure*.
Best and Kellner offer an exploration of questions of theory, politics and identity. They do this through an analysis of a wide range of literary and media texts. Their approach to postmodernism is critical but not hostile.

Eagleton, T., 2003, *After Theory*.
Eagleton's recent work is both a summation of his uneasiness in the face of postmodernism and occasionally a searing critique. It is also a challenge for the future, as Eagleton argues that we must break out of certain orthodoxies in the fields of media and cultural studies – including simply recounting again and again the narratives of class, race and gender.

Jameson, F., 1991, *Postmodernism of the Cultural Logic of Late Capitalism*.
This is something of a founding work in our understanding of postmodernism and its relationships with the capitalism from which it grew. Chapter two is concerned with theories of the postmodern and is one we should all read more than once.

chapter five

Realism

There is not one, but several realisms. Each era looks for its own, that is to say the technique and the aesthetic which can best capture it, arrest and restore whatever one wishes to capture of reality.

— Williams, *Realism and the Cinema*

Verisimilitude: the appearance or semblance of truth or reality; quality of seeming true.
— *Collins English Dictionary*

But important though it might be, fidelity to visual reality was only one aspect of the Realist enterprise; and it would be erroneous to base our conception of so complex a movement on only one of its features: verisimilitude.

— Nochlin, *Realism*

Why realism?

In the previous chapter I considered some of the characteristics of postmodernism and postmodernity. I pointed out that there is a reluctance amongst those who would see themselves as postmodernists to accept big explanations (or grand narratives) about the world. Through consideration of Woody Allen's *Crimes and Misdemeanors,* I noted that all kinds of (postmodern) judgements, especially those concerned with ethics and morality, may be deemed a matter of choice. There are no big explanations or justifications to offer solace or guidance. This has considerable impact, if taken seriously, on the way we make sense of the media, and indeed on the way the media may make sense of the real world. I use this term real without any scare quotes because I happen to believe that there is a real, material world which exists whether I enter a discourse about it or not. But there are those who would point out, with some justification, that I cannot talk about this world which I call real without entering one or another realm of discourse.

There is also a persuasive argument that the material world is sometimes changed, structured, moulded by the ways in which we describe it. Within limits, this may be the case. I cannot change the shape of a house by talking about it, but I can change the perception of that house quite radically if I can convince my audience that the house is haunted, or that it has been the home of a serial killer. The emphasis here is on convincing and does not depend upon whether what I represent to my audience is known to be the case. When we talk about the world, or re-present the world, we do so, usually, in order to make the world real. Whether we are documentarists, feature film-makers, journalists or writers of soap opera, questions of reality and realism will never be far from the surface. The coming of the new technologies, simulators and computer games has complicated the question even more by facilitating the introduction of something called virtual reality. I will return to this concept in chapter eleven. In this chapter, I want to raise some questions which are still very much at the core of media representation of the world – questions about realism. I argue here that realism in the media involves conventions with rules which have to be followed. Furthermore it is a mode of representation which is far from passé, and which is alive and well in contemporary media, particularly movies and television.

The literature relating to questions of realism is weighty and ranges from philosophical approaches to a consideration of questions of aesthetics and politics. As students of the media we will notice that what was once thought of as gritty realism can seem, with the passing of time, to be somewhat staged and conventional, and occasionally rather quaint. The conventions adopted by realism may vary from medium to medium and era to era, but there are some features of realism that tend to persist.

I will be concentrating, in this chapter, on realism in film and television, though I take my first example from the history of painting. The question of what constituted a realist text, whether it was in the form of a painting, a story or a film, was never easy to pin down, even for those who had a generally agreed sense in a given society of what 'reality' was. There is no better guide to the fluctuations and changes through which the conventions of realism evolved than the history of Western painting. If we consider some of the imagery generated by the painters around the period of the Italian Renaissance, we quickly find that, even if there was only supposed to be one 'real' world, it could be painted in several different ways. First, there was the realism associated with the material world. This demanded that the representation produced by the painter seemed 'true' to the audience. But because there has always been more than one interpretation of truth, there has always been more than one kind of realism. Painters of the Sienese School, such as Simone Martini, tended to offer an image of the material world which was gilded, often literally so. Their work was decorative, and seldom represented anything of the textures and blemishes of material existence. Their strength lay in the representation of opulence, or in a material reality which seemed remarkably spiritual. Hence the crucifixions associated with such painters have an air of other-worldliness about them. The Florentines, on the other hand, were much more inclined towards the drama of human existence as manifested in the play of light and shade, the tactile qualities of everyday life, gesture, facial expression and body language. The well-known Roman painter Caravaggio represented the Christ figure as all too human, in stark contrast to more formalized and gentle images, such as those of Fra Angelico. Yet they were both after capturing a sense of reality. Caravaggio's realism is based, first, upon what can be seen. Fra Angelico's realism is based first upon what can be understood. Both produce images which are based upon sources in the material world. Both painters had to look at human rather than

Figure 5.1 Caravaggio (1573–1610), detail from the *Entombment of Christ*, Vatican Museum, Rome

divine models to produce their images. Yet what they saw was very much conditioned by the way they felt about their subject matter, and the ways in which they related to their particular societies.

What this means is that, for all forms of realism, there has to be something beyond the text against which its claims to truth (relative or absolute) can be measured. This task of interpreting the real is one which has been faced by painters, writers and, more recently, by film-makers and television producers. The conventions of realism have grown from the act of interpreting the world from which different realisms have developed. There are those who would say that this may have been the case with painters, but that it is different once the camera becomes involved. The camera, they say, does not lie. You just point it and you are bound to produce a realistic image. From the beginnings of cinema in the late nineteenth century, when the Lumière brothers showed their short sequences of 'real-life' action to an audience in the Grand Café in Paris, to the inventive tableaux and mini-narratives of Georges

Figure 5.2 Fra Angelico (*c.* 1400–45), detail from the *Deposition,* Museo di San Marco, Florence

Méliès, the concern was with verisimilitude – believability. It quickly became clear, however, that the referent on which the realist text depended might itself be open to question. Films with realist aspirations could be made about subjects which were known to be fictional or mythical. However, whether one is representing hell or heaven, a fairyland or a city under the sea, the issue of realism is still important. The audience for the mass media will judge what they see and hear on the basis of a shared concept of verisimilitude. Some forms of realism, it seems, are based upon what we think would be believable if we believed that what was being filmed actually existed outside the world of the film!

The contradiction at the heart of realism is that it has to put forward the same truth claims, whether it is representing the material world or another which is either fictional or unsubstantiated by anything other than faith. Whether a film is a narrative about the Second World War or *The War of the Worlds* or *Paradise Lost*, the key to its realism remains with its believability. The producer of the realist text also has to apply similar criteria to the production, irrespective of whether or not he or she believes that the world represented in the text actually exists. There are also other forms of realism which are concerned with unambiguously showing the world as it is. Such forms originated in the literature and painting of nineteenth-century Europe (Nochlin, 1978). Today, similar forms of realism would include some documentary, news and current affairs programmes. Such forms tend to be based upon a notion of realism which does not depend upon mediation as much as a claim to provide accurate reproduction. They presume that the reality of a given subject or scene will shine through if it is represented with what they see as total accuracy, fidelity, honesty.

The third major category of realism is that which purports to be part of reality rather than a re-presentation of it. I will be discussing the ways in which television has developed this genre as 'reality television'. It is one of the ironies of our time that, as many critics and thinkers have noted, claims to realism in the media have come to the fore as doubts about the reliability or even the existence of that same reality have multiplied. For the moment, it is sufficient to note that there is not one approach or technique called realism which is either applied or not applied in the media. There are realisms, and they are all based upon conventions requiring specific media practices through which we, the audience, make sense of them, and then of the world(s) to which they refer.

What are the formal qualities or conventions associated with realism?

For the realist who wants to show their audience the world 'as it really is', the suggestion that realism is a convention can be a little disarming. There are two points to note here. The first is that all communication relies upon conventions of one kind or another if any communication at all is to take place. Once we recognize that realism in the arts and communications processes cannot be other than a re-presentation, this is hardly surprising. We are then faced with a number of decisions, both technical and philosophical, about how best we can use our chosen approach to realism to represent the world. The second point is that, in the fields of photography, film and video, pictorial representation has come closer than at any other time to a concept of the real as that which can be recognized through simply showing the phenomenal form. The lens, and the way it records images on film, videotape or digitally, allows for a reproduction of its subject matter which is, apparently without any intervention of the kind necessitated by a brush or a piece of charcoal. It provides an image without a code, or so it seems (Barthes, 1977: 16–31). The two-dimensional reproduction of the human form and other aspects of the material world have certainly never been as consistently and accurately proportioned as when observed by and reproduced through the photographic lens. The point to note is that the lens through which we observe the world has something called a focal length. The focal length of a lens both determines how wide or concentrated our angle of vision might be and, in conjunction with the lens aperture (size of the hole letting in light), dictates how much of the image is in focus. A telephoto lens, for instance, operates rather like a telescope and has a very small depth of field. Hence the focusing is critical in telephoto shots. A wide-angle lens has a large depth of field, so it not only shows a broad view of its subject matter, but also provides an image where everything is in crisp focus.

The lens which we have come to think of as normal is one with a focal length which is most closely related, in an everyday sense, to the way we think we see things. It is neither a telephoto nor a wide-angle lens. Yet this 'normal' lens is very selective indeed and is very inadequate when it comes to something like peripheral vision. The very fact that photographs and film and television screens are usually rectangular should tell us something about the problem with what has been called photographic realism. Seeing things through rectangles or the pillbox of the contemporary cinema is an acquired skill, and a convention.

Realism is not only about the observation of the visual world. It is also about the selection of what is observed and then represented. The worlds of fiction and drama present even more interesting and complex possibilities for media producers. They have to face the challenge of deciding whether our understanding of realism is that it is something contrasted to the imaginary, or whether realism is something which should be contrasted with the already experienced. If we have already experienced something (such as skydiving, for instance), this will have happened in one of two ways. Either it will have been a part of our everyday life in the world (we will have jumped out of an aircraft), or it may have been part of our previous media experience (we will have seen one or more films of people jumping out of aircraft). If it is the latter, we actually build our understanding of realism on references to other realist texts rather than the real world. It is only a short step from here to believing that representations *are* the real world.

Another approach to media realism would argue that it has to depend as much upon understanding as upon the faithful rendition of surface appearances. To give just one example, it may be argued that it is not possible to grasp the 'reality' (now I have put some scare quotes around the term) of a war simply by showing men in the trenches. It may be necessary to show the munitions manufacturers who gain from the war, and the bereaved of our own side and that of our enemy, and people living ordinary lives in places untouched by war. It is not, by this argument, susceptible to easy or surface representation. Realism then requires a multi-layered approach to its subject matter and has to be prepared to juxtapose representations in order to achieve a new kind of verisimilitude. In film and television language, this would require the use of montage. Montage allows the juxtaposition of images and sounds in such a way as to provide meanings which neither the images nor the sounds would offer if seen or heard separately. If montage provides a realism, it is a realism of understanding through association. The classic realist text provides a world where understanding depends almost entirely upon narrative structure.

The fact that it is possible to approach realism from more than one epistemological or ontological position is of crucial importance. What it means is that there is much more debate still to be had about the place and purpose of realism in the media. It also suggests that the realist text can take many forms, whether it purports to deal with a fictional or a non-fictional subject.

Recognizing realism

It is important to formulate questions about what constitutes the main features of the realist narrative and what constitutes realist acting and other aspects of the production, such as the décor and lighting. The main vehicle of realism in popular culture in the years after the First World War was cinema, most notably through the feature film. More recently, television has shared this role, though we should not forget that radio is also a medium which offers fictional and other realisms. In the cinema, the realist film came in various guises, from the Italian neo-realist cinema (Bondanella, 2001) through to *film noir* (Selby, 1984) and classical Hollywood cinema (Bordwell and Thompson, 2003).

The realist text (including the realist film) required a sense of what might be called internal coherence – everything from the way the action of the film unfolds to the acting, dialogue and general plausibility, which includes temporal continuity. In the cinema, there are formal qualities associated with the realist text which derive from techniques involving the use of the camera, editing and sound. I have already mentioned how we have become accustomed to treat normal cinematic vision as a view through a specific or 'normal' lens. There have also been debates, again associated with French writer and critic Bazin, about the importance to the realist text of deep-focus lenses. For Bazin, at least, being able to allow one's eye to roam around the image because it is all in focus gives viewers more chance to explore and hence discover the reality before them. In order to do this, a strong argument is made for the importance of the long take in a realist film (Bordwell *et al.* 1985). Many of the earliest 'realist' films were produced by setting up a camera in a static position and then letting whatever was happening pass in front of the lens. There would be only one long shot. It was when two shots could be joined together that the concept of editing was born.

Realism and editing

Editing allowed the film-maker to structure what was being produced with considerable care, to join shots together to make the action flow with apparent naturalness. I will be discussing editing in more detail in chapter eleven. The type of editing most commonly associated with realism is called continuity editing. The main function of continuity editing is to be invisible. That is to say, it is designed as a practice to facilitate the transition from action to action or location to location without jarring or even reminding the spectator that it is occurring. There are specific rules involved in continuity editing which are acquired by us all as viewers, however informally, and which allow us all to 'read' a film without having to reflect upon the way we are doing it. A film sequence may begin with an establishing shot, taken from some distance, then move to a mid-shot where we may see in more detail the two main characters. This may be followed by close-up shots of the two characters as they speak to each other, and cut back and forth until once again we see them at more of a distance. The variations on this basic cutting pattern have been many, but the core structure remains. There are other patterns of editing which repeat themselves in the realist text, and there are certain rules about what should not be done, such as crossing the line and making jump cuts (see chapter eleven and Hayward, 1996: 257).

Defenders of classical realism would say that the invisibility or seamless quality of the editing allows us to be swept along, sucked in by the power of the text. Critics of realism would say that this is precisely the problem – realism induces a false sense of security, at the level of plot, *mise-en-scène*, lighting, acting, shooting and editing (Hayward, 1996: 220). A still significant debate, the backwash of which occasionally ripples around academia, was introduced by Colin MacCabe (1974). He suggested that the main problem with realism was that it could never treat the real as contradictory, because the realist text is organized in a strict hierarchy of discourses, privileging some over others. This hierarchy, MacCabe argued, was ordered in such a way that the narration of a story 'spoke' from a position of unquestioned and possibly unquestionable authority. He also argued that such a text positioned us in particular ways. The realist text was a means whereby ideological domination could be exerted through fiction. David Bordwell (Bordwell *et al.*, 1985) suggested that MacCabe was wrong because he ignored the ways in which we negotiated meaning in a form of dialogue with the text. MacCabe has since modified his position, but the possibility that realist texts might, in some way, carry within them epistemological implications has never been satisfactorily resolved. What we can say is that texts are designed to position audiences (you and me) and that the success with which they do this depends upon the relationship which we strike up with them.

For the Italian neorealist, Rossellini, for instance, realism was precisely designed to make people think. It was a way of opening doors rather than closing them. It is clear that he and MacCabe were speaking of different conventions of realism, with apparently different modes of signification and different intentions. Once again we are reminded that there is not one realism, but that there are realisms with sometimes overlapping and sometimes differing conventions.

Some conventions of realism can best be illustrated by reference to examples. I will first discuss here two films which, in their own time have been seen as realist. I am not concerned here with any detailed critique of the films, but rather with highlighting aspects of their structure, content or form which demonstrate the ways in which the realist cinematic text adopts conventions which appear, disappear and sometimes change over time. These very conventions, in relation to the realist film form, require that there is structure in what is made. There has to be a beginning, a middle and an end; there have to be crescendos, diminuendos and the occasional arpeggios in filmic and dramatic terms. Above all, there has to be an ending, or the promise of an ending. So the realist text is modulated somewhat like a piece of music and the audience is likely to recognize these structural and structured compositions on which the verisimilitude of the movie may hang. Much of this structure depends upon narrative. There will also be a plot, acting and dialogue. The latter two have undergone interesting transformations over the years. Ideas of what constitutes a realist dialogue have produced a whole range of writing and acting, even in relation to almost identical subject matter. Some writers and directors have gone to great lengths to reproduce believable speech patterns, codes of dress and even body language which they consider realist. Others have produced a number of different techniques designed to bring the audience nearer to (illusory) reality, including the use of carefully modulated lighting or no lighting at all except that to be found in the chosen location. What will be clear, as we now consider two brief examples, is that realism, while dependent in part upon verisimilitude, is also dependent upon creating, sustaining or challenging the audience's understanding of the world being represented. It is not necessary to agree with what a text offers in terms of dialogue, acting and so on, in order to accept it as realist. The irony is that realism is often most persuasive when any superficial criteria ('that really looks like a battlefield') are transcended by those which are more complex ('after the film, you knew much more about the nature of warfare and those in whose interests it is pursued') and not dependent only upon surface appearances. This is not to denigrate the majestic efforts which some film-makers have made to simulate forms of reality. It is, however, to suggest that there is a realism of the surface and a realism of depth. The former is based upon looks and sounds in the main. The latter is based on developing understanding.

Two films and a changing realism

The films I will now discuss have been chosen because each, in a different way, is concerned with employment. Each offers a different perspective on its chosen subject matter, and does so utilizing different approaches to the 'real'.

On the Waterfront (Columbia Films, 1954)

On the Waterfront was directed by Elia Kazan and written by Budd Schulberg. It tells a tale of corruption and courage on the New York docks. Marlon Brando's performance remains a benchmark against which young male actors, with aspirations to play the tough but sensitive working-class hero, have to measure themselves. The black-and-white imagery of the film adds to the weightiness of the topic: that of corrupt trades unions terrorizing their members into submission. Brando plays Terry Molloy, a young man of no formal education whose main aim in life had been to box. This he had done, but because of the crooked company in which he was trained, he was forced to throw important fights and ended up just hanging around the docks, working occasionally. His brother, Charley Molloy (Rod Steiger) has had some education, is involved with the union corruption and wears expensive suits to prove it.

The detail of the *mise-en-scène* is very unlike the conventional studio set. We see buildings with flaking paint, docksides with dirty streets, parks enveloped in mist and pollution. The clothes of the main characters are very much of the 1950s, and they are chosen to represent the working-class docker or the corrupt union worker. There is, in the general approach to the subject, an element of naturalism – a wish to show things as they are (or were). The conventions of realism also extend to the physiognomy of the main characters. The worker of 1950 is represented in a way which the worker of 1940 or 1990 is not. There are usually particular modes of emphasis to be found in the ways in which actors are encouraged to stand, walk or speak. The extent to which these characterizations represent actual conditions and behaviour is not as significant as the fact that they were or are acceptable to the audience. The impact of the film at the time of its initial distribution is likely to be somewhat different from the way it might be received now. This is not simply because union corruption or conditions of employment for dockers have changed. It is also because the world in which a realist text is produced is one of the most influential factors determining how its realism is structured and received. In the 1950s, for instance, it would have been unthinkable to use the kind of language which is common in contemporary films dealing with working-class life. Yet it seemed possible for Schulberg to capture something of the necessary speech patterns using what is really little more than a metaphoric representation. The relative verbosity of some of the main characters is also something which is more conventional than real. In the realist text, people make speeches, have dramatic interchanges, share dramatic pauses in ways which are hardly recognizable in everyday 'real' life.

One of the most memorable scenes in the history of Hollywood cinema takes place in the back of a taxi when Charley (Steiger) tries to get Terry (Brando) to go along with the union corruption and reap the rewards for keeping his mouth shut. Much of the power of the film's realism comes from the dialogue, and I quote a small part of it here.

> TERRY: Gee, Charley, I'm sure glad you stopped by for me. I needed to talk to you. What's it they say about blood, it's – ? *(Falters)*
> CHARLEY: *(Looking away coldly)* Thicker than water.
> DRIVER: *(Gravel voice, without turning around)* Where to?
> CHARLEY: Four thirty-seven River Street.
> TERRY: River Street? I thought we was going to the Garden.
> CHARLEY: I've got to cover a bet there on the way over. Anyway, it gives us a chance to talk.
> TERRY: *(Good-naturedly)* Nothing ever stops you from talking, Charley.
> CHARLEY: The grapevine says you picked up a subpoena.
> TERRY: *(Non-commital, sullen)* That's right . . .
> CHARLEY: *(Watching for his reaction)* Of course, the boys know you too well to mark you down for a cheese-eater.
> TERRY: Mm – hmm.
> CHARLEY: You know the boys are getting rather interested in your future.

The dialogue in this film still retains its dramatic power in the context of the film's plot. It is, however, rather tame by the standards of contemporary realism. It is interesting, for instance to compare it with any number of scenes from the TV series *The Sopranos* (http://www.sopranoland.com/). This does not mean that the film is somehow deficient. It merely illustrates the significance of changing conventions in the cinema. Some would argue that the film has gained in power as its claims to realism have become less important. Yet it has to be stressed that when the film appeared in the 1950s, its apparent realism was revealing and shocking. Now it appears to fit into a history of theatre and dramatic performance which is explicable in relation to the particular training of the actors as much as the social realities which they attempted to recreate. The writing of dialogue for the realist text is something which often works to give structure where none may have existed, to give poetry where there may have been banality, to provide dignity where there may have been drabness.

What is also significant, and this is the case with all realist texts, is the way in which the realism that has been created relates to the context in which it has grown. *On the Waterfront*, and the films of Kazan, take on a rather different hue when viewed with this in mind. If we know that the director, Elia Kazan, and the writer, Budd Schulberg, had both been members of the Communist Party of the USA in their earlier years, and had both turned their backs on their former allegiance, we might ask further questions about the intentions of the film. If we know that Kazan, after leaving the Communist Party, had taken out a newspaper advertisement encouraging fellow professionals to inform on known Communists and their sympathizers, it may make us consider the film's realism differently. For in this film, Marlon Brando decides, as a result of his brother's murder, to inform on the corrupt union bosses. His struggle is celebrated through the narrative structure of the film. Informing here may, without too much difficulty, be equated with informing at the time of the Hollywood blacklist. Brando is a hero and Kazan (with Schulberg) has made an indirect statement about his own relationship with the Communist Party. Whether it is honourable or just to equate informing on union corruption and informing on Communist film-makers is another matter for serious discussion and analysis. What is clear is that realism makes use of narrative conventions which allow the producer of the text to say (or imply) much more than any simplistic notion of realism might suggest. It is hard to find a realist text of any worth which is not saying more than a simple summary of its contents might imply. In this sense, realism and ideology walk hand in hand.

The Full Monty (Channel 4 Films, 1987): stripping away the politics, putting on the style

The Full Monty was written by Simon Beaufoy and directed by Peter Cattaneo. It was a major commercial success. The film tells the story of a group of unemployed men in the town of Sheffield in England. Sheffield was once the centre of steel production in the UK, but the film shows a rundown city with deserted or derelict streets and a bleak industrial landscape. The film is a comedy of some considerable merit, centring on the struggle of a group of unemployed men to find a way of raising some money. In doing so they also bring some sense of fun into their lives. They are inspired, by the visit to Sheffield of a group of male strippers, to offer their own show where they will strip in front of an audience composed mainly of local women. In order to do this, they have to do a considerable amount of rehearsing and obtain suitable costumes for the one performance. They also have to overcome their doubts about the wisdom of such a rash act for a one-off payment from the entry fees paid by the audience. There are some sub-plots, which include a budding gay relationship between two of the men, another man who is overweight and losing his sense of masculine identity (and hence virility), and another who has been made redundant from a management position and has hidden the fact from his wife for months. The hero of the film (Gary) is played by Robert Carlyle, who has an added impetus to earn some money, because he is behind with support payments for his son and in danger of losing all visiting rights.

In order to tell its tale, the film has to build a world which is both accessible and understandable to the viewing public. It does this, first, through the employment of a series of realist strategies. These include the choice of locations which signify industrial malaise, including a working man's club and various deserted warehouses. We are also shown a panoramic view of parts of Sheffield, and the selective choices involved in the process of building this media text provide a very particular image of the city. The reaction to this image of Sheffield from those who live there has been interesting. Some have complained that the film shows a rundown environment which does not reflect the development which has now taken place in the new Sheffield. Others find the city to be represented most convincingly. The realism of *The Full Monty* was not uniformly accepted. This suggests that the concept of realism is dependent often upon subjective interpretation of a set of conventions. The film offers us a view (or vision) of a rundown working-class community, plagued by unemployment. The imagery it uses is chosen carefully, but it could be argued that much of the film's realism is a realism of appearances. Where the film deals with personal feelings, the personal interactions of characters and the problems they encounter, there is a strong tendency for it to romanticize its subject matter.

Here we can see how realism may become the vehicle, wittingly or not, for the signification of a host of messages and connotations which somehow ride on the back of realist conventions. We can see the sad walk of the unemployed male, the interior of a council flat with its sparse furniture and cold décor. We can also see and hear the streets of a housing estate. But when it comes to the actions of people, two interesting things occur. First, the characters do not move in real time through their temporal and spatial existence. They appear in scenes. For realism comes to us, at least in film and television, in manageable, linked chunks of representation. These chunks are crafted together in order to convince us that it is possible to make sense of that which we see and that which has occurred but we have not seen. This form of realism asks us to fill in many gaps. Of course, we may have to do this in our own lives, simply because we are not omniscient and omnipresent. Second, the difference between lived existence and the realist text is that the latter gives us so much guidance. Lived existence is very often random, unstructured, without apparent purpose. Existence in the realist text is structured, timed, scripted. I will consider now a key scene from *The Full Monty* which illustrates most of the points I have been arguing, particularly in relation to realism and romanticism, realism and structure, and realism and guidance.

The scene occurs early in the film when Gary and Dave (Mark Addy) are out jogging in order to get in condition for their planned performance. They pass a parked car on the hillside. It has its bonnet (hood) up and we hear the sounds of the driver attempting to start the engine. Dave breaks off from his breathless jog and looks under the bonnet, quickly sorting out the problem so that the engine turns over and the car starts. He speaks briefly with the taciturn driver, recognizing him as once having worked in the same place as him and Gary. The driver does not speak as Dave asks him if he has any work, nor does he thank Dave for his help. It is only when he has rejoined Gary that Dave realizes that the man in the car has connected the exhaust to the interior of the car and is attempting suicide. Dave rushes back down the hill and yanks the man, Lomper, from the car. When Lomper shows little gratitude, Dave shoves him back into the car and slams the door on him. The scene ends with Lomper banging on the window to be released. The dialogue in the next scene is as follows:

Dave: You could shoot yourself.
Gary: Where's he gonna find a gun from round here?
    You wanna find yourself a big bridge you do.
Dave: Yeh, like one of them bungee jumps, only without the bungee bit.
Lomper: I can't stand heights.
Dave: Drowning. Now there's a way to go.
Lomper: I can't swim.
Gary: You don't have to fucking swim you divvy, that's the whole point.

Lomper: Sorry.

Dave: I know. You could stand in the middle of the road and get a mate to drive smack into you right fast.

Lomper: I haven't got any mates.

Gary: Listen, we just saved your fucking life, so don't tell us we're not your mates, alright?

Lomper: Really?

Dave: Yeh, me and all. I'd run you down, soon as look at you.

Lomper: Oh cheers! Ta. Thanks a lot.

The scene is composed mainly of close-ups of the three characters. There is also a view of the out-of-focus Sheffield cityscape with the three figures (arranged carefully for the shot to make it look real, and strangely reminiscent of the studied repose of Seurat's *Bathers*) in the foreground. At this point, the film enters what might be described as a lyrical realist mode. There is extra-diegetic music playing softly in the background as the three men discuss the ways in which suicide might be committed. The gravelly realism of the previous jogging sequence is replaced by a series of shots which are almost sentimental in their intensity and provide a powerful example of the representation of male bonding. The dialogue is also witty, although bleak, and there is something of a lyrical desperation in the words of Gary and Dave. When Lomper realizes that he may have made two friends he is like a young child in his innocent joy. The music on the soundtrack is, by this time, a little more forceful and assertive. The scene ends, however, with a direct cut to a shot of a staircase, at the bottom of which we see a wheelchair. An elderly woman is struggling to climb the stairs and there is no romanticization of the subject matter here. The dialogue is unencumbered with the heavy sentiment of the preceding scene and there is a pathos in the way in which Lomper picks up his mother and carries her up the stairs, with her words in his and our ears: 'I thought you'd gone.'

Both this extract and the previous one from *On The Waterfront* are concerned with working-class males in crisis. Through their specific modes of signifying, each extract offers some comment on the experience of a crisis in the lives of one of the protagonists. In the former, it is a crisis over whether to speak to the police or not. In the latter, it is whether or not to take one's own life. The realism of Kazan is that of black-and-white photography, of eloquent but clearly formalized acting in a cutaway taxicab. In *The Full Monty* we have an outdoor location with sentiment generated by music and humour. The short scene in the house of Lomper is of another genre and modality, of realism with the humour drained away. The context of the representation of the men in *The Full Monty* is that of industrial decline in late twentieth-century Britain. The desperation at the heart of the film is handled through humour and human resilience. These qualities are both wrapped around the codes of realism to convincing effect. The problem is that they exclude from serious consideration any reference to the overtly political. This is a realism of political exclusion. *On the Waterfront* worked in a similar way, but might better be characterized as a realism of projection. Kazan and Schulberg could be seen to be working out their relationship with the social formation of which they were a part through remaking the 'real' world in a particular way.

Much more could be said about both extracts and their place in the films from which they come. The main point to note here is that the harder the realist tries, the more he or she is likely to have to rely on conventions to communicate a message. This hypothesis can be tested out by considering a wide range of realist texts over the years. One example would be the films of director Ken Loach. Over more than two decades, he has developed a technique of improvisation with his actors. In his most recent films, his work has rightly been praised for its verisimilitude. Yet his early work, such as *Poor Cow* (1967), now looks stylized and forced. The conventions of realism do change in important ways over time.

Documentary on television and questions of 'reality'

In the final section of this chapter I want to say something about the ways in which both documentaries and reality television have attempted to offer various forms of realism. Over the last three decades there have been considerable changes in the possibilities open to the documentarist. The first major change came with the post-Second World War invention of the lightweight 16mm cine-camera. Such a camera meant that the film crew could be much more mobile, though it was still necessary for the sound recordist to be connected to the camera by a lead. By the mid-1960s, however, with the crystal control on the Nagra tape recorder and the lightweight Arriflex 16mm camera, the documentary film-maker was free to move around in ways never before possible. Many major documentary film-makers, such as Richard Leacock and Don Pennebaker, produced another kind of realism with their choice of and approach to what were then unusual subjects. It was also in the 1960s that some British documentary film-makers, such as Lindsay Anderson, produced documentaries which clearly were as much concerned with making a personal statement in relation to the chosen subject matter as with any claim to directly reflect 'reality'. Where the film documentary had usually been a one-off affair, often sponsored and made for the cinema, the television documentary would often be part of a series. This meant that viewing documentaries became, for many, part of their regular television-viewing week (Corner, 1996).

Participating in the 'real'

We may now view on television a situation where something which we might call 'new' realism has radically challenged the previous conventions associated with realist texts and offered instead a form of realism which is, in a way, participatory. It is not the first time that claims to draw the audience into the reality constructed have been made. Many newsreels in the past did this, by suggesting to us that 'you are there'. This has now been extended, metaphorically at least, to 'you are there as a voyeur'. The new lightweight technology makes it possible for those who record images and sounds to move around freely and quickly with the subject of their attention, with no serious problems regarding constraints on shooting time.

This technological potential has facilitated the development of a generic form. It may involve the long take once more, but this time it will be a fluid, constantly prying camera eye which scours its subject matter for a point of focus or framing. The presence of the camera is also heightened in this generic form. Such a presence is not to be understood in the way that the French New Wave directors wanted to remind us that we were watching a film and to reflect upon what we had seen. We were often reminded of the camera's presence in such films because someone would address the camera directly.

The new realism, however, parades itself before us as a melding of technique and referent. The camera is part of reality, a composite and integral part. The reality thus produced, it would seem, is shared by the viewer, who is encouraged to suspend any disbelief because what is on offer is offered not as a representation, but as reality itself. We are there as participant observers, often for moments when we know we are intruding on scenes which once would have been regarded as none of our business. Therein lies the pleasure of it all. We sit in the police car (and so often such 'reality' television is about the police at work) and we drive down mean streets. We watch from the car window as officers question young suspects or prostitutes, and then we drive off, unseen but vigilantly present in the car. We are the camera eye and camera ear. Mediation, whereby we might have been intimate observers of a scene played out by others has been replaced. We are now directly involved through our personal 'eye and ear'. This, at least, is the way in which so much of this kind of television has been marketed. This virulent realism is often accentuated by the addition of a pulsating music track playing underneath the action. It seems that even the new realism needs the conventions of more established generic modes to drive it along.

The claims made by reality television are difficult to sustain. It is simply another convention which, rather than showing us something called 'reality', is actively involved in producing it. The conventions of reality television include the same intimate camera presence associated with earlier fly-on-the-wall documentaries. This is given added power because electronic equipment is better able to record images at low light levels, so we also observe a version of reality which is electronically enhanced. What is deemed to be 'real' is then recognized through characteristics of the genre rather than any necessary relationship with the material world being represented. Indeed, many such documentaries are precisely designed to offer the viewer a (re)construction of aspects of the social world which they would otherwise be most unlikely to encounter. From the technology and the approach, an aesthetic is constructed through which a generic form is identified. In one generation we may learn to recognize that which is 'real' because the images are grainy and black and white. More recently, they are likely to be colour-bleached electronic images, or multiple images as signifiers of realist reliability.

The new documentary realism has also provided feature film-makers with new possibilities for claims to verisimilitude. The most notable recent example has been *The Blair Witch Project* (1999), which managed to make an asset of the hand-held, home video kind of shooting technique. Perhaps the conventions of realism have been extended to include the fluid, claustrophobic constraints of a camera which is searching for its realities like a fish in a strange pool – darting frantically, roaming over a strange world in search of recognizable features. If it is established as a convention, it is likely to become a realism of stress.

Realism makes philosophers of us all

The reason why the concept of realism is still such an important one, even in the days of new technologies, is that it raises questions about the nature of existence. Once we begin to question whether and how a text is realist, we are drawn into debates about whether or not we understand the world better by showing things 'as they really are'; about whether or not there is some pure, unadulterated reality out there just waiting to be captured; and about whether a drama or feature film should strive for a realism of appearance or a realism of understanding.

We have also seen that it is possible to debate what constitutes the realist text using very different conceptual and aesthetic paradigms. One approach to fictional realism might be to consider it as ultimately concerned with accuracy of presentation – the 'getting the right buttons on a shirt' approach. Another might concentrate on either recreating speech patterns or using *mise-en-scène* in such a way as to produce and provide verisimilitude. Yet another might suggest that realism, if it is to be more than the mere reproduction of appearance, has to be a mode of representation which stimulates thought and reflection. For this reason, realism has been an approach often linked with social or other movements concerned with questions of justice, equity and politics. The maker of the realist text is often committed to changing the world for the better. On the other hand, many governments, particularly those with authoritarian tendencies, have been or are interested in forms of realism, for the simple reason that they recognize the importance of taking a supervisory role in the re-presentation (or is it construction?) of the real.

Is what we have called realism universal, or culturally and historically specific? The latter is almost certainly the case, though we have to remember not to confuse realism with reality. At the same time, we are drawn back to questions about the nature of our existence, because we need to know whether or not the world is out there waiting to be represented. For those who are in doubt about this, there is much talk about concepts like 'intertextuality' or 'simulacra' (Price, 1997) or the impossibility of knowing or expressing anything outside of (media) discourse. For others the question might be put differently, because they believe that there is a material world which exists independently of its representation. Critics of the basic materialist position would point out that it refers to a world to which we can never have direct access. It is a world which, in the nature of the communication process, has to be mediated. It then becomes difficult to see how we can speak meaningfully of realism, for that to which the realist text refers can never be validated outside the realms of further discourse!

At the end of the avenue of privileging discourse over the material world we find the temple of postmodernism, ironic distancing from material matters and the seduction of political apathy. On the other hand, if we believe that the world is just out there waiting, unproblematically, to be presented to the audience, we may end with dogmatic forms of realism designed to illustrate the truths just beyond our (re)presentations. We need to study and challenge all these approaches, along with the pleasures and seductions which the realist text still offers to both the unsuspecting and the erudite. The study of realism has to be a process of investigation which cannot achieve closure.

FURTHER READING

Lapsley, R. and Westlake, M., 1988, *Film Theory: an introduction.*
This is a classic textbook for the serious student, providing eloquent and clear introductions to the main theorists and their ideas. See especially chapter six, 'Realism'.

Nochlin, L., 1978, *Realism.*
This is now a standard work for students of realism in the visual arts. It is also a productive and, for many, essential complement to works concerned with realism in the cinema.

Williams, C., 1980, *Realism and the Cinema.*
Contains a brief and cogent introduction followed by readings from the champions of cinematic realism. The third and fourth sections of the book are most interesting, dealing with debates about style and ideology and the relationship between specific cinematic techniques and realism.

chapter six

'Race' and the media

Newsrooms are not likely to change the established routines that dictate how events are covered. Despite journalism's trumpeted efforts as democracy's champion, when it comes to race the watchdog is snoozing comfortably in the doghouse.
— Campbell, *Race, Myth and the News*

If there was a God, why he let motherfuckers get smoked every night?
— Doughboy in *Boyz N the Hood*, Singleton, 1991

The quickest way to get on in government, or the police, is to jump on the race bandwagon.
— Richard Littlejohn in the *Sun*, 11 April 2000

Discussion of issues of 'race' in the media is mainly significant because it impacts upon life outside the media. Otherwise it would be little more than a game about whose discourse is the most convincing or appealing on the endless carousel ride of signification which has become one facet of contemporary media and cultural studies. This is not an argument for playing down the significance of discourses in relation to issues of 'race'. It is an argument for recognizing the material correlates and occasional material causation in which discourses about 'race' may be factors. The title of this chapter is not '"Race" in the media'; it is '"Race" and the media'. This is a deliberate strategic choice. It is important that we do not allow our research interests to focus too heavily on merely blaming the media for the racism in society. There may be a case for this sometimes, but the media are actually an integral part of society, rather than something operating outside it. What this means is that, if we look hard, we can find examples of rampant racism in some media and principled anti-racism in others, admittedly a small minority. The variety of emphasis or discursive construction in media messages about issues of 'race' will give us an indication of the spread of prevalent discourses about 'race' which are in circulation at a given time. There is, however, an important middle ground in all this range of media constructions. This middle ground is where concepts of normality are invoked, whether in relation to general social values or specific attitudes to issues of 'race'.

I had two possible approaches to this chapter in mind when I began to think about how best to address issues of 'race' and the media. The first was to stress the significance of living in a multicultural, multi-ethnic community and the ways in which the media are often sophisticated and aware in their representation of that community. In following this line of thought, I had wanted to choose for analysis media examples which demonstrated the ways this new awareness manifested itself. On the whole, this approach was to be upbeat and optimistic. My second thought was to write a chapter which pointed out that going anywhere near matters concerning the representation of 'race' is to enter a political and ideological minefield. It is a minefield in which there are often very real and tangible deaths. Whilst we may sometimes celebrate cultural diversity in our media representations, we are more often having to face the horror of racist violence and murder than feeling any cause for celebration. As both of these approaches seem to be perfectly tenable ways to situate 'race' and the media, it may be more appropriate to address them with reference to the contradictions which they either represent or generate.

Of course, there are many more issues which need to be considered before any serious engagement with questions of 'race' and the media can be tackled. I have already used the term 'we' on more than one occasion. But it is a term which could be said to demonstrate either towering naïvety, unwarranted arrogance or everyday liberal white condescension. It may be that to study the representation of issues of 'race' requires the student or researcher to deal first with some fundamental questions. Is it possible to consider questions of 'race' from a dispassionate, neutral, academic position? Is it possible to make credible statements about issues of 'race' and the media if you are a white, middle-class male? And why do I keep putting the word 'race' in inverted commas?

This book is concerned with ideas and debates. I am not trying to offer, even if it were possible, a potted history of all the key thinkers in each field of media research. What I intend to do here, through the selective identification of examples and debates, is to demonstrate some of the key issues involved. I will also raise several questions which, I argue, need to be addressed by media researchers and media students. They are concerned with concepts such as 'normality', identity and representation. Of course, the previous chapters, with their concern for realism, discourse, the postmodern and ideology all offer potential for considering issues of 'race' and the media. In doing so, it is imperative that we remember that the selection of individual categories for analysis is usually a convenience rather than an ultimately satisfactory or final methodology. One of the problems we face in the analysis of complex media messages is that they are multilayered in terms of the range of readings they may suggest. Another is that the modes of signification of messages differ, as do their generic forms and hence their modes of address. This means, particularly in relation to issues of 'race', that we need to vary and combine our analytical approaches in relation to the task in hand, and recognize analysis as one important part of a much bigger, infuriatingly malleable jigsaw.

Questions of 'race' and meaning have to be negotiated socially. What this means is that there has to be a general agreement about the meanings of specific terms used in such representations. Many of these terms have been and continue to be very contentious. They include, for instance, blacks, young blacks, muggers, immigrants, new immigrants, asylum seekers, fundamentalists, these people, those people, such people and a whole host more. These terms, as individual terms, take on a certain currency in media reportage, but they can only do so once they have been located within recognizable discourses. The media student has to study both the terms and the discourses within which they are located.

Although media discourses are important, when dealing with issues of 'race', one is reminded that ideas and beliefs have material consequences (Althusser, 1971). While it may be possible to pirouette around different forms of popular media and play semiotic games with the discourses they employ, victims of racism are less likely to be convinced about the efficacy of reducing human experience to the sharing of simulacra. When we are considering questions of 'race' and the media, we do so in a very material world, which is full of contradictions. This is not an argument against the study and analysis of media discourses or semiotics. It is an argument against reducing material reality and social relations to little more than signifying games. What we do have to recognize is that there is always a relationship between discourses and the material world, and that the former have a considerable impact on our relationship with the latter. We have noted in the chapter on discourse that a discourse provides a set of possible statements about a given issue. Discourses also organize and give structure to the manner in which a particular topic is to be addressed – in relation to the media, we can say, almost literally, the way in which a topic is framed. This is certainly the case when issues of 'race' are addressed. Discourses have material consequences and correlates.

The social negotiation of meaning is sometimes constrained by those who wish to impose on others a narrow, spuriously essentialized interpretation of the world. For some this may be a question of asserting their identity; for others, it may be about asserting their difference. When identity and difference are linked to questions of ethnicity or dubiously articulated notions of race, then racism is never far away. Here, I want to turn my attention to the ways in which the media address questions of normality and the everyday. The very concept of normality implies, of course, some kind of essential quality. It is closely linked to the concept of common sense – that which we simply know to be the case.

A question of normality

In representing certain forms of otherness, it is often necessary for the media to posit a norm against which to measure the relative undesirability of the other in question. This norm is often presented in terms of 'the way we do things' or the common sense of the time. In recent years there has been much media interest in the UK in the phenomenon of begging. Begging has been going on in London and the major cities of the UK for some years, sometimes engaged in by the homeless, often by those who need cash to feed their addiction. Such begging has never been popular, but it has seldom produced the sustained campaign of hostility which has developed when the beggars are not *our own* beggars. I am referring to the people who come from Eastern Europe (predominantly Romania), and who often beg with their children in their arms.

There are, clearly, social, political and economic dimensions to questions of begging. But none of these is the foremost issue when considering matters of 'race' and racism. The attack against beggars who are 'others' is mounted over questions of personal characteristics. What kind of parent walks the streets with their child in their arms and asks for money? What kind of person begs aggressively? The answer is always the same. It is an alien person. Not one of us. These outsiders are often trying to take advantage of 'soft-touch Britain'. They tend to gather in 'throngs' in order to obtain illegal work, without permits. In Tanderei, Romania, we are told, 'most of the population is supported by an organised begging racket in Britain'. The numbers involved are not clear. How many people constitute a community or a 'township' is not clear. It would require, I assume, some rather successful begging to sustain even a small one. When such begging occurs, then, 'this tolerant, generous spirited nation' will be pushed into actions which are harder-edged, less welcoming and 'even intolerant'. We are thus offered an image of 'ourselves' as soft-hearted, tolerant, generous spirited and ready to turn nasty if our positive characteristics are put to the test. Such logic is a regular feature of some interpretations of the world as seen through 'normal' British eyes. There have been some books on the media where examples have been invented to illustrate the rhetorical points being made. All the data in this paragraph, however, has been gleaned from the editorial in the *Daily Mail* of Friday 17 March 2000. It is chosen as an example of a particular discursive construction of Britishness. Those who analyse the media discourse of the press suggest that the message should be set in the overall context of the paper that produces it. They also suggest that any message has to be interpreted in the context of the overall page layout in which it appears. This is worth pursuing in relation to my chosen example.

The editorial in question appeared on Saint Patrick's Day, and the whole of the rest of page 12 of the *Mail* is given over to a piece written by Leo McKinstry under the banner, 'BLARNEY Or why you Brits mustn't be conned by we Oirish . . .'. Written by someone 'born in Ireland', the piece highlights several virtues of the Irish and reminds the reader of the ways in which the Irish had been held in contempt by the English establishment. Those days are gone, according to McKinstry, despite the attempts by the 'discrimination obsessives [*sic*] at the Commission for Racial Equality' to argue that anti-Irish discrimination was still 'rampant' here. McKinstry provides an impressive and rather convincing list of the ways in which forms of Irishness have permeated British social and cultural life. The fact that success in sport or entertainment is little guarantee that discrimination against a group of people has ceased is not part of the remit of this 'Oirish' writer. He then turns his attention to the present situation in Ireland, a place where, he argues, 'violence, poverty, ugliness and alcoholism are woven into the fabric' of life. The blow is softened, but only slightly, by the suggestion that Ireland has 'just as many dark and brutal problems as any other industrialised country in the Western world'.

The reason, it seems, that the Irish, and their 'growing army of admirers', have been able to make Ireland seem like a rural paradise, is that the Irish have 'the most remarkable gift for language, humour, romanticism'. The piece concludes by noting that, 'We live in an age of illusion and spin, an age exactly suited to the qualities of the Irish character'. Thus we have a first-rate example of the essentializing of an 'other' by someone 'born in Ireland'. The 'new' Irish, it seems, are those who can cash in on their essential character traits, utilize their 'slick patter' to sell to the English their Irish culture. Not so much a devious act as a return to character, we are being asked to believe.

The overall impact of this one page of the newspaper is to offer, by default, a sense of British identity. We have to measure 'ourselves' against these 'others'. The key issue, however, is ideological. Begging with children in your arms, alcoholism and violence need to be tackled through strategies and policies appropriate to a democracy. The question is, how? Discursively, this newspaper seems to be handling them through a limited number of approaches, relying on essentializing and normalizing alleged character traits or national characteristics. Behind such strategies, inferential racism and xenophobia are little more than a hair's breadth away (Hall, 1996; Deacon *et al.*, 1999).

The specific use of language in discourses of the press is something which requires formal analysis, and such analysis has to be based upon theoretical and methodological engagement. Roger Fowler (1990) has offered a clear mapping of this field, arguing that the discourses of the press are always 'structured representations', and that they have built into them values and implicit propositions. This means that such discourses, whatever the newspaper, are always positioned – they have a point of view. Reconstructing the positioned and structured discourses of the press by recourse to their texts is one of the key activities of media studies. It is particularly pertinent in relation to representations of issues of 'race'.

Deviance, deviation, desire

I want to move on now from the ways in which the media structure otherness against an implicit or occasionally explicit notion of normality. For, in line with the kinds of contradiction which one has to expect from the media, they also celebrate some forms of difference, particularly when they are linked with some form of danger. In this section I want to highlight some of the ways in which representations of 'race' have allowed for the celebration of sexuality, (male) strength and exoticism. It is in keeping with such representations that they often exist in a state of tension between attraction and repulsion, though it must be remembered that this is predominantly in relation to an unstipulated but omnipresent white viewer. The exotic, then, is sometimes associated with costume, architecture or culinary delights. It is also associated with forms of physical beauty. These types of beauty have been linked in the past with what has become known as the 'noble savage'. The exotic has also always been linked to the sexual. This has taken its most virulently negative form in the fears expressed by some (white) people about black masculine sexuality. We have to remember, once again, that these fears cannot be said to have originated in media representations. They will have originated in part from social being, from living in the material world. The fantasies of the populace become, in time, the fantasies of the audiences for the media. At one end of the ideological spectrum there may be the amusement and diversion to be had from the exotic romantic novel, based in fantasy and satisfying the sexual imaginings of the reader. At the other we find, with chilling regularity, racist murder as the material expression of other fantasies. The different forms of exoticism find their way into media representations in both benign and malignant forms. The choice of medical epithets here is not inappropriate. At the ideological level, representations of issues of 'race' hover between notions of normality and the pathological. That which is deemed normal may be the measure against which we, with or without the media, can indulge in our various fantasies. In this context, the normal may mainly be concerned with the relatively staid characteristics of the familiar, interpreted against the hoped-for yet feared excitement provided by the 'other'. But it is always an 'other' which can be rejected with psychic or physical force if it becomes too much to cope with. I will try to illustrate this argument by example, beginning with Mills & Boon.

Romancing with otherness

The romantic novel is big business, and is mainly popular with women readers. There has been much research which has argued that such literature offers some relief from the tedium of domestic life and labour. In this respect, the place and purpose of fantasy in the lives of readers is paramount. It is also far from new. Within a range of sub-genres, romantic fiction offers stories of young women who go to distant places to find their true love. I wish to take one small example to illustrate, in condensed form, the qualities which I associate with the benign fantasy. My example is taken from a romance by Mons Daveson, entitled *Desert Interlude*, published in 1990 by Mills & Boon. Mills & Boon is a very successful publisher, with more than 50 million readers worldwide. More than 200 million of its books are sold worldwide per annum. As it points out on its own website, the weight of all its books sold in 2002 would fill more than 160 cargo-carrying Boeing 747 aircraft (http://www.millsandboon. co.uk/index.html).

Before we try the product, however, there has to be something to catch our attention. This is provided in the form of a narrative image, which precedes the reading of the book in much the same way as a trailer tells us about a movie (Ellis, 1982). In part, this narrative image is related to expectations of a generic kind. We will approach a text if we are predisposed so to do. The cover of *Desert Interlude* encourages our latent or manifest dispositions. It shows a man and a woman, both facing the observer. The woman is blonde with a fair complexion. The man, who stands behind her, has dark hair and darker skin than the woman. He has his arms loosely around her and is looking at her blonde hair. The woman is looking away to the left, her gaze unfocused and her hair falling on the man's right arm. Her lips are slightly open and her facial expression, along with the way in which her hand is laid over his, suggests an affectionate relationship. The background is a stylized, brushworked rendition of palm trees and desert. The man is wearing a light-toned shirt which has about it an air, following Barthes (1977), of what could be termed 'Arabicity'. There is just a hint of the exotic in the cut of the sleeves and the collar. The title of the novel is also generically important. In this publication, the generic category of the book is indicated in a typeface larger than the name of the author. So we first read 'ROMANCE' in capital letters. The author's name is also in (smaller) capitals. The title itself offers the reader both romance and the exotic backdrop. A further promise of exoticism is to be found in the male figure.

The text on which I will concentrate is what might be called a taster, and it is printed inside the front cover without page reference or other contextualization. It reads as follows:

'I have brought you here because I wanted to do so. Does that answer your question?'

Aghast at that tone, those words, from this so different Ahmed, Leonie found she couldn't answer for a moment, then she said, 'I don't understand why you're acting like this!' All the anger which she had been feeling on that long ride disintegrated. Somehow she was frightened. But this was the Ahmed whom she had loved.

'Surely you don't mind?' said that grating silken voice. 'You have shown me on other occasions you are not averse to my presence . . . or even to my lovemaking.'

The text contains just enough material to imply a series of possibilities. There is the possible threat we may experience from someone we once loved. Leonie is 'aghast', as we, the readers, are supposed to be. At the same time, it is clear that she has strong feelings for Ahmed, the 'so different' Ahmed. Of course, we will need to read the novel to discover exactly how different he is. Ahmed is annoyed, we will find out, because he wrongly believes that Leonie has spent the night with another man. This suspicion makes him act cruelly towards the heroine and demonstrate a willingness to force her to have sex with him – in other words, to rape her. But the situation is rectified when he learns that she is not guilty of his accusations. This Ahmed is an Arab man with rank and class. He is, as the cover tells us, 'rich, powerful, intelligent'. He is also, as the taster indicates, prone to lose his temper. Yet it is that very unpleasant passion which is also the attraction of our fictional Ahmed. He is also described on more than one occasion in the novel, oddly some might think, as having the appearance of a Greek god. So the reader of the novel will find the exotic promise of the black arched eyebrows of our hero, his piercing eyes and other signifiers of exotic otherness, combined with his chiselled features as though cut from (Greek) marble. There is threat and there is excitement. There is also a balance in signification between characteristics which might be associated with Semitic features and those which might be associated with the Aryan. The fantasy figure of Ahmed provides the sympathetic reader with the stimulus for romantic heterosexual attachment to which is added just a touch of danger. The quality of the story or its telling is not at issue here. I am more interested in the way in which benign fantasy can serve to sustain characteristics associated with a particular kind of otherness. Ideologically, such otherness becomes part of what I have called elsewhere the discursive reserve (Ferguson, 1998). This reserve is passed on through various modes of communication – from everyday conversation to storytelling in a variety of media. It is learned. In its benign form it can be disturbing (some would say this is too generous a reading of an implied rape), but it is contained here within a story which allows any threats to be neutralized by the move towards an inevitable romantic closure. Ahmed is held in narrative check. In such a generic form, the reader may 'enjoy' him for just this reason. Outside the narrative, the same characteristics which may have thrilled sympathetic readers and fed their benign erotic fantasies may become signifiers of suspicion and hatred. It is then that the less than benign sexual fantasies are assembled, called up, worked through (Kovel, 1988). Mills & Boon provides pleasure for millions of almost exclusively women readers (http://www.rwanational.org/Statistics.pdf).

'Race' and *True Lies* – the violence of racist representation

The benign fantasy world associated with issues of 'race' and the media is one which is appropriated mainly by white people, its preferred audience. More malignant types of fantasy can be found in representations which involve degrees of violence or humiliation towards a chosen person or group. Such a person or group will first be demonized, so that any narrative woes which befall them are ideologically justified. If such violence and humiliation can be linked with sardonic humour, then so much the better. The preferred audiences for such a fantasy are likely to be composed of those who are not members of the demonized group. But the plurality of possible audiences is likely to constitute a hierarchy which is itself based in racist ideology. One group of people who might be the victims of racism in one context may, in turn, become the racist consumers of a particular message or narrative in another.

If we consider a movie such as *True Lies* (1994), we can see a popular example of some of the possibilities I have just been outlining. It is a major entertainment and adventure movie, directed by James Cameron, who would go on to direct the even more financially rewarding *Titanic*. It stars Arnold Schwarzenegger and is rich in special effects and a cruel and slick humour. It might be better to approach the representation of issues of 'race' in such a film by considering the way in which it addresses issues of gender. There is in the movie the infamous line, 'Women! You can't live with them, and you can't kill them.' It is spoken in a context where the misogyny is buried under the absurdity of a situation fraught with violence, brutality and instant death. It is a narrative where anything goes, so even misogyny is good for a sardonic laugh. One has to ask, however, who is laughing and why? In this movie, to sympathize with the heroes of the narrative is to become capable of cruelty. That is part of the pleasure it offers – a revenge on one's spoken and unspoken enemies.

The scene in which we first see the villain of the film in action with his companions-in-arms illustrates this well. It is about this villainous character that I wish to write, because he typifies, I would argue, that cruel and unspoken, tacit yet obvious racism which is essential if the movie is to maintain the frisson of vindictiveness which is central to its appeal. The villain in question is named as Salim Abu Aziz. He is played by the actor Art Malik. His character can be publicly subservient and privately violent, capable of immediate and vindictive cruelty, liable to fly into a rage. When we first encounter him, he seems to be a workman in the employ of Juno Skinner (Tia Carrere). He has been watching her discussion with Harry (Schwarzenegger), and he asks her politely and formally if he can have a word with her in her office. Once inside he turns and slaps her hard across the face, calling her a 'stupid undisciplined bitch'. When she interrupts his tirade he slaps her hard again for interrupting. There is little doubt that we, the audience, are supposed to recognize his villainy. This is all, of course, just part of the narrative in an adventure movie. It has parallels with the Victorian melodrama or the traditional pantomime, in that we may be inclined to boo the villain and cheer the hero. But it is also crucial that Malik is seen playing a character who is, in some vague generic sense, an Arab. His behaviour and his politics suggest a man with a mission. At one point he is preparing a video to be sent to the United States government in which he lays out his demands. He is often just a little unshaven or unkempt, and he speaks with an intensity which borders on the pathological. What he says, however, in another context, might give pause for reflection: 'You have killed our women and children, bombed our cities from afar like cowards, and dare to call us terrorists.' The screenplay makes it very clear that the words of Salim Abu Aziz are not to be taken seriously: 'Aziz/Malik drones on . . .'.

The film was released in 1994, at a time when the United States' relationships with Iran and many Arab states were not entirely warm. There is a sense of impending revenge in the movie as our villain is shown as ever more nefarious and cruel. His time will come. The implied audience's revenge will come. Both will occur before the movie ends. The vehicle of the audience's revenge will be 'Arnie', the Austrian immigrant. He will blow the terrorists to pieces along with the whole floor of a building in which they are ensconced. The Crimson Jihad will get theirs. (What could be a more evocative ideological phrase in this era of the end of ideology than Crimson Jihad?) Salim Abu Aziz will also be despatched, but astride a missile which will be assured to blow his private parts away a fraction of a second before the rest of him follows. That, at least, is a possible semiotic reading of the way the movie handles its villains. For this high camp violence is actually a revenge on the Arabs, and it is one which requires the reinstatement of numerous stereotypes about issues of 'race', along with virulent sexism and open misogyny.

The importance of all this for the researcher may be that it provides some hints about recurrent patterns of representation which can be tested out over a number of narrative fictions. Can we say that extreme villainy is best represented in the entertainment movie by recourse to comic violence? Can we recognize a possible pattern in the ways in which villainy, sexism, misogyny and racism are interwoven to provide the potent and vicious pleasure which *True Lies* offers us? Can we recognize the fine division which is somehow maintained between the signification of the politics of an era and the essentialized character of its villains? It does seem possible that, in some circumstances, racism and violence may be the signifying cover for discourses which are concerned with revenge and punishment in a world of *realpolitik*. If you can't get 'them' in the world beyond the screen, you can at least pulverize them in the public privacy of the cinema. That was in 1994.

I have described the racism of the Mills & Boon story as benign, while I would describe that of the world of *True Lies* as malignant. These terms are descriptive as much as judgemental. It is certainly arguable that they have recognizable narrative consequences. Whether these narratives have tangible, material consequences in the daily lives of people is a question which is unlikely to be fully resolved through this text. They undoubtedly invigorate the discursive reserve. They bring romance and violence, sentimentality and destruction, fear and loathing. These are not binary oppositions, however, but dynamic, contradictory and sometimes complementary ideological force fields. Readers of both kinds of text may experience the contradictions and dilemmas engendered by the romance or the adventure. They may also absorb them uncluttered by any contradictory perceptions. But the reading of the ideological in relation to issues of 'race' is seldom either static or mechanical. It is at the points of possible tension in the readings that we may identify the operations of the ideological. Should we laugh or should we be disgusted? Should we feel romance stirring or should we refuse the offer of an escape to a world in which we do not believe? If we are not pathological cases, we may do both. Representations of 'race' often allow us to wallow in our dilemmas as much as to celebrate our differences. They also invite us to put aside 'our' insecurities as we move between fantasies of romance and hate.

True Lies is a movie which will always evoke for me the events of 11 September 2001. A considered and sustained analysis of the complex relationship between this movie and that day should be the task of all students and researchers, all questioners of the media.

Tabloid rage

If it is true that issues of 'race' and the media should not be studied as though they existed in some kind of vacuum, this is something which has not been overlooked by the tabloid columnists. They know very well that the power of a media discourse often resides in the ways in which it can ring prejudicial or ideological bells which are significant in the world beyond media discourse. Whether the reader will hear such bells and how they will respond is not the main concern of this chapter. The main point to notice is that where issues of 'race' are commented upon, a range of other issues will not be far away. These will relate to left radicalism (white and black), nationalism (particularly 'our' nationalism under threat), gay people, religion and careerism (almost entirely that of black people), and appeals to our common sense. Arun Kundnani has made an interesting analysis of some of these tendencies in the British press (Kundnani, 2000). I will consider one column here by way of example. Let me be clear, however, that I am not suggesting that all columnists are racist. I am suggesting that many tabloid columnists operate at a level of intensity which invites cheers and jeers. The tabloid columnist is, by definition, opinionated. The media studies student or researcher should be concerned with the ways in which the opinionated formulate their arguments, the structure of their discourses and the means of signification which they utilize.

Richard Littlejohn's column in the *Sun* on 11 April 2000 is written under the banner 'Britain is not, repeat *NOT*, a racist nation'. It is the main feature in a page which contains Littlejohn's views on three other issues. These include the eccentricities of Prince Charles – an issue which is set alongside a cartoon showing the Prince skiing, wearing a hat and scarf and little else, followed by a butler on skis, carrying some clothes and a drink on a tray. The third story is about the stabbing of British fans by Galatasaray supporters in Istanbul. Littlejohn is clearly disturbed by what has happened, but condemns those in England who would seek revenge on Turkish people in no uncertain terms. He refers to the way in which British-born Turkish people have been victimized as 'an absolute disgrace'. The fourth story is about British car companies and the price of cars in the UK in relation to the amount they cost on 'the Continent'. The main article, however, takes up more than half the column.

Littlejohn begins by quoting from a study in *The Sunday Times*, which suggests that nine out of ten young black men living in a domestic relationship are doing so with a 'non-black woman'. He writes that young black women are 'increasingly finding love with white men', though he does not give any statistics this time. For Littlejohn, this should be a reason for the Commission for Racial Equality to be 'shouting these statistics from the rooftops'. He wants to know why the government is not citing this information as evidence of what he calls 'our proud race relations record'. The logic behind both suggestions requires some analysis, but I will concentrate in a moment on what Littlejohn calls 'interracial relationships'. First, it is important to note that Littlejohn does not want to be seen to overstate his case too soon, so he uses apparently placatory euphemism to prepare readers for his impending tirade. He uses the word 'admittedly' to soften the euphemism: 'Admittedly, not everything in the garden is rosy . . .'.

In order to illustrate the point, Littlejohn cites the case of the stabbing of Chris Cotter, the white boyfriend of black athlete Ashia Hansen. The choice of example could hardly have been more inappropriate. First, Littlejohn is weighing the increase in diversity in personal relationships on a scale with alleged racist attack. I say alleged because it transpired that the attackers had been working with Cotter, conspiring to allow Cotter the chance to sell his story to the newspapers. This he did, before the police arrested him, along with his two attackers. It seems that Littlejohn had rushed to judgement with his example. This is deeply ironic, as later in the same column, Littlejohn warns against assuming that a crime is racist before it has been investigated fully. He also reminds the reader that there are 'black militants' who abuse other black people if they enter a relationship with someone who is not black. He then returns to the main thrust of his argument, making a series of assertions which can be listed as follows.

1. The figures which he cited are not being celebrated because the government is not interested in promoting racial harmony.
2. The government thrives on division and conflict.
3. Because of this the government is always looking for divisions where none exists.
4. For the same reason the government is always 'inventing' new and absurd definitions.
5. These include 'institutional racism' and 'thought crimes'. ('If you don't know you are a racist, how can you possibly deny it?')
6. The motivation behind some of the government's actions stems from 'their own pathological hatred of their own country and their contempt for the vast majority of the people who pay their wages.'
7. The rest of the government (we do not know how many because no size is apportioned to the 'some' in the previous assertion) follow their course of action motivated by blatant opportunism.
8. The government believes in divide and rule.
9. The government believes in 'manufacturing' as many victim and client groups as possible.
10. The Prime Minister is attempting to 'carve up' Britain and destroy national identity.
11. The Prime Minister wants to 'submerge' Britain in a federal Europe, of which he hopes to be president.
12. Challenge the government (presumably on one of the above actions) and it accuses you of playing the 'race' card.
13. It is already doing this if it is attacked for its 'incompetent and indifferent policies for tackling *the flood of bogus asylum seekers*' (italics added).

14. If you oppose the 'promotion of homosexuality' in schools, you are accused (by the government, or some other person or body) of hating gays.

15. The government does this to stifle free speech and opposition.

16. The government is the one playing the 'race' card. The government is not interested in facts.

17. Britain has the best race relations in the world.

18. We must not, however, be complacent.

19. 'We' don't have the racism which they have in the USA or the overt racism commonplace in Europe.

20. The politicians and 'race commissars' would make you think that 99 per cent of Britons were members of the Ku Klux Klan.

21. The government is playing the 'race' card because it is a 'surefire' route to advancement in Blair's Britain.

There is more in this single column, but I will not itemize the points further. It ends with the populist call: 'When is someone going to tell the truth and speak for Britain?'

I chose this single column in order to highlight what I called the 'level of intensity' of some tabloid journalism. The assertions come thick and fast. Rational argument is eschewed in favour of a deluge of emotional and aggressive assertion. I will take just one of these to consider in a little more detail.

> That's why they are always seeking out discrimination where none exists and inventing new and absurd definitions and thought crimes such as 'institutional' and 'unconscious' racism against which there can be no defence.

A piece of investigative journalism worthy of the name would have to provide some documented evidence of the seeking out of discrimination where none exists. Is it done through a government department, in cabinet meetings, in parliament or elsewhere? Is the government actually inventing definitions, either new and/or absurd? If so, when and where do or did they originate and what is the proof for this? Is the term 'institutional racism' one which originated with the Labour government? If so, where is the proof for this? One has to presume that institutional racism is not to be equated with the definition of 'unconscious', but this is not at all clear. Did the Labour government invent a term called 'unconscious racism', and if so, when was it first announced, and by whom? By nominalizing the whole complex interrelationship which constitutes the running of the state into two words, 'the government', Littlejohn is able to fire off accusations which are aimed at something all pervasive which acts without identifiable agency (Hodge and Kress, 1993). The sheer volume of points asserted in what is after all a relatively short column is also worth noting. It may be that such work is intended to be taken rather like a stiff drink – down in one. If the reader pauses to reflect on what is being offered, the effect is lost. What could also be argued, and tested out against a range of similar columns, is that such discourse is fragmented in style, but at the same time is as closed as anything Marcuse could ever have imagined. There is no way in unless you play by the rules of Richard Littlejohn. And once in, there is no way to challenge the discourse, because this is no longer rhetoric. It has become incantation.

The purpose of taking this short example has been to highlight the ways in which issues of 'race' are often laced together with a number of other (usually contentious) issues in popular discourse. The impact of such popular discourse may or may not be racist. It is very likely to work through any contradictions it has itself raised, towards a vitriolic common sense which demands allegiance as the only alternative to deviance. Littlejohn, for instance, does not spare those with whom he disagrees: 'pathological hatred of one's own country' is a condition which, one might assume, needs some form of diagnosis and verification. But popular media discourses relating to issues of 'race' operate through assertion much more often than considered argument. The way to see whether this is the case is to test it out through research. Many of the issues I have identified here tend to repeat themselves as patterns or trends. The job of the media researcher is, first, to identify such patterns and, second, to provide possible interpretations or explanations for their existence. The latter is likely to lead any researcher back into the realms of theory.

'Race' and everyday life

I have written briefly in this chapter about the representation of 'race' in one feature film, a piece of romantic fiction and a newspaper column. I have not chosen to offer summaries of swathes of research where plenty exist already (Gandy, 1998). I have chosen to focus my attention on the more localized manifestations of issues concerning 'race' and the discourses and semiotic systems within which they operate. To say that one is seeking for patterns, trends or structures in media messages is hardly new. It is, however, very relevant in relation to issues of 'race' and the media. It is through a process of textual research over time that one is likely to discover such patterns, rather than memorizing them from a reputable textbook. I have already mentioned the dangers in any media research which resorts to a 'spot the . . .' approach, whether concerned with questions of ideology, racism, sexism or another ism. Researching the media and issues of 'race' may require us to make some hypotheses. A key issue for the researcher, of course, must be whether or not the media are racist. Perhaps it would be more productive to take an approach which looks, initially, at how issues of 'race' are handled, constructed, mediated or told about in the media. From this, it becomes possible to move towards identifying patterns or structures in representations. It does not require, however, a mechanical invocation of basic semiotics. This usually reduces research to little more than decoding of an unproductive kind. It has always been an unfortunate way of approaching the media, to discuss only questions of decoding. As we all know, codes are things which we learn, and if we have not learned them well, we resort to a code book in order to ascertain what is being said. There is not much complexity here beyond cracking or knowing the code. It certainly has implications for the kind of research we undertake. In relation to the media and 'race', it can mean that researchers are there to teach the code (which, of course, they already know) to others who are less semiotically accomplished.

The fact that simplistic semiotics allows an easy identification (for some) of the signifier and the signified ignores the complexities and contradictions which may surround any apparently simple media message. It may also be that any given media message may offer or generate apparently contradictory messages. This may be done visually, audio-visually or as a written text. It may, with the coming of multimedia, allow for the making of messages which utilize many modes of communication at once (hence multimodal communication).

In relation to issues of 'race', we need to develop modes of analysis which recognize contradiction and tension in the range of meanings on offer. There are occasions when the image 'speaks' as part of an ideological harmonic, the written word as another, and the sound as something else again. This may occur as part of a single piece of news on television, or a web page carrying written news, video and audio commentary.

We should not, however, allow complexity, postmodern or otherwise, to blind us to the materiality of racist murder or the conditions under which the poor and underprivileged live out their lives. Whilst some media representations of issues of 'race' may be confused or confusing, there are others which come closer to invective and preciseness of description. On 22 March 2000, the *Guardian* newspaper carried a piece on page three by Vikram Dodd and Jamie Wilson, which reported on the case of Duwayne Brooks, a friend of the black teenager Stephen Lawrence, murdered by a racist gang in April 1993. Brooks has been arrested by the police six times since the murder and six attempted prosecutions against him have been dropped. On 8 July 1998, the police stopped Brooks in the City of London under the Prevention of Terrorism Act. He was charged with possession of an offensive weapon. The charge was withdrawn after his employer confirmed that the knife was part of Brooks' toolkit. The police stopped Brooks in his car on 4 July 1999, and discovered a photocopying tool. Police alleged it was an offensive weapon and charged him with possession of a bladed article. Brooks works for a photocopying company. The case was discontinued within a matter of weeks.

The reason for quoting from this story is not to suggest that the *Guardian* is somehow above the discursive in its construction of media messages. It is to argue that there are some discourses which come very close to the material referents upon which they are based – so much so that we may be reminded of the possibility that some kinds of objectivity must, of necessity, be partisan. To describe objectively means, in this context, to take sides (see also Eagleton, 2003: 103–39). Implicit in the *Guardian's* story is a profound suspicion of the conduct of the police, though this is suggested by the deliberate and telling absence of judgemental prose.

On 26 March 2000, the *Observer* newspaper in the UK carried a story by Ed Vulliamy under the banner 'Bullet that tore a hole in America'. The story tells of the funeral of Patrick Dorismund, a Haitian victim of a police shooting. The language used by Vulliamy is more provocative than that in the previous article. The first four paragraphs are structured around references to the bullet in the title of the piece. In paragraph three he writes:

> The bullet also upset Dorismund's Haitian community in New York, only just recovering from the string of trials that followed the torture and sodomy by broomstick of another of their own – Abner Louima.

This is another example of the way in which the discursive may come to take second place to the material referent which it both describes and constructs. Of course, it is important to note the journalistic expertise with which Vulliamy assembles his work, the tightness of the prose making every word resonate. And it is the case that it is only through (media) discourse that we are likely to have knowledge of what happened. It would be obtuse to the point of perversity, however, to develop our interest as media researchers only in the construction of the discourse.

I have chosen these two short examples with which to end this chapter because, I suggest, they highlight the tensions and dilemmas facing the media researcher. On the one hand, it is clear that much of the construction of otherness, the exotic and issues of 'race' is accomplished through complex modes of discourse and representation. On the other, it is apparent to all but the most solipsistic that people's lived existence, and their deaths, cannot be reduced to the discursive. We have to face the contradictions and dilemmas thrown up at the interface of the discursive and the material. We must also recognize that, as media students and researchers, our relationship to our field of study cannot be that of a 'free floating' intellectual, questioner or researcher.

FURTHER READING

Ferguson, R., 1998, *Representing 'Race'*.
An overview of a wide range of media representations, from popular newspapers to film and television. Some consideration is given to theories of ideology and identity in relation to representations of 'race'.

Gandy, O., 1998, *Communication and Race*.
Explores the concept of race through examining media systems and institutions, communication frames and symbolic representations, and social constructions.

Jakubowicz, A., 1994, *Racism, Ethnicity and the Media*.
A collection of analytical writing, concentrating on Australian media, which covers, among other issues, that of national identity and cultural pluralism.

chapter seven

Gender and class

Myth defies logic in allowing polar opposites to co-exist without discomfort (a similar pattern emerges in mythologies of childhood, with children being viewed at one and the same time as pure innocent angels and devil-inspired monsters). The myths of women's discourse parallel closely the diverse myths of femininity as simultaneously other-centred, gentle and kind, but also prone to jealousy and pettiness.

— McDonald, *Representing Women*

Like race and ethnicity under some historical circumstances, gender is in all societies so crucial a determinant of class relations that it must be asked whether it is theoretically adequate simply to integrate it as a sub-system of class. My tentative preference is to use two different modes of description, according to the task at hand. The first speaks of a class-gender system as a way of talking about specific local relations where the two are methodologically inseparable. The second speaks of gender as a separate system that is inevitably enmeshed in the class system . . .

— Frow, *Cultural Studies & Cultural Value*

The effort to identify the enemy as singular in form is a reverse-discourse that uncritically mimics the strategy of the oppressor instead of offering a different set of terms. That the tactic can operate in feminist and antifeminist contexts alike suggests that the colonising gesture is not primarily or irreducibly masculinist. It can operate to affect other relations of racial, class and heterosexist subordination, to name but a few.

— Butler, *Gender Trouble*

Contextualizing the 'Holy Trinity'

Many contradictions and paradoxes have come to the surface in this book. The present chapter is particularly significant in this respect. I have already pointed out that the distinction between some of the conceptual or analytical fields or categories used in media studies is one of convenience rather than providing a rigid or mechanical analytical tool. In practice it is rare indeed to find a media or cultural studies task which requires only one methodological or conceptual category in order to be completed. Unless one has a theory of the operations of the media which allows for contradiction, tension and movement, one is always going to end up with analyses which are either arid or mechanical. Arid analyses yield little more than the satisfaction of obeying some rules which have been invented in order for the analyses to take place. Mechanical analyses, similarly, follow rules for separate and distinct generic or other media and cultural forms. They tend to work towards preconceived ends and prohibit contradiction or paradox as a dynamic and necessary component of social semiotic and discursive work (Hodge and Kress, 1988: 268).

There has been a move in popular academic discourse away from what is sometimes described as the Holy Trinity of class, 'race' and gender, where all three were invoked as necessary and inseparable companions. There are at least two possible reasons for this. One is a perception that forms of militancy incorporating all three categories have often proved to be either reductive or counterproductive. The argument often centred on the hierarchy of importance attributed to each member of the trinity. They were seldom seen as equals. For the traditional Marxist, class was always dominant. Similarly, the militant feminist or anti-racist championed either gender or 'race' as the core issue to be addressed. How one places oneself in relation to these debates is still of crucial significance. The second reason why this Holy Trinity has been criticized can be identified in my choice of descriptor.

One is reminded here of the text in which so many one-time communists described their change of heart under the title of *The God that Failed* (Koestler *et al.*, 1950). The rejection of radical thought is often accompanied by the hurt feelings of those who feel that that which they have in fact deified has turned out to be nothing but human. This is often a two-stage process. First, the people, or your allies or comrades, let you down. Then you realize that your theory is not as divine as you had hoped and you reject it utterly, often with bitterness. Media studies, however, is not about deification, but about investigation and analysis. Deification of class, 'race' and gender usually means that the three terms have been used as forms of dogma needing no further justification for their analytical efficacy other than being named – either separately or together. While there have been good reasons for some of the critiques levelled at the over-zealous, whichever camp or camps they belonged to, there is also another dimension to them which needs exploration. This is one which might link rejection of class, 'race' or gender issues with political defeatism at the beginning of the twenty-first century, or the wish to turn away from the radical politics of the past. One particularly reactionary manifestation of this approach is that which constantly attacks the concept of 'political correctness'. It offers in its place the reassurance that arguments about ideology and politics are either passé or Stalinist or simply killjoy. It is in this context that students or researchers of the media and cultural studies have to situate themselves.

Perhaps the most important lesson to be learned from the debates, acrimonious and otherwise, which have taken place about the significance of gender and class (and 'race'), is that we would do better to address these issues as a variable cluster, rather than to separate them out for analysis. It is not so much a question of whether they can be discussed together, as whether it is possible to sustain any rigorous analysis without recognizing their constantly evolving, dynamic interrelationship. Later in this chapter I will consider this relationship through a brief textual analysis of a popular Hollywood film. First, however, I will outline some key issues for debate.

Looking for a touch of class

Of all the hokum with which this country [America] is riddled the most odd is the common notion that it is free of class distinctions.

— W. Somerset Maugham, *A Writer's Notebook*

Yes, the rich declared class war and won.

— Moyers, http://www.pbs.org/now/commentary/moyers7.html

Where do we look for representations of class and what do we mean by the term? This is not such a simple question as it might at first appear. It was over half a century ago that the English writer Somerset Maugham commented on the popular (mis)conception that class was not an issue in the United States of America. More recently Bill Moyers disagreed, with the added proposition that class war had been fought and won (or is it lost?). In order to make sense of media representations of issues around class, it is first necessary to establish some basic categorizations. For some, the notion of class is something to do with breeding. If you come from a good (usually well-off) family, you are likely to have some class. In the UK, this kind of class is linked with tradition, education and, above all, charm. It is no accident that some of the most successful representations of 'normal' British life in recent years have centred around images of the British which are steeped in traditions of class domination. I am thinking particularly here of *Four Weddings and a Funeral* (Newell, 1994). This movie managed to perpetuate a whole range of stereotypes, most of which had been updated to offer a kind of street credibility to middle-class English charm. Hence we find that most of the opening of the film centres around the reiteration of the word 'fuck'. That such a term becomes charmingly amusing rather than threatening or abusive says a lot for the ways in which representations of class can appropriate oppositional or alienated speech and turn it into the linguistic middle-class flavour of the month. The apparently bumbling Hugh Grant becomes the charming face of this new middle class for all the world to view. In the film in question, such a sanitized and liberal class is represented as concerned mainly with social behaviour and only incidentally with wealth and power. Of course, the representation of class in the media did not begin in the 1990s. We find endless and multilayered representations in popular fiction, radio dramas, novels, plays and advertising. What perhaps unites these diverse representations is the way in which most remove from the issue of class any serious reference to wealth, power and politics. If such references do exist, they are often in the form of working class cheerfulness in the face of adversity, rather than smouldering indignation in the face of social injustice. Of course, there are exceptions. There have been films which take up such issues in a critical and challenging manner. Nevertheless, the conjecture with which the media researcher would do best to operate is one which suggests that 'class' in the media is a concept which refers to a depoliticized, often romanticized and seldom radicalized conception of societal relations. The representation of class has become, paradoxically, the means whereby class relations are either ignored or trivialized.

Analysis of the history of class relations and media representations is also important here. Early British cinema is populated by cheerful cabbies and flower salespeople, who speak with pseudo-regional accents (mainly Royal Academy of Dramatic Art cockney), and the normalizing of middle-class speech patterns as those belonging to the people who run the show. The eventual acceptance of actors with regional accents into the world of theatre and cinema in the UK did not result, however, in a challenge to class relations. Representing class has always had more to do with sustaining than challenging class relations. It has sometimes been used to sell products, but more often to cement social relations.

In the context of the UK media, we also find representation and normalization of middle-class behaviour and lifestyle as an integral part of many media representations. In a minority of cases, we also find advertising which is specifically based upon class relations or appeals to what might be described as upper-class values. In this sense, questions of class are often more about questions of taste and snobbery than about the Marxist notion of class as a relationship between workers and the means of production. So After Eight chocolates are not passed around after supper in a council house or tenement block, but after a dinner party in a very middle-class lounge. The linking of products with social values is neither new nor surprising to the media student. What is perhaps surprising is the fact that linking quality with middle-class norms has become so widely accepted with so many consumer goods. In this case, the concept of class and the notion of pampering become almost synonymous – a 'touch of class' never did anybody any harm. Where working-class life is evoked in advertising it is usually heavily romanticized, whether in the golden past of bread advertisements (Hovis) or the calm associated with the making and provision of gravy (Bisto).

Let me stress once more that there are exceptions to this tendency. On television in the UK we have our soap operas, and the two most popular and long-lasting (*Coronation Street* and *EastEnders*) are set in working-class communities. These communities are, however, virtually devoid of radical political thought. It is possible to hunt down and view media representations which offer radical views about issues of class from many different countries. Such representations are, however, the exception rather than the rule. The key issue for the media researcher is to establish whether issues of class in the media are only about questions of taste, pleasure and preference – or whether they are also about power, politics and privilege. It cannot be stressed too often that representations of class do not occur as discrete and self-contained references in media texts. They are always intimately related to questions of age, 'race', nation and gender.

Gender and discourse, gender and power

. . . gender performs an invaluable function in analysing
how women and men are made rather than born; these processes
cannot be understood in terms of sex and sexuality as attributes of the natural body.
— Oakley, Who's Afraid of Feminism?

During the 1970s there was considerable enthusiasm for media analyses which were based around spotting the ideological impurities of media texts. In relation to representations of gender, this tended to concentrate on the numerous ways in which women were objectified and stereotyped. There was (and is) plenty of material for the analyst to work upon. It was certainly the case that products as different as refrigerators and automobiles could be advertised with a woman either adorning them or in the vicinity offering a maternal or sexual blessing to the product. It was also possible for contradictions to arise. An example of this was when well-known photojournalist Donald McCullen made a calendar for the beer, Guinness, set somewhere in Africa. The calendar, made in 1986, was a piece of quality advertising and was given away to likely clients to be exhibited in pubs, clubs, bars and anywhere else thought appropriate. Each month showed, either in a group or singly, white female models posing as animals in a landscape. The viewer was provided with a line drawing of these animals underneath the photograph. So the pride of lions offers us the aesthetics of the line drawing as anchorage and the low-key titillation of the semi-clad white models sitting on the grass in various leonine poses. This example is offered as one among many which naturalized women as objects for male scrutiny and which utilized high-quality graphic and printing techniques to provide the enterprise with a little 'class'. Guinness has been a product which, over the years, has been associated with high-quality advertising. In the 1980s, however, during the period of high Thatcherism, it felt able to produce another calendar composed entirely of photographs of rounded glasses or cans of Guinness which were dressed in women's clothing or lingerie. It may sound bizarre, but each image was given the name of a woman (of the month, one presumes). There was, accompanying the image, a more extensive and ambitious piece of anchorage which seemed to echo the captions found alongside the topless models on page three of the *Sun*. So for the month of August, we find Marilyn.

Under the banner title, 'Friends of the Guinnless', the image is one of a can of Guinness, from which the outer, painted surface has detached itself and become a black and gold skirt with a crimson lining. The skirt is being blown up in the air because the can is standing over a grating, as did Marilyn Monroe in *The Seven Year Itch* (Wilder, 1955). The 'flesh' of the can is an orange-yellow and its base is rimmed with black. For those viewers who recognize the reference there is the chance of silent self-congratulation. Perhaps this would have been enough to establish Guinness as sophisticated in its sexism, but there is more to this undoubtedly high-quality graphic work. The text under the image reads as follows:

> You've heard of the Blonde Bombshell? Here's the Black and Blonde Bombshell. We asked Marilyn how it feels to be the object of so many men's desires. 'Boo-boo-de-boop', she said. O.K., so she's no Einstein. But with a body like hers, who needs a brain?

The double entendres play heavily upon the weight of the body. For the month of December there is an image of two thin-stemmed glasses of Guinness wearing a pair of lace-frilled knickers. The month of December for the Guinnless goes under the name of Holly, with the following text:

> Whatever Santa brings you for Christmas, one thing's for sure – you won't find a little cracker like Holly growing on your tree! With a big tasty body like that, you'd need two stockings to fit her in. Still – imagine finding her at the foot of your bed on Christmas morning!

This time the reference to the body is more direct and offers for the male gaze the possibility of another dual reading. December's 'big tasty body' has that rich black Guinness flavour and is, only incidentally of course, the black body of Holly, the fantasy Christmas present for thirsty heterosexual males. It would be churlish, some might argue, to scorn or reject images and advertising copy produced with such panache. The arguments against having a sense of humour can also be invoked against any allegedly sour-faced critique of what is on offer. It is, after all, only a bit of fun. The ideological pressure to accept the normalization process seems to be unstoppable for any 'full-blooded' male. This is the way the world was meant to be, and Guinness is good for you.

These examples are chosen to illustrate the fact that the media analysts who were interested in identifying the modes of signification and discourse associated with sexism, patriarchy and misogyny had good reason to undertake their work. The most sophisticated yet accessible account of gender representation in the media, acknowledging an enormous debt to Walter Benjamin (1970), remains that of John Berger in his concise and well-argued *Ways of Seeing* (1972). There are countless other examples of gender representation in need of careful analysis from a wide range of generic forms – from feature films to popular music, from magazines to sports reporting. Many of the characteristics of gender in the media are still easily naturalized or ideologically structured without seriously being challenged. This may have something to do with a reluctance among contemporary scholars to be seen to be out of touch or simply old-fashioned. I have not written here of the representation of males and masculinity in the media, though this will form a large part of the analysis of the film which is undertaken later in this chapter. Masculinity is never far from the surface in the examples chosen so far, however, because they have been produced, as Berger would remind us, for the male gaze. I have also been concerned indirectly with representations of masculinity and gender when discussing the film *True Lies* (1994). For the media student and theorist, the question remains: how best to make sense of or approach the analysis of gender relations and gender issues in the media?

Gender and the rest of the world

On the one hand, there is the possibility that we live in a patriarchal society where misogyny is alive, well and able to make all kinds of ideological adjustments in order to remain part of the discursive reserve. On the other hand there is the possibility that media representations of such star figures as Madonna and the Spice Girls have resulted in women becoming increasingly empowered and liberated from the shackles of male domination. One way to address these possibilities is to look at the employment prospects and projected wages or salaries of women in different societies (Carter *et al.*, 1998). Another is to consider media representations where claims for liberation and empowerment are made (Fiske, 1989). The former will undoubtedly confirm that gender relations are significantly moulded through economic inequalities. The latter provide a series of important textual bases for analysis, as well as potential data for important audience research. The most (over)worked examples at the beginning of the twenty-first century are likely to be Madonna and the Spice Girls. There will be many more to follow. Claims have been made by some media analysts, who draw upon the work of de Certeau in order to argue for the liberatory or empowering potential of these performers (de Certeau, 1988). Such alleged empowerment is usually linked with a relatively private sense of awareness shared by the relatively powerless. It is a form of empowerment which tends to be more symbolic than politically significant. It is recognizable in a form of critical writing which extols the potential of fantasy over the need for direct political action. This is not to suggest that fantasy is not or should not be a significant feature of social existence. It is, however, to suggest that prioritizing resistance through fantasy over resistance through acting upon social and material conditions is a distant cousin of the suggestion in the North American folk song that you can have pie in the sky when you die. The kinds of resistance which have been given positive recognition by some media theorists following the era of Thatcherism, Reaganism and the collapse of state socialism, have been predominantly of this type. The analysis of class and gender relations and the representation of class and gender issues have to be studied with this in mind. For Fiske power relations can be associated with the pleasure to be had from certain forms of media consumption, particularly for 'the powerless':

> But pleasure is closely related to power; for the powerless, the pleasure in resisting/evading power is at least as great as the pleasure of exerting power for the powerful. Subcultural pleasure is empowering pleasure.
>
> (Fiske, 1989: 117)

It is also possible to develop this argument along the lines that pleasure is an ideological category, precisely because it is about power relations. If power relations can remain either unchallenged or better tolerated because certain genres of media representation make oppression more bearable, then such representations could be said to have therapeutic as well as ideological significance. Empowerment becomes a synonym for 'getting by'. These issues need further investigation and have critical implications for the development of viable research methodologies for the media researcher.

Gender and 'girl power'

Favourite word: Bollocks. It's so expressive.

— Victoria in Spice Girls, *Girl Power*

I will consider briefly here the first 'official' book published by the Spice Girls, entitled *Girl Power* (Spice Girls, 1997). The purpose in considering this text is to highlight the type of statements made for a (then) young audience, and the extent to which claims can be made that such a text is indeed liberatory or establishing some kind of change in gender relations. Whether we are now young students of the media or people who watched as the Spice Girls appeared on the international stage, there is much to learn from the claims made in this already forgotten publication. I do not pretend to offer an all-inclusive or summative form of analysis. My concern here is to highlight the contradictions and claims inherent in a particular phenomenon which enjoyed considerable media coverage at the end of the century – that of 'girl power'.

It is a text concerned with gender representation, or perhaps one might argue, with gender construction. As one might expect in a book aimed at the younger teenage (and even younger) market, there are many colour photographs and the writing is basic and to the point. Definitions of what constitutes girl power are offered early in the text. They range from the specific and earthy ('Girl Power is when you and your mates reply to wolf whistles by shouting, "Get your arse out!"') to the general and aspiring ('Girl Power is when you believe in yourself and control your own life'). Each member of the group is then given a few pages of images and text where they speak to the reader about their interests and beliefs. Emma (also known as Baby Spice) tells us: 'I don't want to be a cutie, I want to be a hot sexy bitch.' She also tells the reader that the Spice Girls are doing it and 'so can you'. This may involve learning to 'shout a bit louder'. The emphasis on more than one occasion is on the importance of taking control and doing it. Girls have a right to stick up for themselves. 'The strong will survive and the wise excel,' says Mel B, and Mel C adds, 'We are what we are. We're not gonna change.' Mel C is not interested in restaurants and would rather be invited to a football match. She says that the Spice Girls represent 'a new attitude. Girls are taking control.'

Geri Halliwell points out that the Spice Girls feel passionate about everything, and adds, 'I'd like to be remembered as a wild freedom-fighter with method in her madness. Life itself is a lesson.' Finally, the book offers a quotation which is presumably attributed to the whole group and is concerned with feminism:

> Feminism has become a dirty word. Girl Power is just a Nineties way of saying it. We can give feminism a kick up the arse. Women can be so powerful when they show solidarity.
>
> (Spice Girls, 1997: 48–9)

The mode of address throughout is direct and informal, playing with the possibility of street talk, but remaining at the level of what might be called discreet vulgarity. This is also apparent in the baby-doll outfit which Emma, the 'baby' of the group wears as she rests with her eyes closed on a bed with the others. The floating teddy-bear pattern on the outfit has the words 'fuck off' printed in a sunny red at regular intervals between the cuddly animals.

The media researcher is faced with a range of issues for consideration in approaching such a text. I have not begun to deal with the ways in which the imagery is interspersed with the written word. A brief semiotic analysis might lead one to suggest that there is much energy in the book and that the anchorage provided by the images is one of youth, feistiness and glamour. The layout of the book suggests the importance of vectors in guiding our reading of the images and written text (Kress and Van Leeuwen, 1990: 20). This consideration would remain, however, a more formal and possibly formalist approach unless it were related to the social context in which the book/text is likely to be used. We need to be concerned not only with how reading takes place, but when, where, by whom and under what conditions.

It might also be possible to approach the text as a piece of commercial production and ask who was responsible for drafting and approving the precise wording. If we take a sentence like, 'The strong will survive and the wise excel', how are we supposed to interpret it? Is it a piece of wisdom from some specific source, or is it an example of the thinking process of Mel

B? Investigating these issues is not a matter of looking for a way to undermine what is written. It is, however, an investigative approach into the origins of texts as well as the social significance of their meanings. This is a text which, outside its appeal as related to a singing group of young women, relates to issues about women's place and purpose in society. It would be possible to read such a text as liberatory in that it speaks of rejecting one's preordained place as a 'girl' in a male-dominated society. Such an appeal undoubtedly has value for some young women as a means of building a sense of identity and self-worth. Indeed British television was conscious of this to the extent of producing Spice Girls special shows where the group performed before a mainly female audience to propagate their views – and, of course, their songs.

It would also be possible to read *Girl Power* as a pragmatic and commercially motivated piece of schlock, designed to meet commercially self-perpetuated needs. Of course, the contradictions raised by such a book, as with the group itself, are related to the extent to which the commercial excludes or facilitates the possibility of female empowerment. It is also valid to ask how we might ascertain the extent to which the members of the Spice Girls were able to assert some kind of feminine control over their representation – beyond the kind of slogans and the energetic charge they brought to their work. If we accept that gender is a socially produced category, the means by which this production process is achieved become of crucial significance. Consideration of gender in the media, as with the consideration of class, cannot escape from the commercial and ideological issues without which there would be no representations to study in the first place. The strength of our analysis does not depend, however, upon the amount of postmodern irony we can bring to bear upon gender representation in the early twenty-first century. It depends upon the rigour with which our analysis and argument follow through from the identification and description of the issues to the conclusions which our methodology and positioning facilitate. Put simply, the commercialization of girl power facilitates the creation of multimillionaires as sometime propagandists for the cause of girl power. For the rest, there is the same fantasy which has been provided by Madonna and, before her, a host of other women performers. The freedom of which the Spice Girls (or the copywriters) speak is freedom from the crassness of everyday sexism and patriarchal domination. This is, or would be, a freedom indeed – and should be a right. The solutions which 'they' offer, however, are simple, simplistic and of short-term significance to all but the commercially successful. Unless, that is, we adopt a methodology of celebration and take our intellectual or material cut of that cake. It is a matter of debate and consequence. With hindsight, we need a contemporary analysis of the phenomena of the individual Spice Girls and Madonna as they are reinvented, restructured, repackaged. Or should we say as they grow and develop? The questions we ask here are positioned and positioning, as are the answers they are likely to generate.

Officers and gendered men

The film *An Officer and a Gentleman* was released in 1982. It was directed by Taylor Hackford. I have chosen to discuss it here because it is a textbook text, combining issues around class, 'race' and gender with considerable cinematic skill. It is also an ideological minefield, offering numerous romantic clichés, a romanticized notion of 'race' relations, a justification of patriarchal power relations and near despair about any hope for the working class. That, at least, is one reading. The critics responded with mixed feelings. For Roger Ebert, it was 'the best movie about love I have seen in a long time' (Ebert, 1997). For Pauline Kael, the film demonstrated the skill and the gall of Hackford as he worked on the audience: 'he fingers the soft spots on our infantile skulls . . . It's crap, but crap on a motorcycle' (Kael, 1987: 381). The film, if you do not reject it out of hand, is undoubtedly well crafted and designed to elicit a range of emotional responses through the careful combination of image, music and plot. In this it is similar to many other 'formula' romances and it had some success, grossing over $129 million in the USA.

The movie also demonstrates the ways in which popular culture provides pleasure, laughter and tears as part of an ideological package, which leaves little room for resistance. It offers instead a fantasy world of relationships, from which certain key features of everyday life have been either excluded or ignored. At the same time, the film does acknowledge certain material conditions of existence, and when it does so they are relentlessly bleak. Complicity with the plot of the film and its modes of address is precisely what is required if the ideological force field which is *An Officer and a Gentleman* is to succeed. Before discussing how this is accomplished, I will outline the main structure of the plot and discuss the importance of the star image personas the film offers.

The main action of the film takes place in and around a Naval Aviation Officer Candidate School in Washington State. It centres on an intake of male and female trainees on a 13-week intensive course, which is both academic and physical. Successful candidates go on to flight school, but only about half will succeed. Across the Puget Sound there is a working-class community, which includes many young women who work in a paper factory. They spend much of their spare time seeking ways to get to know the young officer candidates. Some dream of becoming officers' wives.

After the first month of training there is a regimental ball and some of the young women from across the bay attend, including the two friends Paula (Debra Winger) and Lynette (Lisa Blount). Paula pairs off with Zack Mayo (Richard Gere). One thing leads to another and they fall in love. Paula, the daughter of a woman who had once fallen for an officer candidate and been jilted, refuses to try to become pregnant to trap Jack, unlike her friend Lisa, who is prepared to say she is pregnant in order to stay with Sid (David Keith). Zack, on the other hand, is a loner whose mother commited suicide and whose father is a drunken lascivious sailor. Zack is afraid of commitment, though during the film he overcomes this fear in relation to both his military companions and Paula. Before this can occur there has to be a dramatic denouement. It comes in the form of the suicide of Sid, Zack's friend. Sid hangs himself in a motel bathroom for two reasons. First, because he has 'failed' as an officer candidate and has voluntarily left the training. The main reason for this is that Sid did not want to become a pilot, but was doing it for his father. At the same time, Lynette has turned down his offer of marriage, confessed that she is not pregnant and is clearly uneasy about becoming the wife of a floor manager in a commercial store – Sid's preferred profession.

The denouement is also linked to an important sub-plot. Zack has a stormy relationship with the drill sergeant, Foley (Louis Gossett Jr). Both are adept street fighters, though Zack learned most of his skills when in the Philippines, where his drunken sailor father was stationed. At the end of the movie, Zack and Foley fight on the padded training platform in the hangar while the other officer candidates watch from a distance. Neither wins, but as a dramatic nodal point it allows the bad feelings about Sid's death to be purged and finally makes a rounded person out of Zack (Richard Gere). The film moves towards a symphonic climax when the officer candidates graduate, Zack tells Foley that he never could have done it without him, and the music pulsates with a heavy loading on the bass capacity of the speakers. Zack then watches as his fellow graduates celebrate, gets on his Harley-Davidson motorbike, pauses to watch Foley begin the induction of the next intake and rides off to the paper factory where he collects Paula, to the applause of her working colleagues.

The story is one which could, with a little cleaning up, have been written for Mills and Boon. It is also a majestic example of the utilization of star image and evocative music to drive and enrich the melodramatic and heavily romanticized narrative. There are plenty of bodies to observe, whether involved in athletic or sexual activity. And they are the bodies of 'stars', rather than the bodies of the working class. In lesser hands it could have been only an embarrassment to watch. The key issue from a media studies perspective is to consider how issues of class, gender and 'race' are represented or constructed in the narrative as a whole and at certain key moments. It is to these that we can now turn.

Steers, queers and homophobia

Issues of gender dominate the movie, mainly because so much of it is about what it means to be a 'real' man, and how a woman might accommodate this reality. If a woman follows her traditional, possibly preordained, pathway, she will seek the man of her dreams and hope that he will also be a man of class. If she seeks to be the equal of a man, she will have to learn how to do so much which a man can do. She will have to learn to stop weeping because she is a woman, physically weaker than the men (in this film anyway). She will have to rely on men to help her to become like them. She will finally revert to type and weep as she thanks Sergeant Foley for his support. Another key motif in the film is the need for the one woman candidate we see, Casey Seeger (Lisa Eilbacher) to climb over a high wooden wall which is part of the obstacle course which all candidates use. When she finally does so it is because of encouragement and cajoling from Zack, as he forsakes his chance to break the record for completing the course, and is seen to be doing so by the rest of the squad and Sergeant Foley. In this way, issues of comradeship, team playing, male bonding, inter-ethnic relations and the helpless woman being saved by a well-wishing man, are all melded into one scene. It is this suasive combination which makes it less likely that the masculization (with masculine help) of female success will seem anything other than natural.

Similarly, the reactionary judgements of Sergeant Foley are offered in a context of uncritical admiration for his manliness, his soldierliness and his blackness. We first see Foley in pieces. In the first shot, his shoes appear on the steps followed by his well-creased trousers. The next shot shows his hand on a drill cane. The hand is wearing a large ring, and it is the hand of a person of colour. This is followed by a big close-up of his epaulette from above, then another from the front of his medal ribbons. Finally we see his hat badge and the whole of Sergeant Foley moves into picture. He is an impressive figure, and he lays into the recruits with a linguistic vehemence which facilitates the nearest thing that militarism is ever likely to provide to lyricism. It is a winning performance, but the reason for noting it here is that it facilitates the several homophobic references which are thoroughly naturalized in the film. In speaking to the gullible and still vaguely schoolboyish Sid, Foley coaxes him to use the word 'you'. This is skilfully transmuted into the word 'ewe' and Foley enters a routine reminiscent of all the worst bullying tactics ever perpetrated on a young man by a hooligan. 'You want to fuck me up the ass?' he enquires. Sid is shocked to the core and insists that he is not 'queer'. When asked where he comes from, Sid says Oklahoma. Foley says only two things come from Oklahoma, 'steers and queers', and asks Sid which one he is. If you inhabit the discursive regime of the scriptwriter/Foley, it might be funny, but it is also a bleak legitimization of homophobia. Foley repeats this routine at the end of the film with a new intake of candidates, under the admiring, perhaps adoring, eyes of the new officer, Zack Mayo. In this way we can see how very close homophobia and the homoerotic can come while being apparently unaware of each other. The social construction of gender in the media often facilitates pleasure in male bonding which approaches gay infatuation, while insisting on the need for and maintenance of a thoroughgoing masculine heterosexuality. We see this in the figures of Danny Glover and Mel Gibson in the *Lethal Weapon* films, or the more juvenile characters of Gary (Martin Clunes) and Tony (Neil Morrissey) in the UK television series *Men Behaving Badly*.

In *An Officer and a Gentleman*, the women who happen to be working class are doubly disadvantaged. Unlike Zack, they have not been through college, *and* they are women. They are thus trapped into (narrative) discourses and accompanying lifestyles which seek escape above all else. The escape is not, interestingly, escape *to* a man, but *from* their working-class existence. In this sense it is the male who is the human vector. As the movie approaches its climax, one of Paula's fellow workers sums up her feeling when she points out that the officer candidates change their behaviour towards the end of their training. 'There comes a time, right after they get through survival training, when they start to think they can make it without you . . .'. She then summarizes the bitterness which years of observing this behaviour can generate, in narrative terms at least: 'May they all crash and burn.'

There is not a great deal of male working-class representation in the movie, and what there is, on the surface, is far from salutary. Zack's father is desribed as a drunken whore-chaser. Foley is an African-American drill sergeant with a magnificent physique and a charismatic presence. He is also a reactionary and programmed character, whose life is one of repeating the same script in a more or less continuous cycle. At the end of the movie he is seen speaking to the new intake of recruits about listening to punk rock music and bad-mouthing their country – a slight modification of his suggestion to the previous intake that they have been listening to Mick Jagger. Then there are the young men in the local bar who don't much like the officer candidates in their white uniforms going out with the local girls. They do, you might think, have a point, but the narrative tells us otherwise. For when one of them complains about you 'rich college boys' to Zack, we know better. Zack has had a much rougher time than them. Zack is trying to make his way up and out to where he belongs – or where the narrative tells us he belongs. Male working-class behaviour is also represented in the colour-drained, seedy flashbacks to Zack's life in the Philippines, and in the eagle tattooed on his shoulder. This is something spotted by Foley who points out, as has Zack's father before him, that 'officers don't have tattoos'.

Zack, of course, is the exception. This movie provides the exception to many things. It also identifies the importance of knowing your place and, for the hero of the film, the ability to transcend his likely destiny were he outside this narrative. Foley tries to tell Zack that he is no more officer material than is Foley himself. There is a long line of filmic representation which confirms the class and gender positioning of such characters, the most notable of which would be Burt Lancaster as Sergeant Milton Warden in *From Here to Eternity* (Zinnemann, 1953). But in *An Officer and a Gentleman*, film issues of class are transcended via myth, the myth described so aptly in the lyrics of the title song of the film – being 'up where we belong'. And if Zack can do it, he can also take Paula with him.

The end of the movie is one which is laden with emotion. It not just that Zack has made it through his basic training. It is that Casey Seeger has also made it, and they both know how to be grateful to their drill sergeant. Lynette, the onetime friend of Sid, has also learned a lesson and is so noble that she can lead the applause and provide the last words of the film: 'Way to go, Paula. Way to go . . .'. And it is a way which combines well with the sentiments of the lyrics. Zack comes into the paper factory in his white officer uniform and accompanied by a throbbing music track, picks Paula up and carries her out to a future which we are spared. On the way, her cap comes off, and Paula's copious hair flows around her shoulders. As they pass the camera, we see her look of total devotion as she stares into Zack's eyes. They walk away with the light behind them and, just before the frame freezes, Paula takes Zack's officer cap and puts it on her own head. Fade up the music.

But lest this should seem to be only negative critique, it is important to note that the film has other meanings on offer. Beyond the thrill of watching the two young lovers escape, there are those who are left behind. There is near tragedy in watching Foley begin his reactionary diatribe for a second time. Comedy and tragedy. There is unremitting and sentimentalized tragedy in looking at the crying eyes of the paper factory workers as they see one of their number go off in the arms of a white knight. All they will have left is the possibility of de Certeau's lines of resistance open to them. And for Zack and Paula, the future will involve learning the rules of etiquette and living with other classes for the remainder of the six years of training. But that is beyond the narrative and the narrative suggests persuasively that it is good to dream. It is also persuasive about roles that are there to be filled if you are a man, a woman, a 'queer' or a factory worker. Thus gender, class and 'race' are offered as contradictory, malleable yet unchanging categories. Thus the ideological dimension of a powerful cinematic narrative is confirmed as a representation of that which is necessary rather than real.

Gender and class and women for men

The most compelling critique of realism involves the subordinated positioning of women, not simply in terms of roles but also in terms of narrative structure. Although they may be contested and qualified, arguments about the pervasiveness of fetishistic and voyeuristic relations between a masculine view and a female image as an object of visual pleasure have great persuasive power.

— Nichols, *Representing Reality*

The purpose of this book is to generate debate and discussion as well as encourage media analysis. What has been offered here has left out vast fields of human experience and only hinted at the richness and potential of analytic approaches to gender and class representation. I have not discussed the question of fashion and consumption in relation to gender and class. There are those who have argued that fashion is a field in which young people, particularly, are able to express and experiment with their identities (McRobbie, 1991). The extent to which these fashion changes have been in some way emancipatory is something which requires a careful study of media representations. It also requires some study of the fashion industry in relation to the media and other industries. Once again, there are those who argue that new fashions and new identities have impacted upon economic structures. Where young people have suffered economic hardship, they have managed to have creative fun with clothes and materials that are cheap and accessible through street markets or charity shops. There is undoubtedly some strength to this argument. It is also one which might miss the ways in which the fashion and other industries can adapt to and accommodate this change. Radical thought and radical fashion can always be repackaged and resold. These fashions are, in turn, related to the ways in which issues of gender are re-presented in the media. Hence the relationship between relative economic deprivation and what it means to assert a feminine or masculine identity needs some study. Even if Madonna wore clothes which did not cost much (sometimes), her gender identity was and is formed as much by her bank account as her attire. That at least is a possible reading. It then leaves those with only the clothes and very little in the bank in a somewhat different relationship to their material conditions of existence. The way that the media may plug this gap is by allowing both Madonna, the Spice Girls and the economically deprived to share girl power: to engage in carnivalesque opposition and to revel in shared empowerment. The represented world for the female gender thus becomes a world of fantasy, and it is strictly delimited by age and usually shape. As the Spice Girls tell us: 'We're all mad. We're in a bizarre world so you've got to be mad to live in it' (Spice Girls, 1996: 49).

Gender and class representation cannot but be concerned with issues of power in societies. Where mixed class relations come together in blockbuster movies such as *Titanic* (Cameron, 1997), it is interesting to note the way in which they are structured and hence re-presentable. The young, male, gifted, good-looking, charming, working-class hero has to die. The audience is invited to concentrate on a doomed love affair (suppose the *Titanic* had not sunk . . .?). The young hero is an artist. The young heroine is the model. We are there to look in on them both. We share their hopes and learn from their tragedies.

101

I have discussed other media representations which work to sustain patriarchal gender relations, and the Guinness calendar was only one example among many. The media student and researcher may wish, also, to enter and explore the complexities of the audience's relation with media texts. This allows for an extraordinary range of possibilities for reading and interpreting issues of gender, class and 'race'. The complexities become more layered and sometimes seem impenetrable when psychoanalytic theory is introduced to the study of gender relations. Cohan and Hark provide a first-class though demanding introduction here (Cohan and Hark, 1993).

The study of gender and class in the media embroils us in debates about whether the media lead society in forming ideas and opinions, or whether the opinions are formed first and merely re-presented in the media. Some media representations offer discourses of masculinity in crisis, from *Friends* to *The Full Monty*. Woody Allen produces either serious or comic overviews of (his) gender. Pedro Almodóvar, in movies such as *All About My Mother* (1998) may offer interpretations of gender identity which are confounding, bewitching and often deeply disturbing – but this is to a somewhat limited audience.

Conventional relations between class and gender in the media are still played out regularly in the press, magazines, at the cinema, and on television and radio. For the media student the task is to study the extent to which the conventions of representation of class and gender are established and steady or evolving and tenuous. Answers are likely to be contradictory and inconclusive. Continuous and specific textual study is required, related to the likely conditions of reception of media messages. I will return to these issues in chapter nine.

FURTHER READING

Hill, J., 1986, *Sex, Class and Realism.*
Concentrating on British cinema, Hill deals with the emergence of the 'social problem' film, when topics such as juvenile delinquency, prostitution, homosexuality and 'race' became the concern of film-makers. Contains strong discussion of realism and relevant social history.

McDonald, M., 1995, *Representing Women: myths of femininity in the popular media.*
This text reassesses how women are talked about and constructed visually across a range of popular media. Arguing for the importance of a historical approach, this book examines continuities and changes in dominant myths of femininity, especially in the transition from the modern to the postmodern period. Outlining key theoretical debates in an accessible manner, this book offers a wide range of examples from advertising, women's magazines, popular television programmes and mainstream film.

Stead, P., 1989, *Film and the Working Class.*
Stead's book, from the prestigious Cinema and Society series, works chronologically from the coming of television up to the era of James Bond. He concentrates on films which depict working-class conditions and struggle. The analysis combines theoretical insight with material taken from contemporary trade journals and press. Considers both UK and US examples.

chapter eight

The media and history

Every time history repeats itself, the price goes up.

— Anon.

I should like for us to abandon our whole educational system as it is now constituted. Deliberately abandon, that is; rather than let it vanish, as it is doing through attrition. I would then begin again.

I would make history the spine of the mandatory twelve years of state-imposed indoctrination. Although, ideally, 'reading skill' should be improved, this is not going to happen for the third generation of TV-watchers, as well as computer-masters. Therefore, let us be bold. Let us screen history.

— Gore Vidal, *Screening History*

Forrest Gump *tells us with reflective and condensed bumper-sticker irony (and with something akin to the long view of the* Annales *school of history that deals with 'long-term equilibriums and disequilibriums' through the minute detailing of everyday life and its 'conjunctures'), 'Shit happens.'*

— Vivian Sobchack, *The Persistence of History*

The media fragments things; it [sic] *puts a tremendous burden on educators trying to develop any kind of historical sense, not in a narrow professional way, but any sense of cause and consequence down the line over a period of time. Newspapers and television fragment time into twenty-four-hour units. Or decades. Every decade you've got to have a special issues of* Time *and all that crap, as if that was significant.*

— William Appleman Williams in Abelove *et al.*, *Visions of History*

History is probably the most important and significant academic discipline for media studies students and researchers. This may seem a somewhat heretical claim, but it is one which I believe will stand the test of time. In this chapter I will try to justify the claim by reference to some questions of historiography and by considering selected media examples. The first and, I would argue, most healthy point to note is that historians find it difficult to agree about much beyond the suggestion that 'shit happens'. Whether this involves the recognition of something as basic as 'the facts' is also a highly contentious issue. The concept of a fact has come in for some serious discussion and dispute among reputable scholars. An interesting and provocative overview of some debates can be found in Jenkins (1997). The second point to note is that writing history is analogous in many ways to the construction of a media message. Of course, they are not both made under the same conditions, with the same preparation or the same training. Nevertheless, there is an important sense in which the media producer has to make decisions about structure, mode of address, narrative form, presences and absences, and general intellectual and professional positioning, in relation to subject matter or theme. In this, the media producer is very similar to the historian. Where they differ is, by and large, in terms of the amount of time the historian is expected (and expects) to devote to preparation and research for their work. The exception to this might be when specific media, usually television, employ researchers to assist in the making of programmes which purport to be history in one form or another.

What is historiography and how does it relate to media studies?

Historiography is concerned with the study of the development of historical method, historical research and the writing of history. It is about how history comes to be what it is. For some historians, the past is nothing more or less than chaos. It is history, in the ways in which it is constructed, which imposes some kind of order on that chaos. (For introductions to debates in the field, see Carr, 1978; Abelove *et al.*, 1983; Evans, 1997; Hobsbawm, 1997; Jenkins, 1999. For a more demanding – and rewarding – overview of key debates, see Callinicos, 1995.) One immediate and obvious way in which order has been imposed on the past is through the periodic division of time. Media studies researchers will have seen this most recently with the coming of the millennium. There was a sense that producers, experts, individual citizens and religious leaders were all seeking to mark in some way the change of century. The fact that important or lasting issues in history may not be susceptible to decimal or other numerical analysis is not always taken into account. In the media, this has become more of an issue as the news has moved from being a three-times-daily event, to news on the hour, to twenty-four-hour news. The pressures of time in the world of the media bring about a frenetic and sometimes neurotic sense of crisis-laden historiography. Order must be imposed upon the chaos, and furthermore there have to be experts on hand to comment upon the order they are daily imposing.

Historiography is also about the narrativization of history – turning the past into a (usually good) story for the present. There is always a sense of chronology in history. Historical events happen in an agreed and only occasionally disputed order. But how one tells the story of those events is another matter altogether. Hayden White has summarized the situation thus:

> The events must be not only registered within the chronological framework of their original occurrence but narrated as well, that is to say, revealed as

possessing a structure, an order of meaning, which they do *not* possess as
mere sequence.

(White, 1980: 5)

We know very well that the drive towards narrative is not confined to the writing of history,
but for the media studies student there is much to be learned from the forms of construction
of historical narratives. For White, the question of narrative in history has been important
because with the narrative comes a sense of involvement with that which is legal or legitimate.
Narrative brings with it, it could be argued, a certain sense of authority. This is just as much
the case with the fictional narrative as with that deemed factual. Historical narratives have also
been interpreted as the means whereby the historian is able to moralize about the matter in
hand. Such moralization may not take the form of individual counsel about ways to behave
(though it does do so sometimes), but it is more likely to take the form of a justification of a
world-view. In this sense, history was and is never anything other than ideological.

In relation to history, there are numerous examples which provide narrative accounts of
the past designed to 'place' a particular nation at the centre of social developments, and which
result in the construction of very selective narratives. Marc Ferro has provided an incisive and
sometimes shocking account of the ways in which history has been written to fulfil particular
nationalistic or other aspirations (Ferro, 1984). Ferro is also very aware of the ways in which a
narrative control over the past is crucial to 'legitimise dominion and justify legal claims'
(Ferro, 1984: vii). Zygmunt Bauman has demonstrated in some detail the ways in which the
Third Reich went about legitimizing the Holocaust by spurious appeals to 'history', and by
legalizing and legitimizing its murderous enterprises (Bauman, 1989). Donald Horne has
written of the ways in which museums around the world have used their exhibits to justify
highly selective visions of the world:

> Anachronism (using the word in its original sense) [Anachronism: the
> representation of an event, person or thing in a historical context in which it
> could not have occurred or happened.] is the very essence of tourism: the present
> is used to explain the relics of the past, and then the meanings given to the past
> are used to justify aspects of the present, or to justify beliefs abut how things
> should be changed.

(Horne, 1984: 29)

The invention of tradition is something which has been well documented by a number of
scholars. One of the most interesting is *The Invention of Tradition* (Hobsbawm and Ranger,
1983), in which numerous 'traditional' issues are demonstrated to be of relatively recent
origin. The Scottish kilt, for instance, is said to have been invented in the eighteenth
century by an English Quaker from Lancashire called Thomas Rawlinson. The tartan,
kailyard and, most importantly, the kilt, have dominated media representations of
Scottishness. The ideological significance of leaving such 'traditions' unquestioned is
certainly a matter for the media researcher to investigate. Linked to these kinds of
developments we also find an explosion in the twentieth century of what has become known
as the heritage industry (Hewison, 1987). This has involved another (re)writing of histories

in creative, romanticized and, some might argue, mendacious ways. In the UK it has resulted in the development of specific museums which romanticize or reconstruct the past, often with the help of actors, so that the museum is partly a performance centre, where history is literally acted out before us.

I would hope that the examples so far cited provide a strong indication of ways in which issues of historiography relate to the pursuit of media studies. I would also hope that they provide a salutary indication of the fact that the construction, reconstruction, alteration and occasional invention of discourses of history have been the business of historians and others before Hollywood, Cinecittà and others set to work on historical representation. The rest of this chapter will offer examples of some of the ways in which the media have 'written' specific versions of history in a variety of genres, or the ways in which what has been represented has itself become of historical importance. The examples I have chosen cover a wide field of representation. They are linked by one important factor: they are dependent upon stated or unstated theorizations of history. I will finish the chapter by returning to some of the theoretical debates which have informed both historians and theorists of the media.

Historiography and media representations for children

The number and range of educational broadcasts for children that deal with history is impressive. There are those which are specifically designed for use in schools and there are those of a more general nature, which hope to attract children and possibly their parents as viewers. Then there are the programmes which are first and foremost entertainment, but which also offer historical overviews of the world, or a part of it. These may range from dramas about Robin Hood and the Sheriff of Nottingham to those about Davy Crockett or Abraham Lincoln. For the media studies researcher, all these representations are a rich source of material for productive study (Ferguson, 1998: chapter nine). The construction of the past offered to young people is of crucial significance in their personal, social and educational development. Representations offered to young people are often rehearsals of more general world-views which will become part of the discursive reserve of adult audiences.

I will begin here with a consideration of a programme made by the BBC for 11–13 year olds in the UK. It is part of a series made in the 1980s called *History 11–13 The Middle Ages*. The period covered and the period of the broadcast is sufficiently distant from today to allow, one might hope, for relatively balanced judgements to be offered about it. There are five programmes in this series, each of approximately 25 minutes' duration, and the first is the only one which is entirely dramatized. It deals with the Peasants' Revolt, which took place in England in 1381. The brief description and analysis which follows is intended to demonstrate what I would argue are recurrent patterns in educational and other documentaries which are concerned with moments of social crisis in history. In order to make sense of any critique, however, it is necessary to interrogate your subject. In this case, the subject is, first, the Peasants' Revolt and, then, the genre of educational television. We may, should we so decide, direct our questions in a manner which suggests that there is an objective or true account of the revolt waiting to be made. We may also ask how the television representation on offer might have been different from the way it is and in whose interests it works in its present form. This latter approach is more productive, and it is the one I will follow here.

The context for the programme's content is medieval Britain, in which the lands were owned by the Church and the nobles. Though many of the peasants were no longer slaves in the legal sense, they often had to spend much of their working week producing crops or toiling on the land for their employers. After that, they might keep some of the products of their labour for themselves. They also had to pay taxes to the king to finance the wars which England was fighting in France, where there were armies waiting to be paid. Economic matters dictated that the boy king, Richard, should seek taxes to finance war. The burden of taxation in the form of a poll tax was enough to trigger a revolt from some peasants, mainly those living in East Anglia. They marched on London and demanded to see the king. One of their leaders was a man called Wat Tyler (now an accepted figure in the heritage industry's version of 'our' past). Another key figure is John Ball, a radical priest with some strong socialist pretensions. The peasants met with the king in the open fields of Mile End. There was some kind of fight when Tyler met the king and his nobles, resulting in Tyler's death, with thousands of peasants watching from a distance. The revolt eventually collapsed and the peasants returned to where they had come from. The king reneged on all the promises he had made to the peasants during the revolt and John Ball was hanged, drawn and quartered, and various parts of his body despatched to different corners of the land. (For further information on the Peasants' Revolt, see Dobson, R. B. (ed.), 1984; Price, M., 1980; Webber, H., 1980 – the latter is a populist and conservative interpretation).

Little is known of the precise details of the revolt or the peasants who took part in it. Most of the primary sources have proven unreliable as they were written by chroniclers who were, almost without exception, nowhere near what happened and wrote some years after the event. They were also uniformly hostile to the peasants and more interested in the values of chivalry than the gathering of empirical data. Such is the background against which the BBC constructed its brief drama for schools.

Some records do exist of peasants who were taxed, and of course records exist of some that were hanged. The script for the programme I will discuss took notice of this, and the peasants represented all have some basis in history because a sentence or a named reference exists about their fate. The only exception to this is the wife of one of the key figures, a certain John Wolk. Joan Wolk, however, is a key figure in the drama. The programme begins after the revolt and most of it is a flashback to the attempted collection of the poll tax, followed by the march on London, the appearance of Tyler as the peasants' leader and the return to their huts of John Wolk and Diccon Tripat, his friend. Wolk is hanged and the last shot of the programme shows his leather-booted feet swinging from a tree as his wife, Joan, looks up at him. It is certainly material which might be thought likely to hold the attention of a young school audience in the 1980s.

Putting peasants in perspective

There is no space here for more than a brief analysis of the modes of signification and narrative structure of this programme. I want to comment on the representation of women, the handling of radical ideas, the representation of rebellious leaders and the implied lessons to be learned from what has been shown. Before doing so, I should point out that I recognize the budgetary constraints under which the producers of educational programmes have to operate. This particular drama has a *mise-en-scène* which is constructed around a minimalist realism. The ideological dimensions of the text, however, are neither excusable nor explicable by reference to the production constraints.

Joan Wolk is, as I have noted, an invented character, though it is quite possible that John Wolk was married or lived with a woman. The character portrayed in the drama is something of a stereotype and is given some particularly unpleasant lines to deliver. She does this with a whining voice with constantly falling tones of reproach or dismay. When John Wolk and his friend Diccon Tripat are discussing the teachings of the radical preacher John Ball, their dialogue encapsulates all that is most suspect in the programme.

SCENE 5
(1) DICCON: (WHISPERING)
And Thomas Baker was also talking about that preacher, John Ball.
(2) JOAN: (LEANING FORWARD)
John Ball's nothing but a bottle-bellied chamber-pot.
(JOHN GIVES DICCON AN 'IGNORE HER' LOOK;
HE UP-ENDS THE STOOL AND RAMS LEG FURTHER INTO PLACE)
(3) JOHN: (TO DICCON)
Hold that while I belt it.
(HE PICKS UP MALLET)
(4) DICCON: (WHISPERING)
According to them John Ball said . . .
Here! That's my fingers! . . .
He said . . . (HE THINKS AND PREPARES TO QUOTE)
'Ah, good people, things are not going well in England . . .
(CONTINUED AS V/O IN SCENE 6.)
SCENE 6 INT. ROOM IN TOWER. DAY.
(GUARD BY PILLAR, HALES ON DAIS. RICHARD ON THRONE.
WALWORTH STANDING R. COURTIER PLAYING CAT'S CRADLE.
RICHARD II READING AND EATING CHICKEN LEG. WINE AND
SWEETMEATS BY HIM. HALES OSTENTATIOUSLY EATS A SMALL
PIECE OF WHITE BREAD.)
V/O CONTD:
DICCON: . . . nor will they until all property is shared and Lords and peasants are equal. They dress in velvet and rich furs when we have clothes made out of poor cloth. They have wine and white bread, while we eat black bread and drink water.

SCENE 7. INT. HUT. DAY.
(5) (DICCON NOW SEATED ON MENDED STOOL)
DICCON: They live in fine houses.
JOHN: We have the pain and labour of the fields, and we're treated like slaves.

The fact that Diccon whispers the first mention of John Ball indicates one of two possibilities. Either he thinks this is a seditious matter or he wants to avoid the nagging whine of Joan's voice. Her response to the mention of Ball's name elicits one of her more florid (scripted) metaphors and a look from her husband, with which we are complicit, which confirms his opinion that there is no point in taking any notice of her. It also implies that she had heard of John Ball before Diccon's mention of him. If this is the case, we are left wondering how she responded to the detail of his arguments, particularly in relation to the organization of the Church. But once again, the requirements of the narrative preclude any possible engagement with these questions.

Joan's response leads John to ask Diccon to hold the stool in an absurd manner if he intends to drive the stool leg back into place with a blow of the mallet. John's request to Diccon is perilously close to the music-hall gag based upon an imbecilic misunderstanding – 'See that nail? Take this hammer. When I nod my head, hit it.' It may be apparent to the 11–13-year-old audience that this is coming, or it may be a surprise. Either way, what happens is designed to raise a laugh immediately before we hear the message which John Ball had been preaching. The choice to present this message through the tail-end of a weak joke is significant. If the joke succeeds in making the audience laugh, they are likely to miss at least the beginning of what is said. If they do not laugh, but groan, it will still be apparent that the words of this 'bottle-bellied chamber-pot' are not to be taken too seriously.

The words of Ball are paraphrased from Froissart's chronicles. Froissart, like most chroniclers of the time, was more interested in the codes of chivalry than in checking what might have happened in the revolt. By Froissart's code, the peasants were base and reprehensible in daring even to think of revolting. The sermon is reported at the beginning of Froissart's account of the revolt and was clearly intended as an indictment of the peasants and all they stood for. Before moving to that sermon, I would like to draw attention to the fact that Froissart suggested that the main cause for the revolt was 'the ease and riches that the common people were of'. In other words, the peasants had it far too easy and were thus of a mind to rebel. The writer of the play which we are now considering, along with most 'objective' narrative historians, would not seriously support Froissart's contention. Yet they will quote, selectively, from the sermon which Froissart reports. I have already pointed out that the conditions under which we now hear a highly edited version of the sermon are not likely to encourage the audience to give it serious consideration. It would be neither disrespectful nor a poor comparison to ask whether a schools programme would ever dramatize reportage of the abolition of slavery, the Declaration of Independence or the Sermon on the Mount around the semi-comic routine which John and Diccon are seen to perform. Dobson has suggested that Ball's sermon, as translated by Berners, 'becomes the most moving plea for social equality in the history of the English language' (Dobson, 1984: 369–72). The viewers of this programme are unlikely to think so.

The two friends are shown later in London, where they encounter Wat Tyler. Tyler is represented as a cruel and fanatical person, with glaring eyes and an unhealthy love of power. We do see, also, that the young king (with or without his advisers), treated the peasants with considerable cruelty, and was quite happy to renege on his promises to them when they were in London. But the key message carried in the programme is the ill-advised action of the peasants. This is a history based upon a rebellion/transgression/expiation model. What this means is that it identifies, for young viewers, the fact that there may have been injustice in the England of 1381. It then suggests that, through their rebellion, the peasants went too far, and they would have to pay for what they did. When Diccon is recounting the happenings after the event, he points out that 'Tyler was dead and some of us weren't sorry.' In the mid-1980s, when this series was made, the UK was often in the throes of some industrial dispute. The ideological message about not going too far would not have been missed by either trades unionists or employers. For many teachers of 11–13 year olds, it would certainly have seemed like a counsel of conservative gradualism. This is a history (like most) with a heavy ideological message which needs to be unpacked. It also demonstrates most cogently the ways in which history and media representation become sometimes one and the same thing. Tracing recurrent themes and patterns in the representations of history will often suggest potential models of communication which have found a place in the repertoire of contemporary broadcasters.

History and heritage

My second example is of media representations which began their existence as newsreels in the cinema, but have become of historical and ideological significance. It would be too crass to suggests that today's news becomes tomorrow's history, but there is an important sense in which this does happen. The number of newsreels on sale in large stores which deal with the happenings of specific years is significant here. The newsreels which most of these videos contain purport to give the viewer an accurate representation of the times. In ideological terms, one could argue that they certainly do just that. But the accuracy resides in the availability of the text. That is, we can see the actual newsreels and they constitute, in an important way, primary source material. Their content may be highly suspect and occasionally risible by today's standards, but there is usually no suggestion of this in the way they are marketed. The example I will be considering comes from the Silver Heritage Collection of British Movietone News. Such videos can be purchased in Woolworths or other video outlets and Movietone is unambiguous in its claims:

> It's all here – drama, pageantry and war – covered as only Movietone could cover it. Now you can own and enjoy, with your family and friends, a priceless piece of British heritage.

The tape from which my example comes is volume two in the series and concerns the Silver Jubilee of King George V of England in 1935. In some ways it is a remarkable document. It certainly shows the contemporary audience something of the fashions, demeanour and sense of pageant which were prevalent at the time. The extent to which this pageantry is itself a result of mediation is certainly worth considering. The concept of news in 1935 did not have the connotation of immediacy which we associate with news today. The news cameras were heavy and bulky. They had to be placed carefully and decisions taken about the nature of the images they might render. Thus the images produced inside St Paul's Cathedral, with the rays of light streaming through the high windows into the nave were carefully shot, exposed and edited. But it is in the voice-over that we find our ideological thickener. The item begins with a superimposed title, over images of pageantry. It reads: 'Jubilee Day, May 6 1935', and it tells us that our description of the scenes to follow will be by Eric Dunstan. The choice of the term 'description' is an interesting one, in that it does fairly represent what the commentary will offer. The term is, of course, neutralized in the titles. It does not say 'cold description' or, more accurately, 'fawning description' by Eric Dunstan. The audience is asked to accept what follows as what might be called a 'natural description'. The second superimposed title reads: 'The world rejoices as their majesties drive in procession to St. Paul's.' The music track, which plays martial and patriotic music throughout, is offering a version of 'We are the soldiers of the King', and the description commences. I offer selected extracts here:

> A golden day for the Silver Jubilee and the spectacle of a nation exalted. There are three processions starting from Buckingham Palace. The third is headed by an open carriage in which their majesties ride and as they emerge from the south gate, listen to the tempestuous ovation roared by ten thousand excited voices.
>
> All the more sincere because it is so rare, national exaltation breaks all bounds in expressing that veneration which the British people feel for their king and queen. [. . .]
>
> Has the queen ever looked so beautiful? Certainly, I have never seen such a handsome figure of majesty as Queen Mary presents today. (cheers on soundtrack) And so the drive is resumed.
>
> (cheers, and the sound of the bells of St Paul's)
>
> And now, the bells of the city's noble cathedral, where Queen Victoria rendered thanksgiving for her Golden and Diamond Jubilees, ring out to announce that her grandson comes to make similar homage for his own twenty five years of faithful reign. He comes, King George, with his devoted Consort, hailed by the acclamation of an unnumbered multitude, and heralded by a fanfare.
>
> (Shot of the cross on top of St Paul's, followed by a shot from very high up of the light streaming through the windows and down on to the nave) [. . .]
>
> The service is finished and the King and Queen reappear and take leave of the clergy, watched by members of the Royal Family. You and I, perhaps, were in that great assembly, or lined the route by which their majesties drove back to Buckingham Palace. We stood or sat and watched and waited. And when the King and Queen passed, what did we do? Were our hearts too full for words, or did we shout with the multitude?

Much patriotic music follows and we see the crowds close in on the palace. A song is sung now, and the closing words of it are: 'God save the King is the nation's loving cry'. The commentary finishes as follows:

Closing on this picture of Buckingham Palace, we may reflect that it is the example of noble lives, lived in public-spirited endeavour which really influence humanity – so that the example of the Royal House of Windsor must exercise a glorious influence upon the destiny of generations to come.

The words 'God save the King is the nation's loving cry' are played once more.

It is, perhaps, easier to dismiss this newsreel than it is to study it. I want to stress the significance of such material for the student and researcher of media and cultural studies. At one level, it is significant because it provides us with what seem to be textbook examples of specific and obvious forms of discourse and signification. The choice of vocabulary, the structuring of the sentences, the implicature,[1] the intonation of the voice – all these things are ripe for analysis. The editing when the monarch enters St Paul's is reminiscent of Eisenstein's montage, albeit used to strengthen rather than challenge any beliefs. The roaring crowds on the soundtrack and the delivery of the description remind one of the contemporary British comedian Harry Enfield, who specializes in lampooning certain traits of upper-crust Englishness. Whilst such newsreels may not have thrilled the populace in quite the way suggested by Dunstan's description, however, neither is there a record that they were greeted with howls of derision. An understanding of such material might be of importance to those concerned with audience research. It is a sobering activity to consider audience responses to the media over generations, and to study them in relation to contemporary contexts as part of a comparative project. We may recognize that the royal family has not fared so well over the years. We may also note that the language and sentence structure of commentaries (or descriptions) has been modified considerably. What we might consider, however, is whether there are underlying traits in the relationships of audiences to media which are manifested in times of national crisis or celebration, and whether such trends are ideologically significant. Recent examples for consideration as part of a comparative project could include the World Cup, the funeral of Princess Diana, the last night of *Big Brother*, and many others. It is a serious and challenging prospect to consider the ways in which Elton John's rendering of 'Candle in the Wind' at Diana's funeral will be read some 200 years from now; or how the signifying practices employed during the last night of the Proms in 2000 will appear alongside Movietone newsreels from 1935. In future, media representations and media productions will become one of the main sources of primary data. The media studies researcher and the historian may then find themselves occupying similar discursive fields of contestation and interpretation.

From newsreels to the 'eyewitness'

Contemporary history has presented both the historian and the media researcher with an important and problematic phenomenon: that of the eyewitness. The concept of the

---

[1] This concept is derived from the work of the philosopher, H. P. Grice:

> An implicature is a proposition emerging from something that is said, but not actually stated by the words uttered, nor logically derivable from them. It must therefore be a product of the relationship between utterance and context; and a vital part of context would be the knowledge and motives of the speaker and addressee.
>
> (Fowler, 1986: 172)

eyewitness is significant in at least two ways. The first of these is consideration of the camera as eyewitness. This is a phenomenon which still has important implications because of the news value such eyewitness accounts may offer. The fact that there are cameras (and people operating them) in some of the worst trouble spots in the world suggests that we may be in the position of being better informed than we once were about what is happening. Such a suggestion needs careful interrogation. It is certainly the case that the newsreel camera may offer us information about some of the conditions which prevail in some situations for some of the time. But this does not mean that, because we have seen many hours of violence, explosions, death, mayhem and cruelty, we are better informed. We may be better informed about the forms of representation which are on offer, about the positioning of the cameras and about the generic form which such representations tend towards. This will include the semiotics of violence and the absences which mean that certain conditions are un(re)presentable in the present circumstances. This would include the showing of severed limbs and broken heads.

The generic similarities to be found in the representations of violence mean that stone throwing and the retaliation by the forces of 'law and order' seem to follow a similar pattern in different contexts. For the media researcher, such information is important. But of itself it yields only partial understanding. For the history from which a particular representation has sprung is usually invisible to the camera. Only the most recent manifestation of protest may be recordable. The problem then becomes exacerbated when such representations come to stand in for the history with which they sometimes purport to be concerned. It is precisely because such representation is so devoid of precise meaning, beyond the recognition of a genre, that any anchorage such imagery is given has to be studied with care. One response to the 'eyewitness' camera is to treat it as the bearer of the same old message: history on television as eternal recurrence. The other is to wait and see what is said about what is shown. In the latter case the ideological dimensions of commentary, presentation or other voice-over techniques become of crucial significance. The example already discussed of the Silver Jubilee of George V is a case in point. Without the commentary, or with another commentary, it would surely take on a different status as evidence.

The second way in which the concept of the eyewitness is important is when such an eyewitness is living and available to be recorded on film or video. The immediate responses of an eyewitness to a moment of some importance, whether it be a road accident, the winning of a race or game, or the survival of a terrorist attack, possess identifiable characteristics. On the one hand, they are often the brief comments of those who are elated or in shock, and may often tell us about the outward signs of such physical and psychological conditions. On the other hand, they are the product of media professionalism and have been constructed by those who have to fill time slots with material which is generically recognizable – usually for the news.

The living eyewitness may also become the reflective eyewitness, asked to recall in tranquillity events which are deemed by the programme-maker to be of some significance. One of the most powerful examples of this type of recollection has been found in films such as *Shoah* (Lanzmann, 1985) or the BBC's 1999 series on the Second World War, *War of the Century*, which concentrated on the relationship between the Germans and the Russians.

Such programmes allow for longer than usual statements to be made, and they are often revealing in the facial expression and body language of the interviewees, as well as the actual content of what they say. Detailed study of such representations takes the semiotician into the territory of the psychotherapist. Making sense of such media representations as data for history proves to be one of the great challenges still facing the media researcher and the historian.

It is also very possible that what does not make it into the programme may hold the key to other histories which would tell us much about how and why the world comes to be represented as it does. Such data are not often available to the researcher.

Ireland as victim of a 'garbled past' and as tragic art

I have written elsewhere about some of the ways in which Ireland and its history have been represented on television (Ferguson, 1985). I believe the arguments which I put forward then have relevance and illustrate well two major historiographic trends in television documentary. The first of these I would describe as the 'documentary as ungarbler of the past' approach. The second is the 'history as tragic art' approach. I use both these terms as descriptive and do not intend them to carry inherent positive or negative connotations. Both approaches require the careful selection and presentation of their material with emphasis placed upon fundamental decisions, which include:

i)   choice of whether to have a presenter or a voice-over commentary

ii) whether to feature interviews with eyewitnesses (assuming any are available)

iii) the kind of music used in the programmes

iv) the choice of camera style and lighting for interviews

v)   the choice of camera style and lighting for all outdoor shots

vi) the length and number of the programmes

vii) The selection and treatment of archive footage.

This list includes the major preconceptions upon which it is necessary for documentarists to work. They are all concerned with form and these will have a considerable impact upon the choice and type of content which will be chosen or constructed. Form and content may be problematic for the media analyst concerned with what happens at the point of consumption or decoding, but for many producers they have not presented the same problem at the point of production. On the one hand, we may find documentarists whose overall approach is to ask what the general issue or period to be covered will be and to weave this into their generic preference for a preordained documentary history format. On the other hand we may find those who will first conceptualize a period – or even all of history – as a particular sub-genre of documentary and then use the data (from interviews to helicopter landscape shots) to develop and strengthen this sub-genre. The former could be illustrated by Robert Kee's television history of Ireland (1980), which I will be discussing, or more recently by the way in which Simon Schama represented the history of the British Isles. Simon Schama is a contemporary historian whose concept of historiography is very different from that of Robert Kee. Schama's approach would be seen by many as inventively postmodern. His screen image, however, is still that of the media historian, leaning on tombs, walking in and out of buildings, across landscapes, silhouetted against the seashore. Such, it would seem, is the contemporary fate of the historian televized. That and the wealth and fame which go with it (Schama, 2002).

Two major documentary series were made in the UK in the 1980s, both of which offered histories of Ireland to that date. The first, called *Ireland: A Television History* (1980), was written and presented by the eminent historian and broadcaster Robert Kee. The second, called simply *The Troubles* (1980), was made by a team from the now defunct Thames Television led by Richard Broad, and was distinguished by evocative imagery, emotive music track and deliberately monotonous though radical commentary. I will offer here a brief overview of the ways in which the respective series offered us their meanings. Kee's historiography is set out in the opening of programme one. The opening shot of the series is of an Irish woman, who says:

> Yes well we were always told, not only by our mothers, we were taught it in the school as well you see. All the troubles between Ireland and England, right back from Queen Elizabeth – we were told she was a very cruel queen – to the Irish people and to the Catholics. And you see that's how we get to know through the schools as well you see, about how cruel the English were always to the Irish people.

This is followed by a montage of explosions and mayhem. Robert Kee's voice is first heard as a voice over the scenes of stone throwing and shots of the rooftops of Belfast. When we first see Kee, he is seated in a leather chair in a study, surrounded by books. His link, which takes him from what has been called the 'Voice of God' commentary, to the first shot of him in academic surroundings, runs as follows:

> Some people think it's dangerous to go into Irish history because by looking into past Irish troubles you may simply stir up new ones. But as a historian of the last century said: 'A knowledge of the truth is never dangerous, though ignorance may be so. And even more dangerous', he went on, 'is that half-knowledge of history which enables political intriguers to influence the passions of their dupes by misleading them with garbled accounts of the past.' The past and garbled accounts of it are the root causes of the troubles in Ireland. Ungarbling the past is what this series of programmes is about.

I want to draw attention here to a number of issues which deserve detailed analysis. The choice of the woman to speak at the beginning of the documentary provides what is sometimes called a hook – a means of attracting an audience who may be undecided about whether to watch such a programme. The explosions and blood offer drama to complement the softness of the woman's statement. The tension between these two images is then resolved temporarily by the appearance of Kee. He is professional, confident, competent. His historiography borders on the simplistic, being based as it is on the suggestion that a garbled past is a root cause of major social and political problems. Perhaps more significant is the implicit claim (made explicit in the trailer for the programme, which refers to it as 'the first full television account of the history of Ireland') that this history will set the record straight. No more garbling. It is a discourse which is not so far from the idea that if you saw your history on television, it must be true.

The second example I will mention briefly is a series called *The Troubles*, which was made and broadcast at the same period by Thames Television and was directed by Richard Broad. History as tragic art is still best typified in his work. Broad had previously made an award-winning series called *Palestine: Promise and Fulfilment* (Thames Television). His style is recognizably melancholy and uses voice-over commentaries and powerful music tracks. In the opening of *The Troubles*, Broad used the voice of actor Rosalie Crutchley to provide a sombre and intentionally monotonous pulse to the discourse. The music swells and falls away as we see scenes of derelict buildings and streets wet from rain and without human presence. Such a history manages to offer many radical judgements about how and why the troubles in Ireland came about. Broad had achieved a similarly strong and radical level of analysis in his series on the question of Palestine. The problem, perhaps, is that any radical potential the documentaries possessed was sucked into the melancholy of the mode of address. In *The Troubles*, we finally see the British troops patrolling the streets of Belfast in slow motion. This is, indeed, history as tragic art.

My main point here is not to argue that one form of documentary is inherently better than another. It is more important to note that different modes of address are likely to generate different responses, and that claims to objectivity (whether openly stated or not) need to be treated with interested and positioned scepticism. Audiences (and media scholars) do not stand outside the ideological and hence material conditions of life. Different genres of history operate through different modes of signification, with different potential for understanding the world to which they refer. The study and analysis of the operation of these different modes is the business of the media studies researcher.

Featuring history

The study of the feature film and its representations of history has seen a healthy growth over the last couple of decades. In part, this can be explained by the pleasure which so many films which are based in or on history have brought to so many people. This would include some historians and media researchers. It might also be explained by the fact that the research interests of some historians and media researchers have overlapped more in recent periods than heretofore. An interest in questions of discourse, or power and signification, and the question of how to appraise 'fictional' histories as relevant historical data have all contributed to this development.

Making sense of representations of history as educative entertainment cannot be done without constructing one or more analytical frameworks. I will indicate only a few possibilities here. An important and not unnoticed phenomenon has been the recognition that many representations of 'history' or an 'era' tell us as much about the period when they were made as the period they re-present. Films as different as *Les Enfants du Paradis* (1945) or *Mississippi Burning* (1988) illustrate this well. During the Second World War, when it was impossible to deal directly with contemporary subjects under the German occupation, the French film-maker Marcel Carné made *Les Enfants du Paradis*. It is a fictionalized portrait of the nineteenth-century mime Jean-Gaspard Deburau. The film takes much of its poignancy from an awareness of its conditions of production. The very concept of representing a mime, someone who has to communicate without speech, is itself an indicator of this. *Mississippi Burning* is a film about the civil rights movement in Mississippi in the 1960s. This film was made during a period when to represent such struggles was deemed important and timely. Yet this film has received much criticism for its concentration on the white 'heroes' and the fact that they are both FBI men. Based as it is upon an actual incident, when three young civil rights workers were murdered, there is a sense in which the film simply romanticizes this past. It thus presents a version of history which absolves the white conscience and strengthens the concept of white heroes acting on behalf of the quaking, illiterate, black populace. Though the young civil right workers are represented in the film, they are not given names.

This means that there are at least three different readings necessary if we are to interpret such films. These readings involve considerable reconstructive activity. The first is concerned with the era and events represented in the film. The second is concerned with the period when the film was produced. The third is concerned with the period when the film is being re-read, its contemporary context. A brief but illuminating engagement with these questions can be found in *Past Imperfect: history according to the movies* (Carnes, 1995).

The ways in which film has represented questions of national identity are also part of the contemporary research agenda. It is to questions of identity and otherness that I will turn in the next chapter. I will first consider the ways in which some contemporary debates about the nature of history are relevant for media studies. In doing so, many of the familiar arguments about the nature of reality, the era of postmodernity and the nature of truth all raise their heads once again.

This chapter takes the somewhat unusual step of finishing with a short series of quotations, chosen to elicit debate about the ways in which history might be of significance for the media student and researcher. Whether history is re-presented through historical drama, reconstructed through forms of documentary or called up in support of commodities or identities, is central to much media representation in the twenty-first century. I believe we should consider how some of the complex issues hinted at or stated in the following quotations might relate to specific media examples with which you are familiar. Consider, also, how the utilization of the positions hinted at in these quotations would lead the media researcher to think carefully about how to construct a viable methodology for analysing media messages.

The angel of history

A Klee painting named 'Angelus Novus' shows an angel looking as though he is about to move away from something he is fixedly contemplating. His eyes are staring, his mouth is open, his wings are spread. This is how one pictures the angel of history. His face is turned toward the past. Where we perceive a chain of events, he sees one single catastrophe which keeps piling wreckage upon wreckage and hurls it in front of his feet. The angel would like to stay, awaken the dead and make whole what has been smashed. But a storm is blowing from paradise; it has caught in his wings with such violence that the angel can no longer close them. The storm irresistibly propels him into the future to which his back is turned, while the pile of debris before him grows skyward. This storm is what we call progress.

(Benjamin, 1970: Thesis IX of 'Theses on the Philosophy of History')

Playing with words

It is human beings who play with words; words don't play with themselves. To establish their meaning we historians therefore need to search for the authorial intention; to study the social and political context which created the contemporary form of language; and to steep ourselves in the traditions of the culture. By these historical means, we will be able to recapture a provisional truth, at least sufficiently plausible to command assent for a while from most well-informed readers.

(Laurence Stone in Jenkins, 1997)

A question of objectivity

It does not follow that, because a mountain appears to take on different shapes from different angles of vision, it has objectively either no shape at all or an infinity of shapes.

(Carr, 1978: 23)

The purpose of [the representation of] history

For no matter how ingeniously constructed the past has been in modernist (and other) historical/ethical practices, it is now clear that 'in and for itself' there is nothing definitive for us to get out of it other than that which we have put into it. That 'in and for itself' the past contains nothing of obvious significance. That left on its own it has no discoverable point. That it expresses no intelligible rhyme or reason.

(Jenkins, 1999: 3)

The historian and the media

The rapid succession of superficial problems instantly solved, which is the mainstay of both television fare and the advertising that sustains it, induces the viewer to assume that there are simple and readily available solutions to every problem. The constant reiteration of 'news' presented in flashes and headlines, induces in the public a present-mindedness which finds reinforcement in the other media and in advertisement. The short-range interpretation of events by television pundits and journalists discourages perspective and in-depth analysis. Present-mindedness, a shallow attention to meaning, and contempt for the value of precise definition and critical reasoning are characteristic attitudes produced by mass media culture. All of them run counter to the mind-set of the historian and to the values and perspective historical studies provide.

(Lerner, 1997: 123)

The image will always serve to fuel our imaginations and therefore our visions of history. But its nature is changing: it is no longer a source which can be checked, if only against other testimonies; it is no longer the object of our reading or writing of history. The new technology of the image is changing the dominant position of our imagination and in so doing is transforming our relationship with history. History is again becoming what it always has been: a virtual approach to the past.

(Wenger, 1997: 78)

FURTHER READING

See quotations above.

Benjamin, W., 1970, *Illuminations*.

Carr, E. H., 1978, *What is History?*

Jeleff, S., 1997, *History and Its Interpretations*.
Includes essay, 'The tele-vision of history' by K. Wenger, as quoted above.

Jenkins, K. (ed.), 1997, *The Postmodern History Reader*.

Jenkins, K., 1999, *Why History?*

Lerner, G., 1997, *Why History Matters*.

chapter nine

Others, difference and identity

Most people are other people. Their thoughts are someone else's opinion, their lives a mimicry, their passions a quotation.

— Oscar Wilde, *De Profundis*

It may seem somewhat ironic that just as we discover that not only particular identities but identity itself is socially constructed, we organise political struggle within the category of identity, around particular socially constructed identities.

— Lawrence Grossberg in S. Hall and P. du Gay, *Cultural Identity*

It is a decidedly ambiguous compliment to praise others simply because they are different from myself. Knowledge is incompatible with exoticism, but lack of knowledge is in turn irreconcilable with praise of others; yet praise without knowledge is precisely what exoticism aspires to be. This is its constitutive paradox.

— Todorov, *On Human Diversity*

The study of the media has, from time to time, carried with it a certain kudos associated with contemporaneity and forms of discourse which are at the cutting edge of human development. Whilst this has been and sometimes still is the case, it is also the case that studying the media raises many issues which have troubled intellectuals and educators for many generations before the arrival of what we now know as the mass media. Some of the key questions with which we will now be concerned are those to do with the nature of human identity and questions of 'otherness'. Such questions are informed by a whole range of debates and ideas, some of which I will raise in this chapter. This is not, of course, a purely academic exercise. The media, particularly television and the Internet, now provide access to forms or suggestions of identity and otherness which cover the whole of human existence from birth to death. If a sense of identity was once acquired only or mainly from one's immediate community or family, today it is offered incessantly and in a number of ways through the media. It may be that some beleaguered communities still acquire and sustain part of their identities from their physical or psychic enclosure, but even they are likely to buy trainers or drink Coca-Cola. Identity is now as much the business of the mass media as it is the business of the family, religious organizations or education systems. Issues of identity are not simply

Figure 9.1 Offers of identity provide the wallpaper of daily existence (Topshop frontage)

presented to audiences. They are structured, re-presented, recycled and ordered according to changing sets of criteria, which are susceptible to analysis and critique. They are also formed, in part at least, through the agency of those to whom media messages are addressed – that is, you and me. In other words, we also participate in the formation, sustenance or change of our own identities. I will consider these issues shortly, but first I will consider what some of the main arguments about identity and otherness are, and why they are important in media studies.

Identity and discourse

I have had occasion more than once in this book to point out that the key questions which we have to consider do not refer to unitary or free-standing categories of thought and analysis. It is necessary to state this once again because questions of identity cannot be reduced to any single root cause or primary mover. Identity grows and develops in relation to a dynamic range of social, economic, ethnic, national and religious factors. The first and most important point for the media researcher to note is that identity is not preordained (Hall and du Gay, 1996; Woodward, 1997). For those of us who think that identity is essentially formed, the main activity of media study would be that of confirming or denying the validity of a specific representation when measured against that essential quality. We would then have to learn to recognize the essential identities of a man, a woman, the English, the French, and so on. Identities should be understood as the manifestation of behaviours, of relating to the world. They are in a state of either construction, sustenance or movement. We have to develop modes of description and analysis of identities as part of our media studies work.

Representations of issues of identity need to be understood as more than just re-presentation. They have to be analysed as modes of description which are also modes of construction. In this sense, we could note that questions of identity are also questions of discourse (see chapter three). Identities are both practised and talked about. We all practise our identities in our daily interaction with other human beings. We may also talk about the identity of others. But the overarching and omnipresent providers of (suggested) identity have to be the mass media. Whether it is in relation to what constitutes a football fan, or what constitutes beauty, or what constitutes the political identity of nations, it is the media who form, reform, indeed constitute, these matters. Whether this is theorized through an approach which suggests that the media are agenda setters, or whether the media are seen as ideological state apparatuses, it would be difficult to avoid the conclusion that the media are as much an identity industry as they are a culture industry. It could be argued that identities have become commodities which can be bought and sold, and that they are dependent mainly upon other commodities which can be bought and sold. Later in the chapter, I will be considering some of the specific ways in which identities are on offer to audiences or consumers.

Difference and others

If identity is something which is preordained and essential, then I can simply measure mine against the ideal. If, on the other hand, identity is contingent and changing, one of the ways in which I can recognize myself is in my difference from or similarity to you or any 'other' person or group. Now the concept of difference can be understood as something positive or something negative. Perceptions of difference which are negative are often related to insular thinking, or to insecurity. One is suspicious of 'others' precisely because they are seen as other, and one may attribute to them all the wrongs of the world – from taking one's job to not liking the smell of their food. It is one of the tragicomic ironies of our time that in the UK, curry has become one of the most popular meals, connoting otherness and the exotic. But that which smells good to eat in one context may become a means of identifying the negative 'other' if one is white and not in the mood for curry. Difference is a fragile and sometimes dangerous concept.

Many of the classificatory systems used to identify difference have worked on a binary system. So we have had black and white as one of the most prominent indicators of difference between people. The fact that neither term is a remotely accurate descriptor of the human beings to which it refers has never been a problem for those happy to use such a binary. The desire to classify often transcends the ability or wish to describe or analyse with accuracy. Other significant binaries which have been invoked in relation to media representations would include: inside and outside; in-group and out-group; developed and underdeveloped nations; citizens and scroungers; the employed and the unemployed; the right and the left. The list could be extended and it is certainly the case that working with binary oppositions has been influential in fields such as anthropology and sociology, as well as in the study of media. The oppositions utilized by Clause Lévi-Strauss in anthropology were recognized by some film theorists as productive, and Peter Wollen argued his own set in the once influential *Signs and Meaning in the Cinema* (Wollen, 1972). These binaries included, with particular reference to the films of Howard Hawks: garden/wilderness, ploughshare/sabre, settler/nomad, European/Indian [*sic*], civilized/savage. I mention them here because they form an important part of the often unacknowledged history of the development of concepts of difference with particular reference to the study of the media. While these binaries proved productive as a means of identifying certain narrative and sometimes ideological structures in movies, they were found to be unsatisfactory when it came to handling the complexities of the representation of human behaviour, and the crucially important concepts of contradiction and tension in relation to otherness and difference. (A useful introduction to the use of binaries in the study of film can be found in Lapsley and Westlake, 1988: chapter four). I will return to these concepts in relation to my media examples later in the chapter. I have already crossed over, in my last few sentences, from the question of how we might theorize difference to the ways in which difference is represented in the media. The two are related in ways which have significant ideological implications.

Making a difference?

Those who wish to interpret difference as a positive relational concept see it as a means of identifying diversity and richness. Some forms of multiculturalism have engaged in a celebration of difference which deliberately avoids or ignores any possibility that there may be any universal characteristics in the behaviour and lives of human beings. Kenan Malik has argued that such ideas of difference also lie at the heart of racial theories. He suggests that identities are not something which can be put on or taken off at will, but are based in social existence and relations:

> If we could choose identities like we choose our clothes every morning, if we could erect social boundaries from a cultural Lego pack, then racial hostility would be no different from disagreements between lovers of Mozart and those who prefer Charlie Parker, or between supporters of different football clubs. In other words there would be no social content to racial differences, simply prejudices born out of a plurality of tastes or outlooks.
>
> (Malik, 1996: 252)

There is clearly a difference here between those who would argue that we are free to establish our own identities as we celebrate our differences, and those who would argue that the very concept of difference is rooted in identifiable forms of social existence rather than individual choice. It is an important 'difference' when we come to the study of the media.

Representing the other

The category of the 'other' is very much linked with concepts of difference. As with difference, we may speak of the other in both positive and negative ways. There have been many positive representations of otherness which draw upon notions of romance and adventure. We, as cinema audiences, have seen figures such as Ethan Edwards played by John Wayne in *The Searchers* (1956), or Shane played by Alan Ladd in the film of the same name

(1953). Here we have been offered the other as an outsider figure, drifting in and out of our lives (as audiences) and adding a sense of our potential frailty and their own inner strength. This was an otherness linked to the provision in narrative form of solitary heroes. Such otherness found a more contemporary form in the brooding, glowering solitude of Michael Keaton as *Batman* (1989). I have chosen these examples as a reminder that otherness in at least one of its media manifestations was concerned with others who were, at the same time, one of us. Taken at the metaphorical level, that might have universal implications, for 'our' heroes were only other in their remarkable facility for acts of bravery or bravado. They were with us and came to give us security, protection and identity. Such otherness was, of course, rooted in normality – in the benevolent, strong otherness which was and is irredeemably 'white'.

There is another form of otherness which has been mainly influential in and through the media, and that is the otherness of the exotic. The quotation by Todorov at the beginning of this chapter highlights an important paradox, one which bears the characteristic tensions within the very concept exoticism. Todorov suggests that we can only exoticize that about which we are ignorant. At the same time, he suggests, we find it difficult to praise that about which we know little. This contradiction is often handled, I would argue, by inventing that which we do not know and ignoring that invention when it does not suit our purposes. This means that we can admire the 'otherness' of the gypsy in a Gitanes advertisement, while not wishing to have any of 'them' parking their vehicles near us. It means that we can enjoy the exotic appeal of the Arab sheikh (see chapter six) as lover or horse rider, while despising the alleged characteristics of 'Arabs' in other fields of social existence. I have to stress once again that this concept of exoticism is a white phenomenon. In order to see how it works in the media, one needs to return to questions of signification.

The social semiotics of the exotic

The social semiotic scales in which we weigh the power of exotic signification are not fixed or unchanging. There are some forms of the exotic which can become assimilated into our everyday lives. For the middle classes, it might involve the choice of a Persian rug which will be put not on the floor but on the wall. For some groups of people it might involve the wearing of an earring. Such actions may be the result of a whole complex of motivations, from adding 'spice' to one's life to enhancing the appeal of the body. Whatever the deeper causes for these phenomena (if such deeper causes exist), these changes in human behaviour involve the negotiation of meaning. From the tattoo on the arm of the nineteenth-century male sailor to the tattoo on the neck of the twenty-first-century female model, that negotiation has resulted in a semiotic agreement about what is acceptable as well as what is exotic. Indeed, there are some forms of signification which take their social semiotic cachet from being acceptable to some groups only. In this way, the exotic is commandeered by interested social groups for the purposes of re-establishing or reasserting that group's identity. The same exotic signifiers can be put to different social uses in different contexts. The dinner party where home-cooked crispy Peking duck is served has a different exotic appeal to going 'down the corner for a Chinese'. One is not better than the other – they are different.

Exoticism, in turn, has come to signify a range of alternatives to the norm, which carry with them the promise of the pleasure of the different within the security of that which is normal.

The etymology of the word 'exotic' relates to terms in Latin and Greek for that which is outside or foreign. The contradictions which exoticism has had to endure include two important developments. The first is that that which was once 'foreign' can often no longer be claimed to be so. The coming of multicultural societies and the relative ease of travel for those from wealthy countries have seen to that. The second is that media representations of the exotic have had to rely on more traditional appeals to its meaning, through historically based dramas and adventures. The foreignness of the exotic, in short, has to be repackaged to meet the needs of the time. More often than not, these are commercial needs as much as social ones. Exoticism is still for sale, and it can be practised as well as observed. And the media are there to re-present and thus reconstitute the possibilities and promises of the exotic.

Empirical study is needed to ascertain the extent to which exoticism is offered as a positive or negative attribute of a person or group of people. Such study cannot be measured on a merely quantitative scale. It is certainly the case that the number of times when whiteness is presented as a norm is decreasing in many of the media, but it is only a relative decrease. It is also the case that not all representations of 'other' people are negative, but it is the narrative and ideological weighting which such representations carry which needs to be unpacked, just as much as their frequency or infrequency. Concepts of the exotic are also changeable and changing. For the media studies researcher, it is important to understand the ways in which such changes take place and the modes of signification which they employ. It is here that the question of history is once again of importance. To study, for instance, the ways in which exoticism has been represented in advertising, one would need to have some knowledge of the period in which the advertising originated, its potential audience and the economic environment. Advertising relating to the British and other empires has often been documented in generously illustrated analytical texts (Pieterse, 1992). What these records show are the ways in which the exotic other was viewed (or was it constructed?) from the position of power accorded to the implicit viewer. That means they were made mainly for white eyes.

In the USA there have been many food products which take their minor exoticisms from historical roots. The meanings attached to such products were certainly learned and agreed by at least some of those who saw them. I am referring here to such products as Aunt Jemima's Pancake Flour or Uncle Ben's Rice or Uncle Remus' Syrup. These products offered a subtly balanced mixture of homeliness and otherness at the same time. Of course, it was an otherness only for those who perceived black people as other. Such products were often sold using pieces of manufactured vernacular. Uncle Remus, in 1948, is shown smiling at us with his white hair and beard providing a dignity which is offset by his words: 'Dis sho' am good'. Aunt Jemima (a fictional character invented by a Missouri businessman in the late nineteenth century as a gimmick to sell his self-raising pancake mix) also spoke to the consumer from the box or the magazine. Her words were, 'I's in town honey' or occasionally, 'Every bite is happyfyin' light'. Humour, patronization, sentimentality and the naturalization of forms of servitude were all incorporated within such significations.

Over the decades, Aunt Jemima has slowly changed. She is no longer someone who could (factually) have been a slave just recently liberated, speaking to us (fictionally) in manufactured dialect. She has become younger, lighter-skinned and eventually (black) middle class. Her bandanna became a headband and then no headband. Her assimilation into the mainstream has removed most of the historical fictions and facts from which she grew, and she has lost her exotic appeal, as she has been offered to us as an assimilated figure (Roberts, 1994). The relationship between forms of exoticism and the market are thereby highlighted. One explanation of the changes in the representation of black people in advertisements might be that the advertisers and their employers have become so much more liberal and understanding. Another would be that many of those who had been so caricatured in the past are today's clients. You do not demean those who will buy your product by offering demeaning fictions about their past in order to sell them your products. You show some historically appropriate respect. If necessary, histories can be rewritten or reinvented.

Another extension of these forms of exotic representation has been the way in which the exotic other has been linked to the provision of a service. Waiters who serve beer or coffee, or turbaned domestic staff, have provided exotic and ideological vectors for what might otherwise have seemed mundane products. In today's new ideologically manufactured intercultural media environment, some airlines are at pains to demonstrate their inter-ethnic mix of staff. Others choose to offer only one kind of exotic staff, with the promise of infinite, gentle patience and a fixed smile. Social semiotics, ideology and hence identity operate in commercially driven material conditions.

Orientalism and the media

Some of the advertisements to which I have alluded also draw upon the appeal of Orientalism, a term most often associated with Professor Edward Said and his influential book of the same title (Said, 1978). I have made reference to Said's arguments and some of his critics elsewhere (Ferguson, 1988). I will draw attention here to three aspects of the work and their influences which are of significance for the media studies researcher or student.

Orientialism and ideology

Representations of the Orient, whether in books, paintings, prints, magazines, comics, movies, radio or television, have been observed to follow certain trends. These trends have demonstrated that the Orient is discursively fixed. Its characteristics and the characteristics of its inhabitants remain unchanged and unchanging. Hence we have a whole range of Oriental stereotypes, which Said has noted in relation to the cinema as much as in literature (Said, 1978: 286–7). But Said also makes very clear the fact that, although much of the discussion in his book has been about the representation of Arabs, the Orient and Muslims, there are occasions when people who are deemed Semites may be grouped together easily. He cites a passage from Marcel Proust to illustrate his argument, and it is sufficiently evocative to merit re-quotation here:

> The Rumanians, The Egyptians, the Turks may hate the Jews. But in a French drawing-room the differences between those people are not so apparent, and an

Israelite making his entry as though he were emerging from the heart of the desert, his body crouching like a hyena's, his neck thrust obliquely forward, spreading himself in proud 'salaams', completely satisfies a certain taste for the oriental [un goût pour l'orientalisme].

(Proust in Said, 1978: 293)

The importance and the potential weakness of Said (and Proust's arguments) is that they rely on forms of generalization. When Said writes of the representation of Arabs in the cinema, he is perhaps even more sweeping in his claims. This is not to suggest that such generalizations are ill-founded. Far from it. Hollywood cinema abounds with representations of lecherous, devious, sadistic and treacherous figures (these are the terms used by Said). Yet an emphasis on identifying this type of representation at the general level has often been counterproductive. It has concentrated so much on negative representation that it has fed those who would wish to argue that such representation is accurate rather than a travesty. The danger of too much use of generalization cannot be stressed too strongly here. What is needed is detailed study of the ways in which specific representations are situated, constructed and utilized for ideological purposes in the telling of a story. Generalization should be retained for a last instance which never comes. The refusal of generalization as a category for discussion and analysis allows space for understanding and studying the complex nuances of narrative and other forms of address which may be used in media representations of otherness. Gross stereotypes still find their way into the media and I have discussed some in other chapters of this book. They do not, however, tell us very much about how otherness is sustained in the realm of what might be called the 'ideological ordinary'.

Said has also noted the way in which the relationship between the Middle East and the West is often defined as sexual. Said writes in response to a passage from *Golden River to Golden Road: society, culture and change in the Middle East* (Patai, 1973):

The Middle East is resistant, as any virgin would be but the male scholar wins the prize by bursting open, penetrating through the Gordian knot despite the 'taxing task'. Harmony is the result of the conquest of maidenly coyness; it is not by any means the coexistence of equals.

(Said, 1978: 309)

Here Said is critiquing the work of Patai, but the hypothesis which Said puts forward is one which merits much more investigation. Whether we are speaking at the metaphorical level about the ways in which scholars have related to questions of Orientalism, or whether we are concerned with specific representations in specific contexts, questions of the sexual recur (see also chapter six). Orientalism, rather like the Mills & Boon novel referred to earlier, allows for interpretations of the exotic and, in this case, the Arab, which are both a promise and a threat.

Said has also been a key figure in the debates which followed in the wake of his work and which are concerned with issues of postcolonialism and postmodernism. We may note here only the fact that Said was insistent that human identity was not something fixed and unchanging. It was this insistence which led Said to concentrate so much of his analytic force

127

on those who would construct the Orient as the haven of all that was bewitching and unchanging. It is important to note, however, that such ideological media discourses as those identified by Said are also fraught with contradiction. That which is represented as unchanging is also, paradoxically, unpredictable. That which is virginal is also permeated by lechery. Such are the ideological contradictions through which media representations often operate.

Orientalism as a possible conservative or progressive force field

One other point needs to be noted before turning to broader issues of identity and the media. This is the question of whether or not it is possible to interpret any forms of Orientalism as progressive rather than conservative or regressive in their intentions or outcomes. This possibility opens the door to an engagement with concepts of otherness which are enriching rather than alienating. A persuasive argument for this position has been put by John Mackenzie (1995). Mackenzie is forthright in his position on the ways that the Western arts

> sought contamination at every turn, restlessly seeking renewal and reinvigoration through contacts with other traditions. And both Self and Other were locked into processes of mutual modification, sometimes slow but inexorable, sometimes running as fast as a recently unfrozen river.
>
> (Mackenzie, 1995: 209)

Mackenzie suggests that many of the artists who were Orientalists have been wrongly accused of seeking to portray the East in such a way as to make it more amenable to the economic, cultural and political transformations of imperialism. The nineteenth-century Orientalists were, argues Mackenzie, culturally conservative and technically innovative: 'Far from offering an artistic programme for imperialism, they were finding in the East ancient verities lost in their own civilisation' (Mackenzie, 1995: 67). Of course, there is some distance between the representations of the Orient to be found in nineteenth- and early twentieth-century painters and the movie productions of Hollywood in the late twentieth century. We will also find contradictions, generalizations and sometimes woolly argument in many of the most righteously indignant attempts to critique the representation of the East. If media studies is to be concerned with identifying the ideological dimensions of media messages, and I believe it must do this, then it must do so in ways which tread carefully on ground which was once thought to be the terrain of battle. It turns out very often to be ideological thin ice.

Questions of identity

Questions of identity and difference have come closer and closer to the core of contemporary work in media studies. Identity is no longer a matter confined to those who see themselves as primarily concerned with multiculturalism or Orientalism. It is at the heart of contemporary quotidian existence and manifests itself in everything from fashion to music, from lifestyle to cultural preferences. Now more than ever, we are what we buy, how we dress, how we look, how we are seen. And the media are there to help us along the way in this problematic, symbiotic relationship.

Ever since the arrival of the mass media, the question of identity has never been far from centre stage. At first, it may have been more to do with a sense of national identity as mediated through the press. Then there was the way in which social mores and values were mediated and, within this, the role of men and women and children, and others, were (re)constructed and circulated. While such basic concerns do not disappear, more contemporary manifestations have moved towards the representation of identity through the revelation of that which was once deemed to be private. We may still find representations which deal with the conventional concept of identity as being concerned with the citizen and the normal man and woman. At the same time, however, there are now many representations which deal with those who would assert their identity by being either declaredly different or exposing aspects of their behaviour and appearance to public scrutiny, approbation or vilification.

I am referring here to shows such as *Jerry Springer*, where those who appear demonstrate their identities under stress. The programme has turned the concept of washing one's dirty linen in public into a popular cultural festival. It has also established the possibility for those who wish to assert their identity to do so as performers. Indeed, it could be argued that quotidian identity as mediated performance has become part of the staple diet of many television audiences. Whether it is about identity as manifested through one's house, one's garden, one's clothes or one's performance potential, it is all made to show on television – and such representations find willing audiences.

It is possible that we can learn much about identity and difference from studying such texts. But this may or may not tell us much about the audiences for such texts. One thing is sure: texts can only have meaning if they are perceived by an audience. From such a position, there is no text until it is construed as such through the activity of making meaning. And such meaning does not have to, indeed it may not be able to, reside in the text. This is a persuasive argument, though many texts have indeed made their meaning without necessarily being read, watched or listened to. They are simply 'kept' in the home. In the past, these texts have ranged from literary classics to the *Encyclopaedia Britannica* or *Mein Kampf*. Today, they may include a range of CD-ROMs and DVDs. They carry or have carried social cachet and in doing so they lay claim to their significance, even if unused.

The next chapter will be centrally concerned with audiences and their relationships with the media. The question which textual analysis by the researcher raises is: what is the status of my reading as a researcher in relation to yours as a (or an other) member of an audience? One way of addressing such a question is through social semiotic analysis, which stresses the importance of identifying modes of signification as specifically as possible. Questions of identity then become recognizable through moments or passages of signification. For the rest of this chapter, I will be considering specific media examples which deal with questions of identity and the ways in which particular significations operate. The examples I have chosen are overtly concerned with questions of identity.

Identity: That work of art which we want to mould out of the friable stuff of life is called 'identity'. Whenever we speak of identity, there is at the back of our minds a faint image of harmony, logic, consistency: all those things which the flow of experiences seems — to our perpetual despair — so grossly and abominably to lack.

(Bauman, 2000:82)

Identification: Psychological process whereby the subject assimilates an aspect, property or attribute of the other and is transformed, wholly or partially, after the model the other provides. It is by means of a series of identifications that the personality is constituted and specified.

(Laplanche and Pontalis, 1988: 205)

Identities are often on offer from the media as secondary features of representations which are ostensibly about something else. A now classic example of this type of representation would be the Marlboro cowboy advertisements. Their purpose was to sell cigarettes. They did this by offering again and again a particular kind of masculinity. It was signified through representations of (masculine) silence and contemplation, moments of leathery tranquillity, horses' hooves and the promise of masculine freedom. You did not have to be a smoker to take in the message about what constituted manhood. You did not even have to be a cowboy. The characteristics of the strong silent man were presented in such a way as to transcend professions. Despite the fact that it may sound risible now, such imagery did its work well enough to please the advertisers, and probably got through to more men than would be prepared to admit it. Perhaps the main point to note about such representations is that they worked through the process which Louis Althusser called 'interpellation' (Althusser, 1971). This is simply another term for hailing or calling. For Althusser, this was a form of hailing to an ideological position. It was also, of course, a hailing which was constantly offering identities of one kind or another. This is hardly a new phenomenon, and it is something which is too easily forgotten as we debate the contemporary media scene. The offering of identity has been at the core of narrative structuration every since narrative began. It is argued persuasively by some that questions of identity and lifestyle have overtaken the actual product in importance in advertising (Klein, 2000). Identities are constituted in part through social interaction. But there is much that is also on offer, whether or not it is the subject of debate, from media representations. Sometimes the media representations and the social interaction become fused for a period of time, as with the male identification with the appearance of characters from Tarantino's *Reservoir Dogs*. Such identifications may be based upon fashion in part, but they are also constituted around forms of chauvinism and patriarchy. For most, such identification is little more than fantasy, but in ideological terms, such fantasies serve to sustain patriarchal relations of power and subordination. Identity has also been offered by many more conventional forms of popular culture.

Singing identity

I will take one example here from a well-known musical. Musicals are often staged by amateur theatre groups these days, with occasional revivals on Broadway or in the West End of

London. They may draw a yawn from those who consider themselves part of the contemporary scene. Like any other cultural product, they should not be dismissed merely because we would not choose them as part of our own collection. The film versions of musicals are also shown on television. Such films are recycled very often on festive occasions, such as Christmas, for family viewing. *Carousel* (Henry King, 1956) is the story of a carousel barker, Billy Bigelow, who falls in love and tries to change for the better. The songs in the film are described by the critic Richard Maltin as 'timeless'. They have become a part of popular culture, which appeals to the more mature viewer. It is worth considering what such timeless songs offer in terms of identity, and there is one particular number which encapsulates a whole range of ideological positionings and senses of identity. It is a song sung by Billy and is entitled 'Soliloquy'. It might have been written with Louis Althusser in mind. The lyrics are long, and it is indeed a soliloquy, both spoken and sung, as Billy contemplates impending fatherhood. He begins by suggesting that his son will be someone who thinks his father can physically dominate any other boy's father, and says he will be right to think that. He believes his son will look exactly like him, but is likely to be more intelligent. Billy's wife will teach the boy how to behave, 'But she won't make a sissy out of him. Not him! Not my boy! Not Bill.' Bill will be as tall as a tree and hold his head up high. No one will bully Bill. Billy says he doesn't care what his son does, even becoming president of the United States, as long as that is what he wants to do. He doesn't want Bill to grow up and marry the boss's daughter, implying that his son will marry a 'real' woman.

Then Billy suddenly wonders if he may have a daughter, rather than a son, and launches into a description of her characteristics. At first, he feels that there is little he could do for a daughter, as a 'bum with no money'. He reminds himself that you can have fun with a son, 'but you got to be a father to a girl'. He thinks then of the ribbons she would wear in her hair, and of the boys who would pursue her. He avers that she will not be brought up in the slums and associate with 'a lot of bums like me. She's got to be sheltered and dressed in the best that money can buy.'

This description of some lyrics from a musical from more than half a century ago has to be interpreted in two important contexts. The first is that of the world of musicals and of magical if sometimes tragic musical narratives. The second is our context of reading, where it is likely that such lyrics will be treated either with weary cynicism or sentimental attachment, depending on our own predilections. Either way, the agenda has been set that a man is a particular and essential kind of being, and so is a woman. The earlier reference to Althusser was not facetious. It was Althusser who wrote that our identities sometimes precede our birth in the discourses through which we are constructed in advance of our arrival. If some of the ways in which identity has been offered as musical interpellation seem distant from everyday life, we have only to turn to a range of popular magazines to find much more on offer.

O

I will consider one example. It is the magazine called simply *O*. The *O* stands for Oprah, and Oprah Winfrey is the founder and editorial director of the magazine. The edition of 2 October 2000 has what it describes as its monthly mission under the title of 'Trust Yourself'.

For the media studies researcher or student it is a most complex text for analysis. This complexity relates to the many and different ways in which Oprah Winfrey has become a social force and a role model for many in the USA and farther afield. Oprah's sense of the political is not one of her main strengths. She is, however, a champion of the need to interest people in reading books, and does much work to encourage reading. She is also extremely rich. As an African-American woman, she is caught in the ideological tensions which accompany success in the American way of life. She speaks to ordinary people, but she is herself extraordinary. She is also a champion of looking inside oneself to find the person one really is.

The magazine is glossy and includes advertisements for perfumes, face creams, clothes, haircare, make-up, cars, duvets, watches, jewellery, insurance, travel, digital photo printing, bed linen, milk, yoghurt, furniture, biscuits, credit cards, butter, soymilk, HIV testing, underwear, soap, breakfast cereal, fruit juice, storage containers, meatless burgers, coffee, olive oil and others. There are 318 pages in the magazine, of which 107 carry articles on a wide variety of subjects. Most articles are two pages in length and many contain large photographs or other advertisements which take up page space. Most of the advertisements, covering more than 200 pages, would repay careful semiotic analysis in relation to issues of identity.

Oprah's comments and advice about identity are a mixture of homely wisdom and semi-opaque spirituality. For the sympathetic reader they may offer comfort. For the critical reader they offer constructions of identity where material conditions of existence take second place to inner (and hence inaccessible) knowledge. The purpose of this short analysis is to highlight some of the contradictions which such a magazine raises. It is also to suggest that the study of identity is often most rewarding if it is related to the contradictions associated with material existence and inner peace.

Identity and trust

The monthly mission for *O* is concerned with trust and the concept is given considerable power and leeway in the discourse of the magazine. The reader is encouraged to listen on those occasions when something inside screams out to 'us'. The content of such a scream is identified as being concerned with slowing down, walking away or starting again. The reader is assured that if the inner voice is heeded, 'you give yourself the highest honour – impeccable trust'. The reader is encouraged to stop and listen to her/his inner voice and to ask, 'What do I really need? And when you hear the answer, trust yourself enough to act on it' (p. 41). The magazine offers many quotations as thoughts for a calendar day. For 16 October, the quotation is from Samuel Johnson and runs as follows: 'It is better to suffer wrong than to do it, and happier to be sometimes cheated than not to trust.' For 26 October, a quotation is offered from Thomas Fuller, an English physician: 'Trust thyself only, and another shall not betray thee.' The potential contradictions in these two positions are not explored. Either the reader is thought to be a competent dialectical thinker, or the compiler of the calendar advice thought contradiction an irrelevance. Wisdom just sounds wise.

On page 60 there is a short piece by Phillip C. McGraw PhD, under the title 'Take back the power in your life'. It is about retraining a neglectful husband. In advising an unidentified person about her worries that her husband may be unfaithful to her, Dr McGraw asks her to 'remember that you must let go of your bitterness, not for him but for yourself'. To a woman who is disturbed because her husband always forgets their anniversary, Dr McGraw responds with sympathy: 'Your need is not wrong – it just is. Don't accept less than you deserve.' The contradictions continue to amass as Dr McGraw is identified at the end of his piece as the author of two works, entitled *Life Strategies* (1999) and *Relationship Rescue* (2000). His professional description, however, begins with the information that he is president of Courtroom Sciences, a litigation firm in Texas.

Between the advertisements we find the articles and each one carries a banner in the margin, with titles such as 'Live Your Best Life', 'Dream Big', 'Tell It Like It Is', 'The Working Spirit' and 'Minding Your Body'. On pages 141 and 142 there are some more quotations, this time in the form of tear-out cards. From Marva Collins, we have: 'Trust yourself. Think for yourself. Act for yourself. Speak for yourself. Be yourself. Imitation is suicide.' From Shirley MacLaine: 'I could be whatever I wanted to be if I trusted that music, that song, that vibration of God that was inside of me.' These quotations identify a mode of discourse which is part of a continuum which can move from declarative propositions through rhythmic assertion to chanting of the kind favoured by those in public places who wish to warm up the crowd. (Oooh! Aaah!)

The concept of beauty is also used to generate advice for the readers – advice which has a strong bearing on the question of identity. There is a short selection from the book *The Simple Abundance Companion* by Sarah Ban Breathnac. The selection is printed alongside an image of a slim blonde woman, standing in front of a mirror, looking at her model's figure with quiet approval. I will offer some key phrases from the text: 'Slowly take in your appearance from head to toe.' 'Find ten things that you love about your face and body. Yes, you can do it.' 'Today and every day take as your personal mantra: I am what I am, and what I am is wonderful.'

It is not the purpose of this analysis to praise or blame the identities on offer here. What is important is to note that they *are* on offer and that the offer is made using modes of signification which can be identified and described. Perhaps the qualities which both *Carousel* and *O* share are those which require a softening of the harsh realities of life while we imagine what we might be or who might be our children. Such imagining is based upon a deliberate eschewing of social conditions in the case of *O*. In a magazine which depends upon relative economic success if the reader is to have any share of the products which fill two-thirds of the glossy pages, there is very little about the economic when it comes to identity. Of course, there are exceptions, such as the short piece on Maria Bartiromo, CNBC's financial anchor and 'money honey'. When money is mentioned, it is in relation to an identity which is hard-working, strong, feminine, beautiful and successful. 'If you need a little luck, work harder. I guarantee you will get noticed,' says the 'money honey'. This is fairytale identity and it is significant because it relates to the American dream. You can make it if you try. Such identity attempts to transcend ethnicity. It deals with class identity by simply ignoring it.

I'm worth it. You're worth it. They don't matter. We don't exist.

I have discussed briefly some of the ways in which identity, otherness and difference impinge upon the work of the media studies student and researcher. Whether or not one adopts a heavily theorized approach to questions of identity and otherness, they are stubbornly there every time we consider a media text. The examples I have chosen do not pretend to have covered all the issues. I have avoided discussion of major cultural and popular icons who are primarily entertainers. The days of considering whether or not Madonna has provided a means of empowerment to those who would imitate or draw upon her sartorial creativity are numbered. This is not because such work was of no consequence. It is simply because we have to re-problematize the concept of identity to include the possibility that some identities are far from empowering. We have to consider, bearing in mind the debates about the nature of the postmodern, whether or not identity is something which is a surface phenomenon – linked with what we wear and how we speak, etc. If this is the case, it could mean that one's identity can be 'worn' to suit the occasion. Up to a point, this may indeed be the case. We also have to ask whether or not there is anything more than the surface when we consider identity and representation. This may seem like some kind of metaphysical question to those who would question how we could possibly know more than that which we can observe through what might be described as surface semiotics. It is here that the importance of the discursive comes to the fore.

Studying the media is not just about identifying the way things (representations) appear as texts. It is also, and probably more importantly, about the way in which representations are structured, implicitly or explicitly, into discourses. There are discourses about otherness and alterity which cannot be reduced to any one representation, and hence cannot be read from a single text. Very often these discourses circulate via what I have called a discursive reserve. They are part of the repertoires of speech and signification of those whose lives continue when they are not in direct communion with the media. Discursive reserves are not innate but socially acquired. They may be stimulated and sometimes fed by the media, but they are not dependent upon the media for their existence.

There is, then, a third dimension to the study of representations of identity and otherness. It is the dimension which is concerned with the material conditions of existence of the readers (audiences) of media texts. Those readers may be considering adopting a particular, surface lifestyle as a result of engaging with media texts. They may decide to dress differently, for instance, assuming that they can afford the type of attire which their new identity requires. Or they may adopt particular speech patterns which offer, they hope, either street or salon credibility. In taking such action, there are those who would attempt to construct themselves as 'other', but usually a superior other. On the other hand, there may be those who are the recipients of forms of identity construction in which they have not been asked to participate. Such individuals or groups are likely to be constructed, represented and talked about as negative others.

The concept of identity cannot be reduced to some kind of essential and unchanging quality – our 'true' identity, which we discover when we find out who we really are. Stuart Hall has argued that identity should not signal 'the stable core of the self'. For Hall, identity is a strategic and positional concept. He tends to speak of both identity and identification in the language he once used to describe the issue of hegemony – that is, that it is not a natural state of affairs and that it can be 'won' or 'lost', sustained or abandoned (Hall, 1996: 1–17). Such a conception does not sit easily beside that of the magazine *O*, with its emphasis on listening and looking deep into oneself to discover who one is. It may be that we cannot put on and take off identities at will. It is also the case that we do not inherit an identity which is fixed for the duration of our time on earth.

These issues are important in relation to media studies because, on the one hand, identities are constantly mediated through a variety of modes of signification. They are also important because the media have a hand in the construction as well as the mediation of identity. And they are important because both these processes impact upon the lived, material existence of individuals and groups. The relationship is not always an easy one, and it is fraught with contradiction. Individuals and groups are referred to, by those who are concerned with the media, as audiences. It is to the study, conceptualization and significance of media audiences that we will turn in the next chapter.

FURTHER READING

Du Gay, P., Evans, J. and Redman, P. (eds), 2000, *Identity: a reader*.
This is an important resource, containing as it does extracts from some of the most significant thinkers and writers in the field. It draws on a variety of disciplines, from cultural studies to sociology and psychoanalytic theory.

Hall, S. and du Gay, P. (eds), 1996, *Questions of Cultural Identity*.
An edited collection of readable and stimulating essays which cover fields as diverse as music and identity, and biology and the new technologies. Contains the important introduction by Stuart Hall, 'Who needs identity?'

Woodward, K. (ed.), 1997, *Identity and Difference*.
An interrogation of the concept of identity and whether or not it is an essential or fixed characteristic of humans. Deals, among others, with questions of difference, the body and difference, sexualities, motherhood and the concept of Diaspora and identity.

chapter ten

Questioning audiences

*Studies of audiences often credit them with supernatural characteristics; they are
unknowable but all-powerful. They have to be propitiated. This is the purpose of academic
ethnographies and commercial ratings alike.*

— Hartley, *The Uses of Television*

*People always compare their own television viewing to that of the imagined mass audience,
one that is more interested, more duped, more entertained, more gullible than themselves.*
— Seiter, *Television and New Media Audiences*

*It could be said (with certain reservations, of course) that a person of the Middle Ages
lived, as it were,* two lives*: one that was the* official *life, monolithically serious and gloomy,
subjugated to a strict hierarchical order, full of terror, dogmatism, reverence and piety; the
other was the* life of the carnival square*, free and unrestricted, full of ambivalent laughter,
blasphemy, the profanation of everything sacred, full of debasing and obscenities, familiar
contact with everyone and everything. Both these lives were legitimate, but separated by
strict temporal boundaries.*

— Bakhtin, *Problems of Dostoievsky's Poetics*

What do we mean by an audience?

When the concept of a performance was a localized matter because it happened in a theatre,
hall, palace, stadium, arena or piazza, it was easier to identify what was meant by 'an
audience'. They were the people who were there. They had come to watch and to listen, to see
and be seen. Of course, no one thought that the audience was a homogeneous mass. The
audiences in the Colosseum in Rome, or the audiences for Shakespeare at the Globe, would
include people with different interests, motives, backgrounds and intentions. Very few
commentators at the time would have conceptualized, talked or written about a single
audience, not least because it could have cost them their careers or their lives. There may have
been slaves, plebeians, senators, nobles, aristocrats and many others in the audience that
watched gladiatorial combat or listened to the words of the bard. It might have been said that

the audience was a diverse group, united mainly by their location and only occasionally by their intent or experience. Indeed the experience of an emperor watching a combat over which he knew he had ultimate control or someone selling fruit or other light refreshment in order to make a living would be somewhat different. They were both, however, part of the audience. This digression is far from frivolous. It is most noteworthy that with the coming of the mass media, the mass audience was invented. It was an audience with remarkable qualities of uniformity and some notable exceptions. The exceptions were mainly constituted by those who passed comment and judgement upon that mass audience – the critics and commentators, the moralists and standard-bearers. The uniformity that this mass audience was deemed to possess was primarily based around a number of negative attributes. These included the tendency to be gullible and easily influenced. They also included the inability to decide what was of quality and what was not, what was bad for the development of a healthy personality and what was not. This mass audience was, in fact, a problem for all serious-minded elitists. It had to be guided, protected and occasionally simply told what to do.

There is nothing very new in all this. Concerns had been expressed in the past about the coming of mass literacy, about the ways in which the masses would behave if they could read what they like, see what they like, listen to what they like. John Carey has provided a useful antidote to intellectual complacency about these matters (Carey, 1992). He points out, with numerous examples taken from the writings of novelists, essayists and others in the late nineteenth and early twentieth centuries, that the masses were often held in contempt by literary figures. Wyndham Lewis, argues Carey, provides a more virulent example of this kind of thinking:

> Though he attacks those who control the press, cinema and radio for assuming the public is infinitely stupid, and despising it, they are, he admits, right. Totalitarian regimes are to be admired for perceiving that human beings are naturally subservient, like a horse or a dog or a 'very helpless child', and treating them accordingly.
>
> (Carey, 1992: 193)

While such views would be abhorrent even to many conservative minds, they do indicate an important way in which the audience for the media is so often first construed and then constructed.

How do we obtain an 'audience'?

The field of audience research is one which seems to have generated certitude and doubt in equal measure over the past half century. It is a field which has been concerned most of all with the suggestion that the media have some kind of effects on their audiences. Just what we mean by audiences and what we mean by effects are the key problems which we will need to consider in this chapter. In order to do so, it is important to place the debates about media audiences in some kind of historical perspective. If you read one of the many reputable summaries of audience research, you will find that it is possible to 'prove' many things about the effects of the media, including the suggestion that they have very little effect (McQuail,

1983; Cumberbatch and Howitt, 1989; Lowery and DeFleur, 1994; McQuail, 2002). So we have to choose our research data with care, just as audience researchers need to look long and hard at their research methodology. It becomes clear that the audience cannot be studied in a vacuum, but has to be a situated audience.

There have been numerous attempts over the years to understand the audience by reference to a triadic structure that can be constructed in the following way:

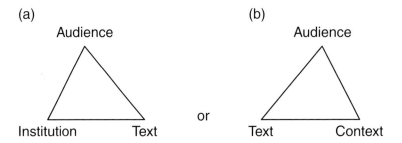

Figure 10.1 Triadic structure of the audience

This figure suggests that, whatever an audience is, it is best understood in conjunction with other important determining factors. In Figure 10.1a these include both text and institution. The concept of text includes all kinds of programmes and artefacts that an audience may encounter. The concept of institution may be interpreted in a number of ways. It may include the institution of production, which would involve a study of the makers, scriptwriters and other workers in the media industries. It may also include the concept of production as being the business of corporate concerns with their own ways of working, organizing and relating to each other. The key point to note is that we are dealing here with a relationship between interdependent factors. The second triadic relationship (Figure 10.1b) includes the concept of context rather than institution. Here we may interpret the audience's relationship to text as being importantly dependent upon the context of both production and reception. In the second version, we would expect, also, to take note of the social environment and economic environments in which audiences exist. In both of these simple models, it is incumbent upon the researcher to consider the audience as something that is contextually based or grounded, rather than something which has an independent existence. If, however, the audience is conceived as having an independent existence, it becomes something about which all kinds of judgements can be made that can be characterized as belonging to or emanating from that audience. The suggestion that the characteristics of audiences may have something to do with the characteristics of the societies in which they exist has not, as a result, always been given priority. Nor has the possibility that in any single audience for a media text there may be different people making different sense of that text. Finally, and frustratingly for some, there is also the possibility that audiences may, on occasion, make the same (or very similar) sense of a given text. I say frustratingly, because this is one of the main assertions of those who would construct the audience as a mass with but one mind. Shared mass decoding puts the question of media effects firmly back on the agenda. But it still does not answer the question about what the audience does with its shared meaning. The correlation of audience views at any one time should never be automatically or uncritically transposed to questions of causation.

Nor can we easily, or perhaps ever, be confident that we have ascertained in a reliable way the views, feelings and understandings of those audiences. Sometimes (rarely), a mass audience may all act as one in response to a media message. It is probably more usual for groups of people to 'place' their meaning making in relation to their social activity, their economic position, their gender and ethnic origin, etc. It is for the media student and media researcher to engage with aspects of these meaning placements in relation to specific instances. What, for instance, can be learned from a detailed comparative study of the audience who took to the road in fright after hearing a radio drama produced by Orson Welles in 1938, based upon H. G. Wells' *War of the Worlds*, thinking that the Martians had landed, and the audience who wept at the death of Princess Diana in 1997? Are there any similarities in terms of emotional response or media influence?

The triadic conceptualizations above have been included here because, I argue, they are often used as a means of acknowledging the importance of situating the audience – and then either ignoring situational factors or playing them down. I have made a number of assertions which need further elaboration and I will do so in an attempt to clarify what is an important field of contestation in the study of the media: that of the constitution and relevance of the media audience.

The audience as a target

Many early theories of communication were constructed around models of the communication process which were somewhat basic. As with so many of the developments in the field of communication, they were often linked to either political power or military matters. The communication process was described in the language of the armed forces. Your communication had to be on target. You had to aim your message in such a way as to achieve maximum effect. The key point was that communication was conceptualized mainly as a one-way process, which was eventually given a little more credibility by including the concept of feedback. What this meant was that communication was still thought of as a linear process, but that from time to time you should check up and make sure you were doing it properly by examining the impact on the target. Feedback was not, however, a concept which gave much respect or significance to the receiver (audience). One of the most influential of the early communication models was that of Shannon and Weaver (1949). They were actually concerned with communication technology rather than the process of human communication in the mass media. In their communication process there was a sender, a message and a receiver. Messages could get through from one end of the communication chain to the other as long as they were not interrupted by something aptly conceptualized as 'noise'. It was a theory with an emphasis on transmission which was appropriated for communication studies. It is worth noting that this emphasis made it easier for researchers to work on their audiences as though they (the audiences) were somehow separable from or outside societies.

Slightly more sophisticated versions of the communication process, specifically developed about human communication, then began to appear. There was the once ubiquitous D. K. Berlo (1960) and his SMCR model (source, message, channel, receiver). Berlo did at least recognize that the receivers of messages possessed characteristics that needed to be treated with respect, including the fact that messages were circulated in specific social contexts. There was also the earlier work of Harold D. Lasswell (1947), which, though easily summarized because of the slogan-like quality of his approach, is quite profound in its implications. Lasswell's work arose from an interest in power and how it was exercised. The Lasswell 'formula', as it came to be known, was important because it was based around the posing of questions: Who? Says what? In which channel? To Whom? With what effect? The less productive outcome of this approach has been that it has encouraged the separation of research work into apparently discrete fields of study, from content analysis, to audience analysis, to effects analysis. It is also based upon a hypothesis which can lead to serious epistemological and ideological logjams. The identification of which medium (channel) is being used for communication is of a different order to the question of the effect the message in that medium is having. In contemporary terms, it might be desirable to add one or two more provocative questions, including 'Who wants to know – and why?' The implied neutrality of the formula belies the fact that such approaches to communication were motivated by state, government, free market or sometimes military interests in the operations of power. The underlying or informing principles of such communication models were always concerned with power and effect. Audiences were targets for communicators. In more recent research there has been as tendency to concentrate more on questions of effect, particularly where representations of sex and violence (and generous funding) are concerned.

The 'effects' tradition

The literature on the effects of the media is enormous in quantity. It is advisable to look for a reputable summary to grasp something of the significance of the different and often major research projects which were funded to ascertain the effects of the media on the (unsuspecting) audience. Lowery and de Fleur (1994) offer one of the clearest summaries of the major projects. Many of the research projects under this general paradigm were very large and well funded. They were also concerned with the production of quantitative rather than qualitative data. The data was often collected by surveys or questionnaires, which were carefully coded so that they could be subject to numerical analyses, eventually with the use of computer technology. A brief and stinging rebuttal of effects research has been offered by David Gauntlett (1995). What Gauntlett generates is a first-class series of questions for further research, all of which need investigating, cross-checking, interrogation. I will cite just two here. The first is the suggestion that effects researchers are misguided because they tackle social problems 'backwards'. What he wants us to consider is that we do not come to understand the problems of violence in societies by going first to the violence we see in the media. We should first, says Gauntlett, 'begin with that social violence and seek to explain it with reference, quite obviously, to those who engage in it: their identity, background, character and so on'. The concept of effects research may then have become redundant. Or, if

Gauntlett's suggestion had been a prerequisite for audience research, the whole effects tradition would have looked radically different, and I suspect would have generated radically different findings. Gauntlett might have added the possibility that understanding social violence is also related to who holds the reins of power, who designs the environment in which people live, and a host of other factors relating to lifestyle expectations and economic contexts. The service which Gauntlett performs is to remind us of the woefully inadequate conceptualization and analysis which effects research has offered of the relationship between the media, the context in which they operate and the possible characteristics of the audience(s).

The second of Gauntlett's ten points which I will mention is the one which notes that effects research (or the effects 'model', as he calls it) has paid little attention to the processes of meaning making (point nine in the original). I will return to this issue in relation to developments in ethnographic approaches to the audience. For the moment, we may note that for the effects researcher, meaning is not 'made', it is 'sent and received'.

Another key moment in the possible understanding of audiences came with the suggestion that audiences actually make use of the media in one way or another. The paradigm under which this interest grew is known as 'uses and gratifications'. The uses and gratifications approach is associated with Elihu Katz (Blumler and Katz, 1974). The emphasis in effects research has remained on asking, 'What do the media do to people?' More than a quarter of a century ago, Katz suggested asking the question, 'What do people do with media?' This simple reversal came for some as a breath of methodological fresh air. Perhaps media research did not have only to be concerned with demonstrating how the mass audience was manipulated and duped. Perhaps they (or it) had minds of their own. The very act of reconceptualization allowed researchers to begin investigations which considered in more precise detail just what people did with the media (Marris and Thornham, 1996: 421ff.).

The sense of liberation which some felt at being able to research and interrogate human response to media output was criticized eventually by those who were sceptical about the extent to which audiences actually did much at all (Lodziak, 1995). The sceptics were concerned that many media audiences simply encountered media messages without any pre-planning or sense of purpose. If we have what might be described as a 'pendulum swing' approach to understanding media research into audiences, then we will interpret these developments as confirmation of our theory. We will think that periods of certainty are followed by periods of doubt; periods when the media are seen to dominate by periods when the audience or the public make their choices freely. There is some work here for the historian of media research. But it is much more productive, I argue, to regard (individual) freedom and (mass) domination as aspects of media culture which, where identifiable, are not fixed and are often locked in tension with each other. Categorizing audiences as free or subjugated is just one of the misguided things we do to try to keep a purchase on an elusive subject.

Do audiences actually exist?

This question is particularly pertinent in an era when many would argue that all we have upon which to base our discussions of the media is a series of discourses and layers of simulacra. Ien Ang, one of the most insightful of the theorists concerned with audiences, has noted that television companies work on the implicit assumption that there *is* such a thing as an audience as a finite totality. This she describes as a necessary fiction because the industry has found its audiences to be 'volatile and fickle'. This fiction is also important because some form of order is necessary to be able to compete, sell and 'predict' audience behaviour. First, you invent your audience, then you attribute characteristics to it, often through expensive market research. You produce fiction as truth:

> A hegemonic, empowering fiction which is positively constructed as true by the creation of simulations of order in the ranks of the audience in the form of ratings statistics and other market research profiles.
>
> (Ang, 1996: 173)

The main purposes in creating audiences, it would seem, are either to protect them or to sell to them – and very often both at the same time. A third possibility is that audiences are created as commodities. This means that the audiences are on sale to advertisers, though it is not the audience that receives the money for its purchase. If audiences can be sold, it is clearly in the interests of advertisers and then of market researchers to keep the 'audience production' process alive and well. It is on the existence of audiences that many television channels, most newspapers and a gigantic proportion of the Internet depend for their very existence. The somewhat controversial question which asks whether audiences exist has a potentially even more controversial answer. It is that audiences certainly do exist, but only after they have been created by those who wish to sell or protect them.

Developing a sensitivity to audiences – is ethnography the answer?

The recognition of the audience as tangible, living people, led researchers to concentrate more on human contact in their enquiries about the media. This contact was sometimes through telephone interviews and sometimes face to face. The very act of allowing people to speak beyond responding to questionnaires was quickly, and sometimes excitedly, dubbed ethnographic. At first this was accepted, but reputable media researchers soon recognized that calling what they were doing 'ethnography' was not wise.

Ethnography is the branch of anthropology that deals with the scientific description of specific human cultures. Major ethnographic research involves the researcher living with a community for a period of time and learning a great deal about how they organize their social and family life, their religious or other practices and a host of day-to-day matters. The researcher would probably also try to detect patterns in the behaviour of members of the community as they interacted with each other, and may have to learn to speak a completely new language before being able to engage with the communities studied. Prolonged periods of direct observation are usually combined with extensive interviews and the keeping of notebooks and diaries – today, this may include video diaries. It is a major and often most productive and rewarding research enterprise. It is also a very long way from some of the work by media researchers which involve two or three interviews with a small group of people.

The undoubtedly important audience research of David Morley and Charlotte Brunsdon (Brunsdon and Morley, 1978) is now recognized as flawed methodologically because the very act of assembling a group of people in a room and asking their opinions breaks with everyday practice and could be regarded as producing 'unreliable' data. (Radical educational thinkers have sometimes pointed out that the same thing happens in classrooms.) More and more media researchers, from Buckingham to Ang, have shown their awareness of these problems in their approach to aspects of audience research (Ang, 1996; Buckingham, 1996). Nightingale and Moores have both offered helpful and constructively critical overviews of a range of 'ethnographic' research (Moores, 1993; Nightingale, 1996). It is fair to say that academics involved in the study of audiences have learned that they are not so much studying 'audiences' as investigating modes of interpretation and media usage in small groups, in usually restricted or constrained circumstances. Studying media consumption and usage has proved to be an slippery topic. Few have pursued their subjects with as much diligence as Marie Gillespie, whose work was based upon being a part of a community in which she had worked as a teacher, mentor and sometimes friend of her subjects (Gillespie, 1994). Gillespie was at least able to relate to the subjects of her study beyond using them as the means whereby texts for analysis were generated.

Ellen Seiter has perhaps given the most sober and useful appraisal of developments in audience research (Seiter, 1999). It is worth quoting at length:

> If done well, ethnographic research takes a long time. There is extensive time involved in entry into the field situation: working out the logistics of getting in, making it past various gatekeepers, securing the approval of the ever more vigilant human subjects research committees at major universities. The researcher must be patient through the process of securing trust, establishing rapport, understanding the daily routines. The fieldwork itself produces mounds of data, in the form of field notes, tapes, interviews. If ethnography is really done right, it requires that the researcher contextualise media in a wide range of practices and institutions, which have conventionally been studied by sociologists, psychologists, economists and others.
>
> (Seiter, 1999: 134)

This summation is also a lesson in humility. To define and research an audience requires much more than a journalistic glance at a home or two, an observation of a family watching television for an hour, or a brief interview which is then transcribed and quoted as though it were irrefutable proof of something or other. We may forget that the quality of the ethnographer's data may also be skewed or altered because the ethnographer is somehow existing within it. What we have discovered over time is that finding out about how people relate to the media is complex and not easily susceptible to the very judgements which many funders and media practitioners seem to demand.

I will cite just one more example which relates to this type of research because it raises questions about methodology and ethics, as well as pointing towards some potentially fruitful lines of development. The research was undertaken by Valerie Walkerdine (1986). Walkerdine describes her encounter with the Cole family. She had gone to their home because she was involved in a research project concerned with the education of six-year-old girls. As far as the parents were concerned, Walkerdine was there to speak with their daughter about matters concerned with education. Hence they were relaxed as far as their own behaviour was concerned. It so happened that the family was watching the movie *Rocky II* (Stallone, 1979) on video. It was this which acted as an impetus for Walkerdine to reconsider her purpose in being there. She realized that she had accidentally put herself in a position where the possibilities for small-scale audience research were considerable. She realized, also, that such an approach had a strong voyeuristic potential. The behaviour she was able to observe depended upon the family not actually knowing why she was there. In other words, there was a certain amount of (admittedly unplanned) deception going on. Walkerdine's own approach was situated within a discursive and psychoanalytic paradigm. The insights which she generated are of considerable importance and the piece argued for the importance of subjective experience and self-interrogation in the interpretation of data. This is a long way from quantitative or content analysis, and it is likely to yield much richer results if pursued by those with the necessary training and commitment.

My concern is mainly with the relationship between researchers and audiences. There are some problematic and as yet unresolved issues here. If we want to know what members of an audience think, we are faced with a paradoxical situation in that they may not be the best people to answer that question. At the very least, those who are being interviewed will construct responses based upon a number of variables which are unlikely to help. If you are a researcher, they will want to know who you are. They will want to know what will happen to what they say. They will also have some kind of image of themselves as they are and perhaps as they might be, all of which may impact upon they way in which they respond in an interview situation. The researchers, intentionally or not, may be creating an ethos where what they identify is the way that a certain group of people behave when they are constituted by the researchers as that small group of people. How they might have behaved otherwise may remain a relative mystery. The alternative would be to deceive your subjects – either by pretending to be there for another purpose or simply by spying on them. These are deeply problematic suggestions and I mention them here only to highlight the fact that we have to read the data gathered in interviews and small-group observation with extreme caution and sensitivity. Another problem is that research subjects are likely to be guarded if they hold opinions which they think the researcher might find offensive. This is one of the reasons why approaches to critical discourse analysis can be so relevant to audience research (Fairclough, 1995; Cameron, 2000). It is also a reason for the careful preparation of researchers who will be dealing with their subjects face to face.

Changing audiences?

The ways in which we designate our object of study have a considerable impact upon the kinds of study we undertake. I have noted that research into mass audiences tended to produce and then reproduce those audiences. They were attributed with characteristics, most of which were less than complimentary. Eventually, and often with reluctance, academics and researchers had to admit that they too were members of a range of audiences for the media. The insistence that researchers are impartial or scientific observers made the admission of audience membership an embarrassment. It was notoriously difficult for an educator to confess to having seen an episode of a soap opera, without heavy qualification: 'I happened to be in the room and the television happened to be on.'

All this was to change as a new generation came along who were not ashamed of their love of the media, and were even prepared to celebrate their media consumption. For some it seemed necessary to move from the 'I just happened to be in the room' approach, to a celebratory, compensatory orgy of theoreticism. Others were more modestly content to continue the process of theorizing their enjoyment. Distinguishing between these approaches is a challenging activity for the questioner of the media and this raised a new set of issues. If it was now acceptable to be associated with the media and popular culture, did this mean that researchers in the past had got it all wrong, and that the popular media had been producing high-quality material all the time? There was not much evidence of a long, vigorous and enlivening debate about value in relation to the celebration of the media and popular culture. There was an attempt by a whole range of theoreticians and researchers to suggest that audiences had a special relationship with the media. It was one which allowed for multiple decodings of media messages. This is a powerful argument and there is much evidence that messages can be read in more than one way. There is less evidence that messages can and will be read in a multitude of different ways. We need to establish both the possibilities and constraints of polysemy or multiple decoding through developing appropriate research methodologies. We also need to investigate the possible discursive or material conditions which would be more or less likely to generate a certain reading of a specific media text. It is simply not good enough to say that not all audience members decode the message in the same way. This has been best and most productively conceptualized by Stuart Hall, developing from the work of Frank Parkin (1971). Hall's three positions from which a reader may decode a (in his case televisual) message are: 'dominant hegemonic', 'negotiated' and 'oppositional' (Hall, 1980). This delicately argued piece is often reduced to agreeing, accepting in part or opposing a particular message. I have now characterized it in the same way, but here I can only urge the reader to go to the original text. Having said that it is an important piece, which is already proven by the very considerable influence it continues to exert, there are a couple of caveats which seem appropriate in the context of this chapter. It is basically a tripartite scheme. It does not deny the possibility of multiple readings, but it has not contributed directly to our understanding of how multiple readings might be possible. Quite the reverse, for many media students end up by classifying media messages unproblematically as either dominant, negotiated or oppositional – when what we are actually talking about is reader positions.

Another development, which is often linked with postmodernism though is in no sense dependent upon it, is the conceptualization of the media audience as aware, alert and often ironic decoders of media messages. The healthy development is that this audience is less often conceptualized as an undifferentiated mass. It is now much more recognized that there are many different media audiences. We may all be part of different audiences for different reasons at different times. Only rarely can we be said to be part of one enormous audience. And even if we are ever part of one great audience, this does not mean that we will be making the same reading of a specific media message. Enthusiasm for opposing the conceptualization of audiences as dominated or helpless masses has, however, led to some other questionable developments.

Carnivals and audiences

The words 'carnival' and 'carnivalesque' have been invoked as explanatory, sometimes mantra-like terms by those who construct the audience as more active and less mere recipients of media messages. This has been particularly true of interpreters of working-class audience behaviour. Popular television shows and all-in wrestling have been favourite topics for consideration. My purpose in raising these issues here is neither to praise nor condemn. It is to suggest that as a researcher or questioner of the media, it is essential to consider critically the arguments for and against different conceptualizations of the audience.

The terms carnival and carnivalesque were first introduced when media scholars read the work of Bakhtin on Rabelais. Mikhail Bakhtin (1895–1975) was a Russian literary theorist and philosopher, whose writing has had a considerable influence on contemporary understandings of the novel and theories of language. He was writing at the height of Stalinism and he spent some time in exile. Because of the persecution he suffered, some of his works were published under the names of friends (Voloshinov and Medvedev). We are not so much concerned here with these important details, but rather with the crucial influence which Bakhtin's work on carnival has had in the fields of media and cultural studies. Or we could reconceptualize the issue as being about the ways in which media studies, for instance, has selectively appropriated elements of Bakhtin's writings on the carnival because they served an identifiable purpose at a specific historical conjuncture.

Bakhtin wrote his influential work, which engaged in part with carnival, as a doctoral thesis, which was published in English under the title *Rabelais and His World* (Bakhtin, 1984). Rabelais wrote in the Middle Ages. He was a monk and a physician, but his real loves are reputed to have been scholarship and drinking. In his writing, both his loves are clearly apparent. The work for which he is (in)famous is *The Histories of Gargantua and Pantagruel*. Before anyone who studies the media becomes infatuated with the concept of the carnival they would do well to read both Rabelais and Bakhtin. The context in which both produced their works is also of critical and revealing significance. Carnival – and very often writing about carnival – is a serious business. Rabelais has given his name to a particular kind of humour, characterized by vulgarity and excess. Carnival is also a demanding business, and it is not the same as contemporary notions of carnival, which are little more than parades, beauty contests and a chance for a few people to dress up and collect for charity. The carnival of which Bakhtin writes is one where hilarity is shared by all and where there are no spectators. The laughter of the carnival is often macabre as well as grotesque, and death as important a component as the celebration of life.

The purpose of this brief outline is to highlight some of the powerful and important characteristics of the carnivalesque to those who are participants in its processes. It is, however, a considerable series of jumps to move from the all-embracing life-and-death-affirming carnival of medieval times, via the interpretations of that carnival by Bakhtin, to the work of those media theorists who consider today's audiences to be engaging in carnivalesque activity. The issue for the media studies researcher is to ascertain whether this is a sustainable and productive line of development. Medieval carnival provided temporary liberation for those whose lives were bleak and oppressive in ways we may find difficult to comprehend. It required, very often, forms of total abandonment, as the 'normal' codes of behaviour were temporarily abolished or reversed.

John Fiske wrote, in 1989, of a television show called *The Price is Right*, in which the contestants were nearly all women. The show, according to Fiske, required these women, with much noise and cheering, to guess the price of commodities – to demonstrate their ability as shoppers. For Fiske, this was a means whereby knowledge of the skills of consumption, usually silenced by patriarchy, could be celebrated. Fiske argues that we should be tracing two forms of liberation in the audience's enthusiasm: noisy acclaim for usually silenced skills, and the opportunity for women to be noisy in public as an escape from the constraints and confines of good sense and decorum (Fiske, 1989: 139). In another publication from the same year, Fiske offers the following sound judgement of the physicality of carnival:

> Carnival is concerned with bodies, not the bodies of individuals, but with the 'body principle', the materiality of life that underlies and precedes individuality, spirituality, ideology and society. It is a representation of the social at the level of materiality on which all are equal, which suspends the hierarchical rank and privilege that normally grants some classes power over others. The degradation of carnival is literally a bringing down of all to the equality of the body principle.
>
> (Fiske, 1989a: 83)

The constant question which audience studies has to interrogate is the extent to which claims made on behalf of the carnival are sustainable or not in relation to contemporary media and contemporary society. If they are, then the audiences for *Jerry Springer* or many reality television shows may be identified as participants in the carnivalesque. But the carnival did not occur several times a week, with regular repeats for those who missed it. Nor could it be watched in the privacy of one's home. Participation had to be total. There are clearly important differences here which need exploring. There is also a less than carnivalesque possibility: that what was once a profound manifestation of the human condition and human oppression through a celebration of bodily functions and laughter has become a hollow celebration of capitalism's oppressions by those without hope. If the latter is the case, it might throw a different light on Fiske's eagerness to find examples of the carnivalesque in a show like *The Price is Right*. The questioner of the media has to decide which of these constructions of the audience is in need of further research – or whether there may be other audiences yet to be constructed or identified.

Poaching and wigs and wishful thinking

The other important figure whose work has been adapted or appropriated for research on audiences of the media and popular culture is that of Michel de Certeau, whose most influential work is entitled *The Practice of Everyday Life* (de Certeau, 1988). As with the work of Bakhtin, we are dealing here with a complex and stimulating intellectual. My concern is that those who question the media should recognize the complexity and subtlety of the thought on offer and avoid any easy equivalence between that complexity and claims made on behalf of constructed or imputed audiences. De Certeau argued that there is a new silent majority of 'non-producers of culture', who are both marginal and in their own way culturally active. This group is not homogeneous. On behalf of the immigrant worker, de Certeau suggests:

> Confronted by images on television, the immigrant worker does not have the same critical or creative elbow-room as the average citizen. On the same terrain, his [*sic*] inferior access to information, financial means, and compensation of all kinds elicits an increased deviousness, fantasy or laughter.
>
> (De Certeau, 1988: xvii)

There are echoes clearly ringing here of Bakhtin and the carnival. There is a lyrical sense of appeal in this, as in other conceptualizations which de Certeau puts forward. It seems unkind to ask whether he means all immigrant workers, some immigrant workers, and, if so, how many – and how does he know that? But we should ask. De Certeau develops a series of theorizations which are, in a way, celebrations of the indomitable spirit of the oppressed. He writes of peasants and workers, and the tactics they may adopt in order to practise their 'art'. He cites the example of what is known in France as *la perruque* (the wig), whereby the worker disguises their own work as that of the employer. By using scraps of material, the worker who 'indulges in *la perruque* actually diverts time from the factory for work that is free, creative, and precisely not directed toward profit' (de Certeau, 1988: 25). The worker, according to de Certeau, uses cunning to demonstrate capability and creativity. This act of 'putting one over' on the employer is seen by de Certeau as a confirmation of solidarity with other workers. As with the carnival, however, 'the wig' is not so much a fundamental challenge to the order of things as a subversive embracing of them:

> The actual order of things is precisely what 'popular' tactics turn to their own ends, without any illusion that it will change any time soon. Though elsewhere it is exploited by a dominant power or simply denied by an ideological discourse, here order is *tricked* by an art.
>
> (De Certeau, 1988: 26)

The questioner of the media might note here that ideological domination is based upon the retention of relations of power and subordination. De Certeau seems determined to celebrate a subversive resistance which does not expect a change in those relations.

I will mention one other important and influential theorization among the many put forward by de Certeau. This is the concept of 'reading as poaching'. It was a mistake, according to de Certeau, to assume that the public is moulded by the products imposed upon it:

> To assume that is to misunderstand the act of 'consumption'. This misunderstanding assumes that 'assimilating' necessarily means 'becoming similar to' what one absorbs, and not 'making something similar' to what one is, making it one's own, appropriating or reappropriating it.
>
> (De Certeau, 1988: 166)

De Certeau argues strongly that we must never take people for fools. He also argues that reading is not simply a passive activity. He goes further than this, however, and makes claims on behalf of many (unnumbered) people:

> Today, it is the socio-political mechanisms of the schools, the press or television that isolate the text controlled by the teacher or the producer from its readers. But behind the theatrical décor of this new orthodoxy is hidden (as in earlier ages) the silent, transgressive, ironic or poetic activity of readers (or television viewers) who maintain their reserve in private and without the knowledge of their 'masters'.
>
> (De Certeau, 1988: 172)

The reason why these claims are so significant is that they have been used, often without further thought, by those who wished to reverse what they saw as the unhelpful and incorrect assertion that people were or could be dominated by the media. De Certeau seems to be gesturing towards a massive and silently subversive audience. This pleases those whose main motivation is to demonstrate that 'people' (a category just about as problematic as that of the audience) are active participants and presumably active decoders of the media. For those whose interest in questioning the media is also linked with social justice and social change, these assertions look like a convenient way of celebrating the status quo. It is, it seems, possible to flatter the oppressed (the mass audience) from a secure position, to celebrate subversive but ultimately inconsequential transgressions.

Audience research continues to develop and many audience researchers continue to reflect on their practice (Nightingale, 1996). For those of us concerned with questioning the media, it becomes apparent that questioning the 'audience' is also important. What we are also likely to discover is that in order to engage with this interrogative activity, we also have to develop our own understanding of and position in relation to the structures of power and subordination in our societies. It means that we must develop the courage to interrogate our own identities, politically and psychologically. How an audience is conceptualized discursively has a formative influence on how it exists materially. How we perceive the relationships of power and subordination in our societies will impact considerably on the ways in which we approach the study and conceptualization of the audience. These relationships are both fluid and volatile. The future and relevance of audience research is likely to depend as much upon our theorizing about societies as upon the choice of a particular methodological paradigm.

One final caveat can be suggested here: it is as unwise to imagine (and that is what we would be doing) that there is ever a single and unproblematic audience waiting to be identified, as that there is or is ever likely to be a clear and unproblematic 'public sphere' in which that audience operates or has its being.

FURTHER READING

De Certeau, M., 1988, *The Practice of Everyday Life.*
This is a complex and interesting book, which has been much used and abused. De Certeau has many critical things to say about intellectuals, but these tend to be overlooked by those intellectuals who wish to celebrate their readings of what he has to say. All media students should read this book and make up their own minds about whether it is about liberation or the opposition of the helpless and deluded.

Hall, S. (ed.), 1997, *Representation: cultural representations and signifying practices.*
Although this collection is not specifically about audiences, it does ask its readers to put themselves in the position of part a particular audience and to ask themselves some interesting and difficult questions. The chapter entitled 'The spectacle of the "Other"' is pertinent and challenging.

Nightingale, V., 1996, *Studying Audiences: the shock of the real.*
This is a sane and well-written overview of important developments in audience research. It includes a critical overview of two decades of research into the television audience. Nightingale traces how central tenets within audience studies were challenged by discourses of postcolonialism, fan activism and new theories of writing, arguing that audience research is necessarily a complex activity.

There is a new online journal called Particip@tions, concerned with audience research (http://www.participations.org/volume%201/issue%201/1_01_contents.htm). This is one where you can not only read but also join in the debate.

chapter eleven

The new technologies

Where a calculator on the ENIAC [Electronic Numerical Integrator and Computer] is equipped with 18,000 vacuum tubes and weighs 30 tons, computers in the future may have only 1,000 vacuum tubes and perhaps weigh 1.5 tons.

— *Popular Mechanics*, March 1949

Technology is a way of organising the universe so that man [sic] doesn't have to experience it.

— Max Frisch

The challenge is to analyse how new technologies can be used as instruments of both domination and democratisation, and to suggest how they might be reconstructed and employed for creating a more egalitarian and ecologically viable society, empowering individuals and groups who are currently disenfranchised.

— Best and Kellner, *The Postmodern Adventure*

The questioner of the media faces their most important challenge in considering the new technologies. They cover a field as vast as any in the history of human science and technology, with implications for future lifestyles, work practices, leisure activities, knowledge acquisition, learning and teaching strategies, medicine, travel, communication modes and the very survival of the human race. The new technologies also account, it would seem, for endless gadgetry, the computerization of domestic utensils and motor vehicles, and Christmas crackers (if you happen to use them) containing musical devices able to play 'Silent Night' ceaselessly two months later in garbage bins. This applies to you most, of course, if you live in certain parts of the world and have a certain economic status. But the poor also feel the impact of the new technologies and there is no escape. There are many who argue that the new technologies have ensured that there are fewer jobs in their communities. Others would suggest that the new technologies have added another layer of unattainable desires to cover the already considerable material deprivation they have to endure. The world is now divided, it would seem, into technophiles and technophobes. But there is also another category, which is that of the questioners, who recognize the positive potential in the new technologies, but fear the negative. This chapter will explore just a few of the tensions and dilemmas which consideration of these issues generates. It will become apparent that the new technologies have stimulated optimism and pessimism about the future in roughly equal proportions. The new technologies have also developed alongside the growth of media conglomerates and the power of a new generation of media moguls. This latter development is the one with which I will begin.

Questions of ownership and control

The 'new technologies' refer to the coming of digital media and satellite technology. This, and the rapid growth in the speed, size of storage capacity and sophistication of software programs for computers, has meant that communications have undergone a vast quantitative change in the last 50 years. More people are now able to communicate faster and farther, with cheaper equipment than was conceivable only a few years ago. The nature of the communications which are possible depends upon the hardware and software available, as well as the various means of ensuring that messages can travel from their sources to their destinations. All of this means that there are vast markets to be exploited, with the possibility of selling access to transmission and reception alongside the necessary equipment to make it happen. The new technologies are a capitalist dream, and they have made (and lost) many fortunes. These technologies have also formed a productive and very remunerative bridge with the past. DVDs are available of old movies. CD-ROMs are marketed which contain the great works of philosophy. CDs are available, at very little cost, of the popular music of yesteryear. Leisure activities are the potential source of vast wealth. Computer games are a multi-billion-dollar industry, as is pornography, on and off the Web. The question of who owns the companies that make the hardware and the software and controls the distribution of communication potential is of crucial significance. It is in the hands of a surprisingly small number of conglomerates.

There have been, in recent years, mergers on a scale never experienced in the history of capitalism (http://www.thenation.com/special/bigten.html). AOL/Time Warner together command revenues of $36 billion, AT&T $66 billion and News Corporation $11.6 billion. The latter is part of the Murdoch empire, which also owns newspapers in the UK such as the *Sun*, *The Times* and the *News of the World*. Fox News is also part of News Corporation. The fact that these newspapers and this news channel have taken particular stands – for instance, in relation to the Iraq War of 2003 – suggests to many that the power of ownership is not merely economic. The monopoly or alleged monopoly control of the Microsoft company has impacted upon most home computer users, whether we were aware of it or not. The main details of ownership are freely available on the Internet (http://www.wired.com/wired/archive/6.12/microsoft.html). What they demonstrate is that the new technologies and the more mature technologies of communication are part of an ideological warp and weft. Although there is freedom for the diligent researcher to move around on the Internet and find multiple viewpoints on a host of issues, for the average net user the pull of the more powerful communicators is relentless. The major news corporations define the world on the Web as well as through the other media. Patterns of ownership and control also highlight one of the most ironic aspects of contemporary technological development. It is that in an era argued to be that of postmodernity and postmodernism, when totalizing is rejected and fragmentation favoured as an explanatory concept, the power of capitalist conglomerates increases all the time. How we interpret these developments will have a considerable bearing on our understanding of the likely role which the new technologies can or should play in societies of the future.

The World Wide Web and the media

I will consider now some of the debates which have evolved with the development of the World Wide Web and the personal computer. I will also consider the relationship of the Web to the other major media, such as film and television. I will then discuss the extent to which it may be possible to think of the Web as a medium in its own right.

As a preface to all this, it is worth restating some basic information about the origins of the Web and the Internet. In 1969, the Advanced Research Projects Agency, a Department of Defense in the United States, announced the development of a network of computers which could connect with each other from a distance. Initially it involved just four computers and became known as 'Arpanet'. The important point about the network was that if part of it was destroyed, the rest of it could still go on operating. The horrendous destructive capacity of the nuclear bomb was the main impetus for this work. I mention this only to highlight the fact that major communications developments have seldom been motivated by a wish to improve human understanding and link the world in communicative friendship. In just a few decades, we have gone from the concept of post-nuclear communication to a worldwide web of communication, which includes sending and receiving mail, with or without sound, image and video messages, sending and receiving music and other multimedia presentations, and sending and receiving feature films. There are hundreds of millions of people involved in this process. In 2003, it was estimated by the Annenburg School of Communications that 59 million people used the Internet in China alone. This communication network is fast, vast, reliable and, at the moment, relatively cheap. According to Microsoft Network:

> the Internet has doubled in size every 9 to 14 months since it began in the late 1970s. In 1981 only 213 computers were connected to the Internet. By 2000 the number had grown to more than 100 million. The current number of people who use the Internet can only be estimated. One survey found that there were 61 million Internet users worldwide at the end of 1996, 148 million at the end of 1998, and 407 million by the end of 2000. Some analysts said that the number of users was expected to double again by the end of 2002.

The Internet has been likened to a highway system which has made possible a package delivery system – the World Wide Web. Once the Internet was privatized in 1995, it opened the doors to vast commercial potential. It also meant that advertising began to appear on the Web. It is now a gigantic commercial vehicle, as well as a potential tool for communication and the sharing of messages around the globe. A number of accessible approaches to the history of the Internet are available at http://www.isoc.org/internet/history/. These developments have been well documented in many places and they raise important issues for the questioner of the media (Slevin, 2000; Winston, 2000). The first and most serious is simple enough – where do we begin? The second is to ask how we might best develop methodologies for the study of the Web.

The vastness of the Web has stimulated many writers to speak in metaphors when commenting on its structures and uses. Writing in 1996 Harvey Hahn described the Internet in terms of exploration and encounters with other people who are always there but never seen. He evokes, through reference to an unidentified stranger, the spirit of *The Little Prince* (Saint-Exupéry, 2003):

> He looks at me for a long moment.
>
> You only *think* you see me. I don't really exist. Anyway, for what it's worth, there's a map of sorts. Don't lose it and you can take it with you wherever you go.
>
> He points behind you to a single piece of paper lying on the ground. You turn around to pick it up and by the time you turn back he is gone. You look down. In the centre of an otherwise blank piece of paper, is a big 'X' and the words 'You are here.'
>
> (Hahn, 1996: xliii)

This may be all very well for those of us who wish to approach the Internet with our hearts, but if we wish to take our intellects along, there are a few other questions to be answered. With the arrival of vast and successful search engines such as Google and Alta Vista, it was no longer necessary to feel so absolutely lost as was once the case. Nevertheless, it is certain that the Web is so vast that even the simplest search can lead the investigator down some extraordinary pathways. This is facilitated by the development of dynamic HTML (hypertext markup language), which means that we can flit (or navigate, if one feels more structured) from web page to web page in little or no time. Let us try just one example. I will attempt to demonstrate some of the conceptual configurations and dynamic meandering which a search can produce. It is an exercise which all those who wish to question the media should carry out regularly.

On 13 October 2003 I made the following search, using the search engine Google: I entered the word 'poverty'. This produced 14,500,000 access 'hits'. I will not comment further on the scale of this response, but it would take some months to read through them all if that was what I wanted. From a brief scan of likely pages, I chose one entitled 'Poverty; Welfare; Ethics – Literature on Portrayal of Poverty and Welfare' (http://ethics.acusd.edu/Applied/Poverty/poverty.html). On this page I found numerous pieces and chose to read one by Thomas Byrne Edsall, entitled 'The Return of Inequality' (http://www.theatlantic.com/politics/ecbig/edsalleq.htm). Having finished the piece I was interested to see that it came from something called *Atlantic Monthly*. I went to the home page of *Atlantic Monthly* (http://www.theatlantic.com/issues/2003/11/) and my eye was attracted by a piece entitled 'A Post-Saddam Scenario', written by Robert D. Kaplan. Having read this piece, I was interested to note that Kaplan is the author of a book called *Warrior Politics*. I clicked on this link and found from the advertising material that Kaplan is also a Senior Fellow at the New America Foundation. My curiosity impelled me to go to the website of this organization. There I decided to return to the original topic of my search and I entered the term 'poverty' in the search engine of the New America Foundation. I decided to read the first of the 204 references that came up. It was a book review by Peter Bergen, dated 20 August 2003, of Walter Lacqueur's *No End to War* (Lacqueur, 2003). I was interested in what Bergen had to say, so I went briefly to his website, where I found his biography and a recent photograph. From there I returned to his review. You will have noticed that I have avoided, for the moment, mentioning anything about the content and form of the material I located.

The search process I have just outlined is not uncommon, irrespective of whether one is searching for information on poverty or football scores. It involves an initial entry, followed by a massive choice of where to go next. How that decision is taken may be dictated by time, expediency, interest or simply the personal whim of the (re)searcher. Once a decision has been taken, one is led to more and more specific and focused material, or to another vast array of possibilities. The Web opens up and closes down its tentacles rather like the contractions and expansions of a giant electronic octopus. It may be, as in my case, that I end up reading a review of a book of which I would otherwise have been unaware. Or I might have gone along with this metaphorical octopus until I was simply too tired to travel further. The octopus does not tire. For the unsuccessful or unfocused Web user, it seems that searching is nothing more or less than a war of attrition with an apparently infinite data bank.

There are two key points here. The first is that the Web offers choices of a size and range that would have been incomprehensible to the user of the largest reference library in the recent past. The second is a related point: because the choice is so vast, it is most unlikely that any but the most diligent researcher will ever follow it through. There is simply not enough time. So 'research' includes the element of chance, which is manifested through whatever catches your eye or ear. The Web provides a form of freedom which allows the fortuitous to dominate the expected. It also facilitates a form of enquiry which is non-linear and multi-focal. Optimists might say that this will generate more lateral thinking and the possibility for knowledge to be extended along with new skills of cognition. Pessimists might counter that the Web merely encourages a flighty and superficial encounter with anything and everything. For psychologists, this presents a series of complex issues in relation to aspects of learning development. The search example I have recounted relates to those who are interested in motivated searching/surfing. For many, it may be the case that once a series of favourite websites are found, they are bookmarked and used repeatedly. Others may occasionally venture out from their familiar sites into navigational forays, which are exploratory rather than investigative. For the questioner of the media, it presents a methodological challenge of considerable proportion. How can we approach the study of the Web when its mode of use is so difficult to pin down, and many of its web pages so ephemeral?

In order to address some of these questions, it is necessary to impose some kind of conceptual order on one's enquiries. In the space of one chapter, my own imposition will not cover all the vast potential which analysis of the Web suggests. I will centre on what I consider to be the main priorities for the questioner of the media.

Web pages and interest groups

Millions of Web users are fans – of films, television, sport and music. They use the Web to go to, and sometimes to design, web pages about their enthusiasms. Most websites of this kind are linked to others with the same or similar interests. I will take as an example the websites related to the popular television series *The Sopranos,* created by David Chase. I choose this single example because it illustrates well the links between the more conventional medium of television, the Web and the commercial interests such as branded commodities which are so crucial to much contemporary popular culture. At the time of writing, *The Sopranos* is in its fourth series, with a fifth promised. It follows the fortunes of the Soprano family – an everyday story of New Jersey mafia folk. The series has been characterized by high production values, first-rate performances and plots which deal with a range of issues, from family loyalty to parenthood. It is also a series which contains much violence and bad language, which offends many and attains a kind of lyrical or poetic quality for many more. It also contains a considerable amount of nudity and sex. The series has deeply offended the Italian American Council. It has compared the representations of the Italian-Americans in the series to Shakespeare's Shylock or the television series *Amos 'n' Andy.* The Catholic Church has made no public comment on the series, but many Catholics regard it as high-quality television.

The producers of the series, HBO, has its own *Sopranos* website (http://www.hbo.com/sopranos/). It is technically impressive and contains many video and sound clips, as well as advertisements for a wide range of products associated with the series. These vary from neckties to bathrobes and sweatshirts, from shot glasses to food gift sets. The site itself offers interviews (written and on video) with the stars of the series, and information about the individual episodes and the fictional characters. There is also an 'authoritative' family page where you can read details of most of the main characters (http://www.hbo.com/sopranos/cast/index.shtml). It is a fine example of the ways in which the Web facilitates a virtual world in which there is no line drawn between fiction and reality because they are one and the same. Paradoxically, it does not mean that you have to believe it – rather that it requires an extension of the suspension of disbelief so essential to the cinema.

This somewhat lengthy introduction to the *Sopranos* site is designed to facilitate certain questions about the relationship between the Web and what I have called the more traditional media, such as film and television. To these we should add the media of magazines and comics. In order to study and question this Web communication, we need to ascertain if it requires a different approach methodologically. For instance, we need to decide if there is any fundamental difference between reading on a web page that a member of the cast, Federico Castelluccio, came to the United States with this family in 1968 at the age of three and a half, was awarded a full scholarship to the prestigious School of Visual Arts in New York City in 1982, where he earned a BFA in painting and media arts, and reading the same information in a magazine or newspaper. If there are differences in the mode of communication – and there are – we have to ask if and how they change what we know about Castelluccio because the source of the information was different. The Web message may be multimodal. The question is whether the 'decoding' or engagement with this form of communication requires a different kind of semiotics because of the different and more complex ways in which we can navigate the site, rather than, for instance, flipping through the pages of a magazine. Whatever our answer to these questions, the onus is then on us to pursue our study or investigation in such a way as to test out our approach. It may be that websites related to television series can be semiotically separated from a comparable paper-based fanzine. But though we may not have pages to flip though, the very fact that the software used to navigate such sites is known as a browser raises questions about the mode of utilization invited. There is the possibility that this dimension of web usage is simply an electronic version of the status quo. But the case has yet to be appropriately made either way. This is the business of the questioner of the media.

Cyberspace and identity

When we consider questions of identity in relation to the Web, there are several ways in which this new technology has facilitated significant change. Identity has been enriched and liberated (or possibly constrained, emasculated and subjected to delusions) through the coming of cyberspace. Cyberspace is a term first coined by the author William Gibson, in his 1982 novel *Neuromancer*. The Merriam-Webster dictionary defines it as 'the on-line world of computer networks'. For Gauntlett, it is 'a more literary term for the internet', and 'refers to the conceptual space where computer networking hardware, network software and users converge' (Gauntlett, 2000: 220). The experience of Web browsing and use has been indicated at its most mundane in my previous examples. Entering cyberspace can indeed be a great waste of time, a diversionary pastime and an endless source of trivia and pleasure. It is also a bottomless well of experience waiting to be explored and a research database of phenomenal proportions. The concept of cyberspace and its companion, virtual reality, has polarized intellectual opinion about the value and significance of the Web. Virtual reality is perhaps easier to define than cyberspace. It involves the simulation of an environment to which we respond in such a way that we (almost) believe we are having a specific experience rather than a 'virtual' one. A popular image of virtual reality is that of the user standing and wearing specially designed headgear, which provides sound and vision inputs and can thereby generate physical sensations of speed and space. It is not a common experience. Cyberspace, the conceptual experience of Web use, by contrast, is a daily occurrence for millions of people. Both terms have become part of everyday language and are used, like the term postmodernism, without much sense of specificity.

Kevin Robins has provided an excoriating critique of what he would argue are over-optimistic interpretations of the potential of cyberspace. He is particularly incensed by Sherman and Judkins (1992) and their

> feverish belief in transcendence; a faith that, this time round, a new technology will finally and truly deliver us from the limitations and the frustrations of this imperfect world.
>
> (Robins, 1998: 136)

Robins argues that we have to recognize there is no 'alternative and more perfect future world of cyberspace and virtual reality' (Robins, 1998: 137). The fact that it is possible to adopt different identities on the Web has been celebrated by the optimists, while at the same time it has allowed paedophiles to 'groom' children by pretending to be children themselves. Meanwhile the celebrators extol the virtues of pretending to be beautiful or strong as you create an identity for yourself (Krueger, 1991). There is an almost naïve belief here in the virtues of pretending to be other than you are, rather than any suggestion that you might change who you are.

There is also something to be said for the importance of exploring the potential which the Web offers for the play of imagination. My concern in this book, however, is to consider the kinds of questions which we need to ask as we approach various media and their modes of utilization. A more detailed exploration of MUDs and MOOs would undoubtedly generate a whole range of questions about the practice of adopting a 'new' identity (MUD = Multi-User Domain or Multi-User Dungeon – online role-playing environments; MOO = An Object-Oriented type of MUD – allows users to interact with programmable objects).

Two other key figures in debates about identity and the Web are Howard Rheingold and Sherry Turkle. Both have entered into the cyberworld with positive aspirations and an awareness that change is not always equitably distributed. Turkle, like Robins, is also aware of the danger of cyberactivities becoming a substitute for activity in the material world:

> If the politics of virtuality means democracy on-line and apathy off-line, there is reason for concern. There is also reason for concern when access to the new technology breaks down along traditional class lines. Although some inner-city communities have used computer-mediated communication as a tool for real community building, the overall trend seems to be the creation of an information elite.
>
> (Turkle, 1996)

Turkle is also an enthusiast of the potential for identity 'play', believing that entering the cyberworld does not have to mean a rejection of the material one:

> Virtual personae can be a resource for self-reflection and self-transformation. Having literally written our on-line worlds into existence, we can use the communities we build inside our machines to improve the ones outside of them. Like the anthropologist returning home from a foreign culture, the voyager in virtuality can return to the real world better able to understand what about it is arbitrary and can be changed.
>
> (Turkle, 1996)

There is a utopian aspiration in much of this writing. This is something which requires close study, both of the behaviour of 'virtual personae' and that of the creators of such personae. We know too little at the moment. Turkle writes of a 'twenty-one-year-old college senior who defends his violent characters as "something in me; but quite frankly I'd rather rape on MUDs where no harm is done"' (Turkle, 1996a: 185). We may agree with this sentiment but wonder whether the suggestion that no harm is done is the case for the actual recipient of the virtual rape. Virtual personae are not the same as dramatis personae. The latter are observed and the former have to be adopted. There is much more to be argued through here, and it is our business as questioners of the media to do so. But there is more to cyberspace activities than MUDs.

Howard Rheingold writes in his introduction to the influential *The Virtual Community*:

I have written this book to help inform a wider population about the potential importance of cyberspace to political liberties and the ways virtual communities are likely to change our experience of the real world, as individuals and communities. Although I am enthusiastic about the liberating potentials of computer-mediated communications, I try to keep my eyes open for the pitfalls of mixing technology and human relationships.

(Rheingold, 1994: 4)

Rheingold's approach has always been thoroughly participatory. He tells stories of the friends he has made in cyberspace and of the assistance he has been able to get from them in times of emergency. His book and the work which has followed from it are a testimony to utopian aspirations, tempered by occasional warnings about possible problems:

The telecommunications industry is a business, viewed primarily as an economic player. But telecommunications gives certain people access to means of influencing certain other people's thoughts and perceptions, and that access – who has it and who doesn't have it – is intimately connected with political power. The prospect of the technical capabilities of a near-ubiquitous high-bandwidth Net in the hands of a small number of commercial interests has dire political implications. Whoever gains the political edge on this technology will be able to use the technology to consolidate power.

(Rheingold, 1994: 278)

Rheingold argues that the potential is there for us to revitalize the public sphere, but the potential is also there for the Internet to become an instrument of tyranny. For those who wish to study the new technologies, these questions need to be addressed as part of our research activities. They should not be held separate according to which intellectual or other camp we see ourselves occupying. This is an aspiration yet to be achieved.

Information access

Herbert J. Schiller was one of the most consistent advocates of a critical position in relation to the new technologies. He was a sociologist with a concern to identify patterns in the ownership and control, as well as studying the distribution, of means of access to information. About the former he commented:

A new condition now exists, though it is barely acknowledged! What distinguishes this era is that the main threat to free expression has shifted from government to private corporate power. This does not imply that the state has lost its taste for controlling individual expression. It means instead that a more pervasive force has emerged that now constitutes a stronger and more active threat to expression.

(Schiller, 1996: 44)

The power of Microsoft has been mentioned earlier in this chapter. Schiller also notes the importance of advertising to the sustenance and development of the new technologies. But the other quite fundamental issue in relation to the new technologies is the question of access. Any recent map of the distribution of access across the globe makes it abundantly clear that distribution is unequal. The cost of access to the Internet also means that large numbers of the world's poor will probably never go near a computer. These stark and sobering facts are often forgotten in the debates about the significance of the new technologies. And in countries where Internet access is improving, it is almost always the well-off who benefit directly. It is hardly surprising, therefore, that some would argue that the new technologies contribute to the widening of the gap between rich and poor. The democratizing potential of cyberspace is thus severely curtailed.

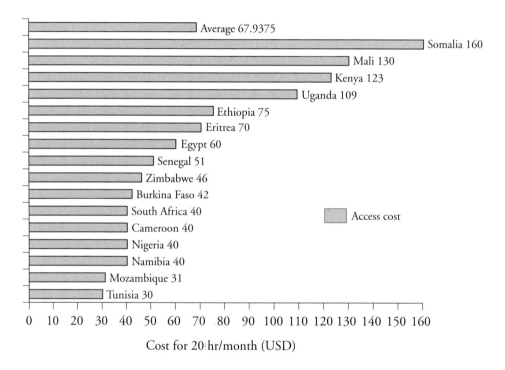

Figure 11.1 Dial-up access costs

Of the approximately 816 million people in Africa in 2001, it is estimated that 62 million had a television, 20 million had a fixed telephone line, 5.9 million had a PC and 5 million used the Internet. It is interesting to compare this figure to the situation in China quoted earlier. When we speak of the information age, we should always remember to qualify our statement with reference to the hundreds of millions who will not have access to this new phenomenon. In the richer nations, there is also much to be studied. In US public schools, the ratio of students to instructional computers with Internet access improved from 9 to 1 in 1999 to 7 to 1 in 2000. However, differences by school characteristics persisted. For example, the ratio of students to instructional computers with Internet access was still greater in schools with the highest concentration of students in poverty than in schools with the lowest concentration of poverty (http://nces.ed.gov/pubs2001/InternetAccess/).

Access to the Web is clearly an important issue. In itself, however, it is still only a beginning. Those who have access do not necessarily spend a great deal of time availing themselves of more than the tiniest fraction of what it makes possible. Acquiring information is not always such a tempting prospect for the person in the street. This is not intended as a reproach. It is merely to note that being excluded from an aspect of communication does not mean that, when it is available, Web users will rush to broaden their outlooks and discover more about the world. This is an open question and one which is difficult to evaluate. Hidden behind it is a more problematic issue about whether we who use the Web might have responsibilities as citizens as well as having freedom to enjoy ourselves. I suspect that for many, the suggestion that we have responsibilities which we should fulfil in part through our participatory productive use of the Web would be seen as an outrageous infringement of civil liberties. But for those who do wish to become politically active, the Web offers a wide range of possibilities for participation both online and offline. Oppositional groups have a mode of communication through the Web which was unheard of in the past. Once again, the interesting issue for the questioner of the media is to wonder why more advantage of this means of communication is not taken, whether one is organizing a local meeting or an international protest. Websites can be both sources of information and organizational tools. This has been demonstrated in the anti-capitalist demonstrations of the last three years, in the anti-war movements around the world and in many specifically party political sites. An example of successful and well-publicized campaigning on the Web has been that of the 'Zapatistas in Cyberspace' (http://www.eco.utexas.edu/Homepages/Faculty/Cleaver/ zapsincyber.html). Recognizing the existence of such sources of information and argument brings us back to some of the issues raised at the beginning of the chapter, and it is to these I will now turn.

Web study, website analysis

It is important, if we are to question the Web, to consider the ways in which it is organized, owned, structured and accessed. But it is also important that we are able to develop modes of analysis of specific websites. The poetry and rhetoric about the Web needs to be superseded by a wish to keep what we are using under critical and material review. Is there a social semiotics of the Web? Can we find useful ways of identifying the ideological dimensions of a given website? To what extent might we be drawing upon the methodologies from film and television studies and discourse analysis? How does one begin to analyse a web page which offers a number of links to other sites? Can we analyse each screen, with its potential for scrolling as a discrete unit, or must we develop modes of analysis which recognize that Web usage always involves movement from one screen to another?

The answers to all these questions are both frustrating and challenging. In most cases they would be of the 'I am not sure really' or 'it all depends' kind. The challenge here is not to be put off in a task which is, at the moment, lagging way behind the speed of technological development. The temptation to be avoided is to try a mechanical application of existing methodologies, such as image or narrative analysis. What is clear is that questioning the Web will require a multiperspectivist approach. Douglas Kellner developed this concept in relation to cultural studies (Kellner, 1995: 98). Drawing upon a range of thinkers from Marx to Nietzsche, Kellner suggests that the more interpretive perspectives one can bring to a cultural artefact, the more comprehensive and stronger one's reading may be. Of course, the fact that we try to adopt a number of interpretive perspectives will still leave us needing appropriate methodologies, for one does not dictate the other. What we will need is a more dynamic method for approaching our 'texts'. I put the term in inverted commas here because the multimodal text is one which requires constant redescription. This is because it can exist, on the Web at least, in a number of different forms.

A web page may be composed of one or two typefaces, set on a neutral and untextured background. It may also contain animations which are activated as soon as one logs on to the page, and the facility to scroll or navigate in three-dimensional space by moving the computer mouse forwards, backwards or sideways. If our analysis is to be dynamic, it must allow us to work through real time and with certain relational concepts. The fact that a web page may present us with a wide number of hyperlinks means that we may have to analyse it with an 'if *a*, then *b*' approach. We will almost always be working with clusters of signification rather than a single signifier. These clusters may include sound, motion and the written word, as well as still images and graphics. We may need to develop the means of plotting or mapping the patterns of exploration involved in website use.

The clustering of signifiers is also one which brings with it content. This is something I have avoided until now in my descriptions, but only because I believe it to be too important to simply gloss over. The means of communication open to website designers can be used for explaining the structure of the atom, finding accommodation, guiding people through their tax returns or child pornography. How the user relates to these topics will be just as significant for our analyses as will our understandings of the principles of web design. It has long been accepted in relation to forms of communication as different as easel painting and legal documents that form and content are strongly related to each other. Questions of appropriateness are often invoked by designers in relation to their projects, but we have to remember that appropriateness is not a fixed quality of design or communication, but is related to content and context. The fact is that one can find on the Web a wide range of designs and structures which are tailored to the needs or imputed needs of the user. If I go to a heavy metal site such as http://mmusa.rmhi.com/hmm/php/game.php I will find an invitation to upload an image of myself and drag and drop a range of features such as facial hair, shades, studs, collars and a host of other accoutrements, while listening to heavy metal guitar hammering my tiny computer speakers. The visual background, as with many heavy-metal sites, is grey and black. The typeface at the top of the page is gothic, in black, red and white. I am invited into a cultural environment in which form and content are married with the technologies of hyperlinks – I can always move on to more heavy metal or music sites.

Compare this with the official Sir Cliff Richard site (http://www.cliffrichard.org/); a semiotic analysis would yield interesting readings. The background of the homepage of Cliff

Richard's site is a regal purple. There is a friendly letter from Sir Cliff, in white sans serif type on the purple background. I can listen to extracts from many of his hits or watch some as tiny videos. The toolbar across the top of the page includes an invitation to a forum. If we go there, we find that it is a moderated forum because 'When it first appeared, it was unmoderated and this, quite frankly, proved unacceptable.' The questioner of the media might wish to pursue some of these issues to find out what it is that is being implied. They might also follow the link to Imaginit, the company which designed the website, and see what else it has done and for whom. The latter is a matter for empirical verification. The former, concerning the moderation of the site forum, would require data, analysis and interpretation.

I will return now to my opening example, where I used the word 'poverty' for my search. It is clear that the kinds of results I followed through were influenced by my interests. The results I found all required a considerable amount of reading time, and often came from sources where they were available as print material. Much of the material concerned with politics, economics and social issues may be available in more than one medium. The analysis of the written pieces I cited would hardly be dependent for their meanings on the fact that they happen to be on the Web. The context of my finding them may be important if you are interested in my Web behaviour, income, job status, etc. But the arguments put forward in the pieces I quote seem relatively untouched by the medium.

I have also suggested that signification via the new technologies such as the Web is 'clustered' and, by implication, that all significations can be clustered and reclustered in communicative forms which are relational and take place through time. Specific features of these clustered significations may take the form of more conventional written text, while other features may include sound, still images and video. Future questioners of the media might wish to find out whether there is more communicative power, in the age of multimodality, in the written word or in other forms of signification. It may be that cyberspace has facilitated new ways of conceptualizing the world and our knowledge of it.

What this chapter has attempted to demonstrate is that the new technologies, particularly the Web, have indeed had a significant impact upon the ways in which we live. I have also suggested that some critics are less than enamoured of these new technological developments, though I have also argued that we need to guard against moving towards any kind of polarization of position between technophobes and technophiles. The new technologies are here to stay. The questions we need to consider are whether they provide potential for change and growth or for continuation of the status quo through the assimilation or modification of existing relations of production and exchange. There are clearly implications in all this for the development of media studies and for the questioning of the media. If one may be forgiven the use of an expression from another significatory moment – the answer to these questions is something of an open book.

In the next chapter I will be turning my attention more specifically to the ways in which digital technology has facilitated giant strides in the possibilities for production as an activity for questioners of the media.

FURTHER READING

Gauntlett, D. (ed.), 2000, *web.studies*.

Gauntlett, D. and Horsley, R. (eds), 2004, *Web.Studies*, Second Edition.

Gauntlett states his case with an enthusiasm bordering on hubris. He argues that media studies was middle-aged, stodgy and nearly dead and that web studies is the new media studies for the digital age. Many relevant and forceful arguments are offered, though time will tell whether media studies is quite as dead as Gauntlett believes. Media students should read it.

Slevin, J., 2000, *The Internet and Society*.

A sane and measured appraisal of the relationship between the Internet and society. Probably of much more lasting value and certainly an interesting text to compare with Gauntlett's.

Turkle, S., 1996a, *Life on the Screen*.

Of the many examples now available, Turkle's provides a clear and empirically based overview. Her writings on questions of identity and the Internet may or may not stand the test of time, but they offer a fair and lucid exposition of the more enthusiastic user's perspective.

chapter twelve

Practical work in media studies

production: the act of producing
practical: of, involving, or concerned with experience of practical use; not theoretical
— *Collins English Dictionary*

There is nothing more practical than a good theory.

— James C. Maxwell

It is something of a commonplace to suggest that those studying media production are disinclined to spend their valuable time on matters concerned with theory and analysis. It is also an unwarranted assumption. It may be true for some students for some of the time. But most students I have known are willing to engage with both theory and production if and when they are deemed to be of interest and significance. This book has been concerned, up until now, with questioning the media. The transition from the act of questioning to the act of production is important and it should never be one-way or fixed. It does not matter whether we are trying to theorize our own cultural practice or put our cultural understandings and analyses to practical use. The key point is to see both activities as related and integral. Whether we are a questioner of the media because we are following a higher-education course, studying for other examinations or simply an interested person, there are good reasons to become involved in production. This chapter will spend some time trying to identify what those reasons are. But first I will provide an overview of the various activities which I would wish to designate as production.

There are many reasons why anyone or any group might become involved in production in relation to the media. For some of us, it may be an activity which is undertaken for the challenge and the sheer pleasure it provides. For others, it is a means whereby we hope to produce something which demonstrates our talent and paves the way for future career development. For those of us who are interested in questioning the media or studying specific media, production may take the form of campaigning and propagandizing, or of analysis with a view to developing understanding. All these different approaches may result in the activity of production.

In the spirit of this book, there are two things which I will not attempt to do. The first is to tell anyone how to make 'things', whether they be digital video, sound, multimedia or other products. The second is that I will not offer a guide to passing examinations. This does not mean, I hope, that the chapter will not be relevant in relation to both. Books which are specifically oriented towards production require data, checklists and procedural outlines. Much of the data in relation to equipment is likely to be obsolescent before the publication appears. Some of the most useful information in this respect can be found in a wide range of consumer magazines and in the instructions which accompany equipment and software. There are also some very useful books which provide general overviews of approaches to practical production, particularly in relation to digital video (see Gross and Ward, 2004).

This chapter is structured around a series of themes and topics and it is designed to raise as many questions as it answers. It is written in a somewhat different generic style, as it moves from everyday practical issues to theoretical ones and back again. This is because I believe it to be essential that practical work should be accessible, discussible and practicable. I have not tried to be prescriptive, but have aimed to identify areas for potential development which we may all wish to engage with as part of our explorations, analyses and questionings. The themes and topics are as follows: making movies to study movies; shooting and editing; emulation as a technique for developing understanding; the still image; and electronic words. This choice is certainly not intended to be exclusive. It may seem somewhat eccentric, but it is based upon many years of encountering what I consider to be the main issues in relation to practical work and the study of the media.

Making movies to study movies

The only 'ism' in Hollywood is plagiarism.

— Dorothy Parker

There is no issue in the field of media study which is likely to generate more passion and bile than the relationship between media studies students and the professionals. I will say a little more about this in the final chapter. On the one hand, there are professionals who scoff at the student who speaks what is interpreted by some professionals as theoretical gobbledegook. On the other, there is the professional response to student or other work, which varies from patronizing acceptance to grudging and often unacknowledged envy of the multi-skilled young media student. Meanwhile, as students, we may be trying desperately to make a good movie to impress our peers and potential employers. There may be some of us, as students, who will do just about anything to become a professional communicator or director. There may be others of us who see practical work as a vehicle for critique of the injustices in society and the debilitating production values associated with the free-market economy. The situation is fraught and often serves to generate many crossed communication wires, with individuals or groups being judged for things they have not done and did not intend to do. The very least we need to do in relation to practical work is to appraise it first according to the criteria by which it was produced. This in itself is a useful analytical skill to nurture. The reason is that many, and probably most, media products do not state explicitly the criteria which were applied in their production. These criteria have to be (re)constituted through a variety of means, such as interviews with production staff, reading publications on production, studying budgets and viewing figures and, of course, by analysing the media text. Just as we might wish to do this when we interrogate the process of professional movie production, so we need to establish ways of interrogating ourselves if and when we decide to make something. Let me stress once more that my motivation here is to make practical production a means of studying and interrogating the media. It is not to train movie-makers or artists. It is just possible that the approach I am suggesting might accomplish this difficult task, but it will be a side-product rather than a central aim.

It is very difficult to become involved in the making of movies unless we come together with other people. It is one of the ironies of our age that this was much easier to accomplish when we did not have the necessary tools and potential skills to carry out the task in hand. In the earlier days of the cinema, there were many film societies which people joined in order to make a film or two. The equipment was basic and often expensive, and it was rare for any group to be able to afford any synchronous sound in its productions. Now we have the world at our digital feet, and it is much less likely, indeed almost an embarrassing thought, that we might spend our spare time in the organized pursuit of production. The technology has, it seems, encouraged certain forms of isolationism. And yet, there is no escape from the fact that one of the least studied and most significant aspects of movie-making at all levels is related to the ability to interact with other people.

If we study the interpersonal dimensions of movie-making, we will have a range of activities to take on board. These will include the behaviour of those who seek funding for making a movie and those who provide such funding. There will also be the ways in which power is exercised through the interpersonal. This is one thing which is very difficult to simulate. When we do simulate the movie-making process, it is rare to include in the simulation the possibility of being fired, having a nervous breakdown, growing ulcers and losing at least as many friends as we ever make. Nor would we wish, even for the development of understanding, to have to simulate the endless hours of waiting around which are part of the average commercial film-making experience. The bigger the production, the longer the waiting around, though there is perhaps the comfort of knowing that you are being paid for it. It is also very difficult to comprehend the amount of power exercised by established producers and directors. Alfred Hitchcock was reputed to have said that all actors were cattle, to which he happily responded that he had merely stated that they should be *treated* like cattle. Many producers in the past were willing and able to flaunt their knowledge and ignorance in order to ensure that their movies were completed on time and on budget. In recent years, we have had the Coen brothers providing one of the many perceptive commentaries on the behaviour of movie producers, with *Barton Fink* (Coen brothers, 1991). There is a vast literature available, some of it reliable, which recounts the ways in which directors, actors, editors and film crews conducted themselves during the making of specific movies. A demonstration of the enormity of human energy and disastrous decision-making involved in movie-making can be found in such books as *Final Cut* (Bach, 1985), which tells the story of the making of *Heaven's Gate* (Cimino, 1980). Bach begins the book by reminding us that it was Orson Welles who stated that a poet needs a pen, a painter a brush and a film-maker an army. This thought is an interesting complement to our own faltering attempts to produce digital movies.

This apparent digression is not intended to dissuade anyone from making movies for pleasure or for the purposes of study. It is, however, intended to ensure that we keep a healthy perspective on such work. For some of the time, like it or not, our practical work can have the same relationship to making movies as playing cowboys does to going out and getting shot. With this in mind, however, I am still a passionate believer in the importance of engaging in practical work as a means of developing our understandings of cinema and the movies. But what should we do?

On the importance of plagiarism

Dorothy Parker may have been right about plagiarism in Hollywood, but borrowing other people's ideas is one of the best ways for students to learn. The great advantage for the student or anyone not seeking a mass audience is that, for the purposes of study, one can borrow every cinematic device and try it out for a while. The coming of digitization has made this all the more possible. A less provocative way of describing such activity would be to call it skill acquisition through the temporary appropriation of a means of expression. This may include work which deliberately sets out to produce meaning in a specific genre. It is the cinematic equivalent of discovering modes of address in writing. So we may attempt to 'speak' *film noir*, melodrama or fly-on-the-wall documentary. Each of these activities will require us to interact with other people. If we are students, we may have our peers to work with. Otherwise we may have to rely on family and friends. As we talk people into working with us, we will be operating in a modest but parallel universe of discourse to that occupied by professional film-makers. Rather than emulating the professional film-maker, however, we will be shamelessly exploiting their approaches to see how they do it. I am studiously avoiding the use of the word 'amateur' in the context of these activities, because that is not what they are about. They are about a pleasurable and demanding reflexive practice. We make to learn, rather than learn to make. The results of such work are likely to contribute to a specific genre, sometimes disparagingly called the 'student film'. The best audiences for such films are likely to be other students or investigators of the media. The least sympathetic are likely to be movie-makers or cinema-goers.

What's in a shot?

The problem with any exploratory work is that it is likely, almost by definition, to be incomplete. We can, for instance, experiment with the possibilities of taking shots which conform to accepted standards and practice, such as long shots, close-ups, two-shots, big close-ups, etc. From this we can learn some of the basics about framing. But what we also need to learn is that shots not only fall into categories which are specifiable, but that they can also be composed. If we possess a digital still or movie camera we can spend hours experimenting with the possibilities of composing shots differently. We can also use the digital camera to produce storyboards for any project we intend to undertake. This is a valuable exercise, but it is also likely to highlight some important differences between still photography and moving-image photography. Planning a shot in relation to the moving image involves, in effect, a whole range of shots in one. Either there will be movement within the frame or the camera will move. Experimenting with what happens in both cases is something like practising a riff in jazz or a phrase of poetry. It has its place and can be very valuable, but it is not an end in itself. In order to understand the full potential of a shot, we need to place that shot in some kind of context. It will be either the context of a narrative or a montage. A shot placed in a narrative context can quickly take on a meaning that might not have been apparent had we studied it on its own. It is for this reason that we need to be sceptical about publications which purport to tell us about the 'meaning' of a high-angle or low-angle shot – usually suggested, respectively, as making the subject small and inconsequential or threatening. The general signification attributed to such shots may be right on occasion, but it is not a universal law. The other point is that shots are put together in scenes and sequences which, in turn, become part of a narrative. Once this occurs, a given, situated shot may tell us more than it could ever do on its own. It has been noted by many writers that a successful narrative scene usually tells us more than a summary of its content would suggest. When Al Pacino goes to the men's room in a small Italian restaurant in *The Godfather*, part one (Ford Coppola, 1972), we see him walk across an unremarkable floor to a door. But what that shot means depends upon much more than what is in it – for we know that in the men's room he expects to find a handgun in the cistern. We also know that if he is discovered trying to find the handgun he will be killed. In this way, an unremarkable shot can be one which makes the pulse race. So meaning and context are hand in glove. Our own practical work can be an act of discovery and exploration which identifies just how the meaning and the context can be produced. What we may suggest from these examples is that there is something to be learned from experimenting with the formal properties of shots, but that we will only be using our knowledge to full effect when we are able to situate them in a context whereby their meaning can be enriched through narrative placement. In other words, we will have to go beyond experimenting and make a movie! The main motivation here would be, in the spirit of this book, to discover what happens 'if'.

Shooting and editing

I have written about the possible significance of exploring the shot as a means of pursuing our questioning of the media. I have also noted that this is something which has a limited value until a specific shot is put in a specific context. I will say something now about the significance of using shooting and editing as a way of exploring how meanings can be made.

Without wishing to sound too staid or restrictive, I would offer first the suggestion that it is far easier, when working with the moving image, to break established rules than it is to obey them. I have worked over many years with students as we have struggled to make a short sequence of film or video which simply obeyed the rules of continuity editing. It has never been easy for us to find out how to shoot and reshoot a sequence, varying the angle of the camera or the focal length of the lens – just so that there are some simple shots to cut together. Many times our objective has been to discover how cutting on the action works. Our work was always done within a short narrative or a sequence with a narrative purpose. It was never an arid exercise. One of the most common responses from those who undertake such work is the expression of a sense of respect for the craft of film-making.

Shooting for continuity editing requires a basic script and storyline. It requires us to prepare and shoot a series of shots which include covering the same action from more than one angle or position. It also requires us to consider the importance of continuity when we have to shoot a given action many times. We have to avoid glasses of liquid apparently filling up between shots and inanimate objects apparently moving their positions. Those who perform in front of the camera will also discover how it is necessary to develop the skill of repeating the delivery of lines, facial expressions and movements, as well as making sure that they are standing or sitting in the same position at the beginning and end of each action.

Our motivation would be to discover through our practical activities how a series of production variables come together and interact in order to signify meaning. These would include, as a minimum, the control of sound, light, acting and shot composition. For the theorist, this might require some complex description and analysis. For many in the profession, it is all about what 'works'. I would argue that these are two different ways of describing the same phenomenon. Unfortunately they represent too often the polarities which exist between theory and practice. Practical work concerned with the moving image and sound is frustrating because we have to alternate between acquiring specific skills, such as pulling focus or panning smoothly, and recognizing that theorizing is something which is not usually done while we are involved in practical production. Indeed it can been argued that theorizing is best done retrospectively. Motivation should come first. This does raise serious questions for consideration: can or should we use the medium of our choice to demonstrate a theory, or should we be more concerned with what it is that we wish to represent in terms of a media message? Can or should we ever attempt to separate form from content in what we produce? It is my judgement that we are much less likely to be able to 'demonstrate a theory' than to acquire the techniques associated with specific genres. But to use a genre successfully usually means adopting a theoretical stance in relation to the subject matter of our work!

Shooting for specific genres is likely to pose different technical challenges and constraints. We are helped up to a point by many of the newer digital cameras. They offer different screen formats and the possibility of shooting in colour or black and white. We are likely to discover the need for a good tripod and the need to practise the most effective way to put it to use. Many of the points being made right now are, of course, laughably simple. The problem with shooting movies is that it is the laughably simple which is often overlooked. Some of what we may learn from shooting might be at the level of psychomotor skills. Other learning may be somewhat more visceral and a most useful complement to the theorizing activities involved in questioning the media.

From continuity to montage and back again

Editing sound and the moving image has never before been so accessible and affordable. Many computers come with preloaded editing software, such as Microsoft's Movie Maker or Apple's I Movie. In schools, colleges and university departments, we are likely to find professional editing software such as Final Cut Pro and Adobe Premiere. Many readers of this book may already be familiar with such software. It is not uncommon today for enthusiasts to become sophisticated users. They have no problem with cutting, laying tracks and introducing optical effects into material. Many are self-taught because there is simply neither the time nor the staff available for them to receive tuition. The days of using film stock have all but disappeared outside of the feature film industry. The days of the videotape are also numbered. In the future, we will all have the (potential) capacity to shoot and edit digitally. This is by way of introduction to some issues which will have an impact upon our practical editing.

Continuity editing is the practical outcome of the wish to simulate a seamless reality. In this reality, events happen with a smoothness which facilitates the production of the realist text. The technique is designed to be, if not invisible, non-intrusive in the extreme. It is a convention and the transition between shots is the key moment of erasure. When the spectator has accepted this convention, the world of cinematic realism is attainable. One of the best introductions to continuity editing can be found in Bordwell and Thompson's *Film Art* (2003: chapter seven). To experience practically the construction of this 'reality' is something which no form of analysis can provide. But continuity editing is not the only kind which is available to the questioner of the media. There are three others, and each offers important potential for exploration. I will mention briefly cross-cutting and deep-focus editing, and then turn my attention to montage editing.

Cross-cutting is used when two parallel and interlinked sets of events are unfolding and we wish to show them at the same time. We are most likely to be aware of this convention in relation to adventure or suspense movies when one set of events (possibly a hero in serious trouble) is intercut with, for instance, the police racing their way toward his location. Eventually, the two sets of events come together, usually but not necessarily at the same location. We may wish to devise and shoot something like a pre-credit sequence to try out this type of editing. Deep-focus editing is a technique where there is less cutting from shot to shot, but in each shot the maximum amount of the image remains in focus. This was championed by some as a vehicle for what the theorist Bazin called objective realism (Bazin, 1951). This approach to editing and realism was certainly effective when watching a giant cinema screen. Whether it has the same impact in relation to the television screen is a debatable point. It is nevertheless an interesting experiment to deliberately shoot some material with a large depth of field (maximum amount of focus) and shoot the same material with the opposite (choosing who or what will be in focus for each shot or part of a shot).

The final type of editing which I will discuss is that of montage editing. It is a mode of editing which is based upon a different logic than that which seeks to create a seamless reality (verisimilitude). Montage editing is about collision. It is about putting shots together in such a way as to generate a meaning which is not inherent in any of the individual shots. It was first exemplified at length by the Soviet film-maker Sergei Eisenstein. The classic example of this convention is to be found in Eisenstein's *Battleship Potemkin* (1925) and I will cite the example chosen by Victor Perkins in his *Film as Film* (1972). The movie is, in part, about a mutiny in 1905 of the sailors aboard the battleship *Potemkin* (Cook and Bernink, 1999: 319). There is a point in the movie, after the famous Odessa Steps sequence, when the sailors turn the guns of the battleship on the town's military headquarters. There are images of destruction, followed by shots of three stone lions. The shots are cut together in such a way as to suggest a single sleeping lion sitting up. It is clear from viewing this sequence that some meaning is intended by Eisenstein. The impact of the sequence was and is considerable. The problem, perhaps, is just what it is supposed to mean. It could be taken to signify the awakening of a noble beast (possibly the proletariat) or an indignant beast (the military and the tsar?). What is clear is that the meaning taken from such a montage sequence will depend very considerably upon the positioning of the audience. Revolutionaries would be likely to make a different reading than tsarists. I mention this example because it can stand as a metaphor for so much that has happened as montage editing has developed over decades. All montage sequences are likely to juxtapose shots in such a way as to elicit meaning. At its most productive, montage can act as a stimulus for thought and understanding. At its least productive it can become a means whereby anyone who knows how to do it can put any shots together in any order and leave the audience to work out what has happened, because the maker has no idea what it all means. Somewhere between these two deliberately provocative extremes, we find montage editing used to considerable effect in some narrative movies. The irony, perhaps, is that its greatest use in the twenty-first century is in the production of advertising on television and in the cinema. Cutting together a sequence of apparently unrelated but graphically stimulating shots, particularly when driven by a pulsating music track, seems to retain an appeal for many audiences. Music videos have provided a regular and stimulating outlet for this type of work. For the questioner of the media who happens to have access to digital editing software, montage editing is a challenge in at least two ways. The first is that it provides us with the possibility to refine our editing skills as we choose and juxtapose images and sounds. The second is that it provides us with a semiotic conundrum, because we are able to produce texts with indeterminate meaning and with relative ease. The challenge in relation to practical work is to find ways of bringing such a powerful potential for meaning making under sufficient control. Perhaps one of the best ways to explore Eisenstein's approach to montage would be to design an advertisement based entirely on the collision of shots, but with an identifiable purpose to each collision.

Emulate: to attempt to equal or surpass, especially by imitation
(*Collins English Dictionary*)

There is little doubt that emulating the work of professional media producers can provide a useful stimulus for our practical work – sometimes. Emulation motivated by the desire for pleasure is not, however, the same as emulation which is motivated by the desire to question and understand. The two are not mutually exclusive. I am arguing in this book, however, for the importance of questioning the media – in this case, through production. If we are motivated by the desire to outperform the professionals, we are seldom likely to succeed. If, on the other hand, we seek a reflexive understanding of the production process, we are likely to place emphasis on the understanding it generates as much as the text it produces. This distinction is one which has caused many polemical debates over the decades. It is a debate which we need to enter as we approach our own practical work.

Working with still images

In an era when multimodal discourse is becoming recognized as a key mode of contemporary communication, it is important to remember that the separation of any one mode of communication is more for descriptive convenience than use as a sustainable communicative tool. In other words, when I write about using still images, I am usually referring to still images plus at least one other mode of communication. The most common of these was identified many years ago by Barthes (1972), when he pointed out that we never see an image without written anchorage to accompany it. There may be some exceptions, but they are few and far between. The analysis of an image (and hence the production of an image) always needs to be undertaken in context. The image of a hunt meeting, with the caption, 'The People's Right to Choose', or alternatively, 'A Meeting of the Unemployed', demonstrates clearly how the text which accompanies an image can work rather like another shot in a film montage. The image and text clash to produce a third meaning. When questioning the media, this is a productive and illuminating avenue to explore.

Electronic words

> *The emergence of cyberspace will most likely have – already has had – as radical an effect on the pragmatics of communication as the discovery of writing.*
>
> — Lévy

It seems appropriate to close these considerations of practical work with a return to the present and likely future of writing. One of the most accessible means of reacting, responding and generating meaning open to those who wish to question the media is the use of the computer. In conjunction with the use of the World Wide Web, the computer offers the most radical potential for responding to the media which has ever existed. Lévy has summed this up well:

> The modes of expression available for communicating in cyberspace are already highly varied and will become increasingly so in the future. From simple hypertext to multimodal hyperdocuments and digital video, to interactive simulations and performances in virtual worlds, new ways of writing images, new rhetorics of interactivity will be invented.
>
> (Lévy, 2001: 224)

With this new potential we can see how it is possible for responses to the media to be generated by individuals or organized groups. It is true that there is seldom airtime allocated for alternative or analytical viewpoints. It is equally true that the practical application of keyboard, graphic and digital editing skills provides a powerful communication base which can often reach larger audiences than publishing could ever find outside the world of bestsellers.

This new world of digital production and manipulation can give cause for concern. There have been prominent academics, such as Neil Postman, who have made a deliberate oppositional strategy out of turning their backs on computer technology. They are usually convinced that computer technology will not encourage clear thinking or writing ability. I believe they are wrong to reject computers, and anyway it is not a successful strategy. We know well enough by now that the biro did not become a tool of revolution. Nor did it result in the poor rising up to write – except shopping lists and credit card slips. It may be the same with computers, but this is a conditional and contingent hypothesis. Biros and computers retain the potential for phenomenal productive use, given appropriate conditions and motivation. We have to remember that when media are invented they are put to use. The issue we face when we question the media is – who is to be the user, for what purpose, and who is to be the used?

There is an impermanence and, for some, a playfulness inherent in the new media. Some would suggest that the days of the written page as we now know it are numbered. I find this difficult to believe, but it is clear that there are radical changes occurring in the relationships between writing, the media and the arts. The computer screen, the speed of computer operation, the digital image as a volatile image – all these things contribute to a new world of practical potential, as summed up by Lanham:

> Even as pixeling a written text onto an electronic screen radically destabilizes and volatilizes it, so painting on an electronic screen launches the image into an existence forever *in potentia*. Electronic painting exists to be transformed by the viewer. The image you see is but one readout of a digital code that can produce hundreds more. Apply a contrast-enhancement program and you have a different picture; a Fourier transform and you get yet another. The Arnoldian ideal of fixed perfection simply dissolves. Again, as with literature, the entire supporting structure of criticism must be recomputed.
>
> (Lanham, 1993: 107)

When we enter the domain of practical work, we will be haunted by simplicity and complexity in equal measure. We will need to acquire the skills which enable us to produce the image or sound or written word that we desire. Sometimes this will mean going over fundamentally basic matters, such as knowing which button to press and when. At other times, we will find ourselves musing on the nature of communication, art and permanence in an age of rapid change. We may also find ourselves considering whether or not the whole business of the new technologies and approaches to practical work is simply a means of ignoring the widening gap between the material rich and the material poor, as we enter and play in our virtual realities. This chapter has tried to raise some of the issues for your consideration. I believe that practical work, in relation to the understanding of the media, is a necessary means of ensuring that we experience and work through the contradictions and tensions which the world and the media together have presented us with.

FURTHER READING

The diversity of references here will, I hope, provide an indication of the richness and potential of the field of practical work.

Gross, L. and Ward, L., 2004, *Digital Moviemaking*.
The fifth edition of this book provides guidance and advice for the would-be director and digital movie-maker. It is a useful and at the moment up-to-date reference work.

Lanham, R., 1993, *The Electronic Word*.
Lanham is a scholar with a belief in the positive potential of the digital age. His enthusiasm is infectious and he has made an original contribution to our understanding of television, reading and education. He is also an advocate of reconceptualizing the process of writing for the digital age (see also http://ccat.sas.upenn.edu/jod/texts/lanham.sample).

Rosenblum, R. and Karen, R., 1979, *When the Shooting Stops . . . the Cutting Begins*.
Something rather different is this entertaining and informative account of the process of film editing, written by two editors with some classic credits to their name.

Wayne, M., 1997, *Theorising Video Practice*.
Wayne's book is rooted in theory, which has been related over some years to the practical production work of his students. The illustrations are all from students' work and the theory is socially aware and challenging.

chapter thirteen

In defence of media studies

What are my credentials for writing such a book? Allow me to introduce myself. I am one of those people The Wall Street Journal, *CBS News, and* Spy *magazine love to make fun of: I am a professor of media studies. You know what that means. I probably teach entire courses on the films of Connie Francis, go to academic conferences where the main intellectual exchange is trading comic books, never make my students read books, and insist that Gary Lewis and the Playboys were more important than Hegel, John Dos Passos, or Frances Perkins. All I do now, of course, is study Madonna. The reason I chose the media over, say, the Renaissance or quantum mechanics is that I don't like to read, don't know much about history, and needed desperately to find a way to watch television for a living. This, anyway, is the caricature of people like me.*

— Douglas, *Where the Girls Are*

Well, it's not a problem to me that lots of young people want to do media studies or communication studies of one form or another. I think that's very sensible. [. . .] There's clearly a great need and a great demand, and lots of people who want to do it. I have no problem at all with the more practical courses that actually tell them how to do it – tell them what's going on; teach them about communications, and most of all teach them how to communicate. How to write, how to speak. Almost whatever job anybody gets these days, any graduate, they are going to need those communications skills. So I have no problem with that at all. I have a problem that they become so academic and so abstruse that large chunks of them are full of a kind of 'newspeak', a kind of gobbledegook. Semiotics – *time and time again. A sort of whole new discipline, if you can call it that, which I think is absolute junk. [. . .] . . . academics mostly trained in other things who have gone over to this because it's the fashionable thing to move in to.*

— Polly Toynbee on *Afternoon Shift*, Radio 4, 21 January 1998

Media studies is a trivial, minor field of research, spuriously created for jargon-spinners and academic make-weights. Students learn nothing of value because the subject doesn't know its own purpose, is unimportant, and because most people teaching it don't know what they are talking about. [. . .] This paper regards a degree in media studies as a disqualification for the career of journalism.

— *Independent*, leader page, 31 October 1996

How not to study the media

The three quotations which introduce this closing chapter do, at least, provide some indication of the levels of fury, ignorance, downright malice – and humour – which mention of media studies can elicit from a range of sources. Polly Toynbee thinks that semiotics is 'absolute junk'. I think Polly Toynbee is speaking from a surprising position of profound or feigned ignorance. The *Independent* thinks that it would be a mistake to employ someone with a degree in media studies. I think the *Independent* is writing from a position of middle-class pique rather than one based upon serious research or any regard for the place and purpose of media studies in any contemporary society. Polly Toynbee thinks that academics 'go over' to media studies because it is the 'fashionable thing' to do. I think Polly Toynbee, along with many other otherwise apparently intellectually able people, is offering judgements which are not based upon empirical research. She lives, it would seem, in a world where it is just so easy to move into media studies that anyone with half an inclination can do so at the drop of a semiotic phrase or two. Susan Douglas, a media professor from the United States, is much more convincing, human and intellectually sound than either Polly Toynbee or the *Independent*. She is what Alf Garnett would have called 'yer actual media professor'. So who are we supposed to believe or take seriously?

There are many examples of overheated media or overheated individuals writing in the media which could be cited. It would be possible to go on writing about them in the generic form which has been indicated by one newspaper and one columnist – that of inferior invective. But that is not what this book has been about. Instead it has been about the issues with which media studies, including semiotics, are concerned. These are issues relating to the way we live, the way our lives are explained to us in media representations and the extent to which we become involved in or active in relation to these and other issues. It is also a field of research and intellectual enquiry that is, happily, full of controversy and debate. I say happily because one of the main strengths of media studies is precisely its capacity to challenge our individual beliefs and values, and its ability to challenge the beliefs and values of those individuals or groups who hold positions of power in our various societies. It is a field of study where intellectual complacency has not yet become the order of the day. There are, of course, some exceptions. There may be some thinkers who are so busy savouring their own contributions to the celebration of the media that they have forgotten that media studies is about power as much as it is about pleasure. It is also a field where pleasure, power and politics are not discrete categories, but ones which constantly overlap and intermingle. One of the aims of this book has been to examine some of the ways in which this can occur. The important point to note is that our concern has been with debates and issues. It has not been about trading insults or about bile-laden sound-bites.

The debates and issues which inform the study of the mass media are interesting and important. There will be, of course, agreements and disagreements in any worthwhile study of the media. It would be a pointless and somewhat totalitarian study if all it required was the learning and regurgitation of an accepted 'position' on everything from advertising to biopics, from news broadcasts to adult comics. The disagreement, however, needs to be part of a process of investigation and analysis. It should never be reduced to sniping from preordained pre-established positions at anyone who seems a worthy (or easy) target. Nor should disagreement become an unthinking and rather self-satisfied means of avoiding difficult issues. The debates within media studies and the research upon which they are (sometimes) based are challenging, and they involve all of us. It does not matter whether we are students of the media, journalists, broadcasters, teachers or, acting in our roles as something which we all share but are often embarrassed to recognize, citizens.

Why all the hostility to writings about the media?

What is it that makes so many people in the media so hostile to media studies? This is a question which is unlikely to be answerable in any definitive way. There are, however, at least three possibilities which we could explore. The first relates to the concept of anti-intellectualism. The second is related to the refusal to recognize and respect the fact that some ideas or theories can be difficult, but that this is the same for most academic disciplines. The third is concerned with why some people have a problem with the suggestion that media studies is an academic pursuit worthy of respect.

Anti-intellectualism is a recurrent feature of popular discourses. It is mainly concerned with having a laugh at the expense of the 'intellectuals'. It is also hostile to any kind of theory or complex thinking, preferring to rely on common sense as a guide in all matters related to the media. Many critics of media studies have suggested that it is a field which is jargon-ridden and often impossible to understand. Such criticism is, in the main, to be found in the press rather than in academic journals. This is not surprising and is not always without foundation. Some texts in media and cultural studies are indeed difficult and some do use jargon. The task for the student or researcher, clearly, is to try to differentiate between that which is necessarily difficult and that which is needlessly opaque – a task not confined to the study of the media. We have to remember that the word jargon has at least two meanings. One definition is concerned with the use of specialist language, the other with jargon as the use of pretentious language or even gibberish. The latter is not justifiable in any field of academic endeavour.

Difficult languages or difficult ideas?

All specialisms, including media studies, use jargon and they are not usually the subject of hostility and derision. If I say to anyone who has done some basic geometry that the square on the hypotenuse of a right-angled triangle is equal to the sum of the squares of the other two sides, I am not likely to be greeted in the media with howls of derision if overheard by someone who is ignorant of the basic principles of geometry. If, on the other hand, I say to a media studies student that the diegesis of a *film noir* is likely to be structured in relation to setting and mood rather than generic form, this is enough to induce apoplexy in some unsympathetic quarters. But we have to distinguish between the use of specialist language in order to facilitate clarity of thought and exposition, and the use of jargon and linguistic contortion for a variety of other (usually dubious) reasons. One of the core activities with which any media researcher or student has to be involved is that of constantly appraising both media messages and writings about the media. In relation to the latter, this requires the constant questioning of the ways in which writers formulate and express their arguments. Critical appraisal of the use of one's own and others' language is a crucial part of the activity of the media studies researcher and student. In order to study the media, we need to develop our powers of description. The description of the front page of a newspaper or a scene from a feature film requires the development of certain skills and sometimes a specialist vocabulary. There will be occasions when this vocabulary is necessary in order to identify particular aspects of a media message. We may need to know what 12-point bold Times New Roman looks like, and that it has a name. We may also need to know that a particular scene in a film contains several zip pans and a long dolly. At the conceptual level it may be necessary, for our critical work, to describe in detail the way in which the same scene from the same film operates ideologically through dissimulation and the use of cinematic metonym. These examples are offered only to illustrate the fact that we do not have to try to invent all our terminology when we engage with a specific discipline. We may occasionally discover a gap where we feel it is necessary to coin a phrase or neologize. For most of the time, however, media studies involves us in acquiring and becoming proficient in the use of any necessary specialist terminology. (An example of the ways in which complex language can be used to obscure rather than clarify meaning was provided by what is now known as the Sokal affair. See Sokal and Bricmont, 1997.)

Media studies and populist attacks

Another possible explanation for the hostility to media studies is the fact that it is such an easy target. Senior politicians can always expect media coverage of a scornful attack on those who study soap opera. There is an easy elitism in the condemnation of popular cultural forms. Popular culture, for popular journalists, is something which they are licensed to write about. The rest of us can have a bit of a chat about it. If, however, we decide that the media and popular culture are worth studying, we are either getting ideas above our station or trespassing on the territory of the journalist. The virulence with which some journalists denounce media studies sometimes suggests a form of professional insecurity. The scorn poured upon the study of soap opera is seldom extended to the study of the news or documentaries, the nature of knowledge as presented in quiz shows, the advertising business, the representation of national identity in sport, the treatment of issues of 'race' in the media or the relationship between audiences and their pleasures. The ways in which science and issues of health are represented in the media are also major areas for study which are sadly neglected. These and many other issues are the business of media studies. They are not so easily subject to ridicule because they happen to be very important fields of study and investigation.

Why study the media? The issue of prevalence

The beginnings of a shopping list of aspects of the media which are worthy of study has just been hinted at. Some of the issues have been discussed in this book. We could all make up our own list of reasons for studying the media and invent different approaches to such study. I suspect that one point we would all have in common if we were to draw up such a list would be the prevalence of the media in our lives. On this point it does not matter whether we feel warm and secure or hostile and alienated in the company of the media. Either way, they are there and they are part of our personal and social existence. Given the prevalence of the media, I believe it is the hostility to their study that needs to be justified.

There have been those who have argued, often from an elitist position, that we should simply ignore the media, and get on with studying more important things. What this usually means is that we should be studying *other* media – 'better' newspapers or 'better' novels, films or music. While I wish to place the question of quality at the heart of appraising the media, I think it is unwise to rush to a premature judgement of any media form. The novel itself was greeted with some derision in its earlier days. The idea that the populace might be able to read and write was also a source of considerable worry to some in positions of power. The Greek philosopher Plato was even worried about the use of semitones in music. How he would have coped with the blues is a matter of stimulating conjecture. We can no more abolish or turn our backs upon the media than we can the invention of the wheel or the alphabet.

The question is, rather, what our own approach to study and questioning of the media is likely to be. This book has been written from the perspective of someone who critically accepts the presence of the media as a source of multiple pleasures and pains, challenges and mind-numbing platitudes. This extraordinary mixture is, of course, always part of the life of any society where communication is allowed to involve dialogue and the development of critical thought and action. It is the omnipresence of the media in our lives which is perhaps their main distinguishing feature. For some people, the study of the media is something to be undertaken with a sigh, as one assumes the burden of making clear to the uninitiated just how they are being taken for a ride. For others, the media and popular culture are about enjoying the moment, about living in the twenty-first century. I have attempted to argue that studying the media has to involve us in an extended engagement with questions of pleasure, power and politics.

The new technologies

The speed of technological change and the coming of what are often called the new technologies also strengthen arguments in favour of the study of the media. I have noted that these technologies, including satellite broadcasting, the microchip, fibre-optic cable and digital television, are likely to have as fundamental an effect on the material organization of societies as the coming of printing or the Industrial Revolution. They bring together questions about the role and purpose of the media with questions of employment, lifestyle and life prospects. The new technologies provide the capacity to transmit unimaginable amounts of information around the globe at great speed. This information may take the form of television or radio signals, but it is not only television and radio programmes which traverse the globe daily. The new technologies also provide the means whereby vast amounts of money are moved in an instant as the battle for profit (or is it wealth generation?) is fought out in cyberspace. Media studies requires us to study and question the ways in which economic as well as cultural power is exercised through the media.

The new technologies have an effect on our job prospects, as well as offering a kaleidoscope of leisure possibilities for those who have access to and can afford such services. The question of the nature of the kaleidoscope of possibilities is also the business of media studies. Rather than offering blanket condemnation or praise for the changes which are taking place, media studies researchers and students need first to study and question them. This, as we have seen, involves an engagement with a variety of media and genres which rely on the new technologies for their existence. It includes the Internet and email, as well as a wide range of CD-ROMs and DVDs made for entertainment and educational purposes. It also includes an apparently endless array of television programmes, repeats, new productions, dubbed and not dubbed, bleeped and not bleeped to remove possibly offensive language, and a host of other representations. Because of the new technologies, these representations and communications services are available globally (subject to economic status, of course), and their impact upon our lives is part of the concern of media studies. Not to study such important developments and media representations would be an act of gross irresponsibility.

The previous two chapters have shown that computer technology has also made a considerable impact upon the ways in which films and television programmes are made – from shooting to editing, recording to special effects. These changes are also having a radical effect upon the employment patterns in the industries and in the other sectors of industrial societies. The new technologies, or perhaps we should say the technological and economic changes we have seen in the last two decades, require serious attention, which will demand more from us than unproblematic references to courses that teach us 'how to do it' or superficial scorn for the subject of semiotics.

Protectionism

I have suggested earlier that some people believe we should simply ignore the media rather than study them. There is another group, however, who consider it their duty to keep the media under close scrutiny in order to protect the vulnerable public from the corruption which they would otherwise suffer. In the United Kingdom, there is, for example, the National Viewers' and Listeners' Association, which was established in 1965 'to promote the moral and religious welfare of the community by seeking to maintain Christian standards in broadcasting' (Whitehouse, 1967: 194). The (then) Rt Hon William Deedes, speaking at the first Convention of the National Viewers' and Listeners' Association said the following about television:

Our minds have been slow to get to grips with the new social dimension [which television represents]. It is in this – I will not say wilderness, but sparsely occupied territory – that your association began its voyage. A comparison with the Pilgrim Fathers is not perhaps far-fetched. You set sail in a frail craft towards unknown territory; there are Red Indians on the war path and a serious risk of being scalped.

(Deedes in Whitehouse, 1967)

I offer this as just one example from a whole range of possible sources concerned about the deleterious influence of the media in our societies. Here it is television being pronounced upon. Elsewhere we can find everything from comics to popular songs being attacked by a wide range of critics. All are united in that they wish to act *in loco parentis* for the rest of society. It must be, in some ways at least, reassuring to know that you are in the right and can tell everyone else what they should condemn or avoid. Sometimes there may be good arguments for such protectionist approaches. They should not, however, be confused with the subject of media studies. Media studies requires investigation, which is neither prudish nor raffish. The comments of William Deedes may be of more interest to the media studies researcher as an example of a process of naturalization. Here the exploration of the Pilgrim Fathers is legitimized in relation to the dangers of what he calls 'Red Indians'. The media studies student might dare to ask whether there was anyone to protect the 'Red Indians' from the zeal of the Pilgrim Fathers.

Conceptual approaches

As the study of media and cultures has progressed, there have been various efforts to offer some kind of conceptual coherence to the field. This has included the recognition of a network of relationships within and through which the media operate. This network of relationships has usually included the media product or text, the audience for such a text, the ways in which the text is produced and the economic foundations of the production process. It is generally recognized by those involved in the study of the media that utilization of any single component of this network is never enough if it is done without reference to the others. This has not stopped, however, the development of various fields of expertise (some might say 'camps') from which different kinds of research and analysis have been undertaken (McRobbie, 1997; Hansen *et al.*, 1998; Deacon *et al.*, 1999; Tudor, 1999). Those who believe in the central importance of a political economy of the media may say that there is a place for textual analysis, just as textual analysts may genuflect in the direction of political economy. One of the key challenges faced by those who would study the media is how best to hold in productive tension a number of conceptual and analytical approaches. The field is essentially eclectic. This means that it requires those who work in it to develop a level of tolerance of and an ability to listen to those with whom they do not agree. Where disagreements cannot be resolved, debate is still essential. It is one of the main strengths of media studies that it allows for the constant reappraisal of established theoretical and conceptual positions (about, for instance, the place of the press in society or the nature of realism), along with critical consideration of more recent developments (from postmodernism to the idea that consumption may be an act of resistance to capitalist domination). It cannot be said too often that without debate and argument, media studies becomes nothing more than another orthodoxy to be learned, rather than a volatile and stimulating field to be explored.

It will become apparent, if we continue our questioning of the media, that engagement with conceptual issues cannot be separated from a range of theoretical positions and research methodologies. The study of the media is not something as straightforward as something you either do or don't do. The media can be analysed from a variety of positions and in a variety of ways. The least reliable way to study the media is to adopt what is often called (particularly by the media) a 'common sense' approach.

We may, of course, adopt a purely formal approach to the study of the media. If we do, let us say with television documentary, we may discover that the documentarist uses a hand-held camera, powerful zoom lenses, equipment which is extremely lightweight and light-sensitive, and capable of the selective recording of sound. We may also discover that documentaries often contain several long takes and make use of 'witnesses' or 'experts' interviewed in close-up, and in big close-up when dramatic effect is desired. Such an analysis can, of course, allow us virtually to ignore or at least to relegate in significance the subject matter of the documentary. Conversely, there may be analysts who would approach a documentary about a specific subject through almost exclusive reference to that subject. If the subject is civil war or domestic violence, most of the analysts' discussion will centre on the issues perceived as the content or subject matter of the documentary, disregarding the modes of signification which have been utilized. For media studies, neither of these approaches would be adequate if pursued exclusively. The structuring of any media message has to be understood as being in a relation of tension with its content. They are inseparable and should be studied as such. We have to develop our conceptual understanding of the media in such a way that these factors, along with the context of production and reception of messages, become an integral part of the dynamic of media study.

Critical approaches

Once it has been established that our conceptual approach to the media is important, we are faced with a new set of choices. These relate to a range of critical and theoretical arguments about the nature and purpose of the media in a given society and period. But what does it mean to be critical? It is easier to address this question if we first identify what a critical approach is not. It is not a continuous carping or whining activity based on cynical elitism. Nor is it an attempt to spot the deficiency in a given message from a preordained 'critical' position. Examples of the latter have included the 'spot the sexism' or 'spot the racism' approach to media messages. Such activity is usually a rather mechanical exercise, and is often counterproductive. The term counterproductive is potentially problematic, however, because it reminds us that the researcher or student is likely to take up a position about their object of study, rather than remaining a neutral observer. This, in turn, means that the question of objectivity in study and research becomes an issue. Can or should the study of the media be an objective process? For me, objectivity in relation to representations of the social world is not a neutral quality but is, paradoxically, likely to be partisan. After all, we all have to argue for our truths today – unless we believe that they have already been handed down and what we need to do is live by them. Arguing about the nature of a truth should not be confused, however, with a refusal to accept that there is data to be studied. We are likely to be able to pursue our initial studies more effectively, however, if we concentrate our efforts on identifying the position from which a particular media message is constructed, rather than arguing (at first) about its objectivity. This can be assisted by identifying a range of possible analytical and conceptual approaches and testing them out in practice. It also helps us to identify what we mean by taking up a position.

There are those, as we have seen, who would assert that semiology is junk. In order to appraise this position, we would need to read some of the key texts in the field and then consider their potential for offering frameworks for analytical work. Toynbee's position seems to be linked with an approach to the media which sees them as the innocent carriers of data. Hence she suggests that it is a good thing to have courses in the media that tell you 'how to do it'. But the whole point of media studies is that it is interested in *questioning* how we do it. This means that it is necessary to know what might happen if the rules or guidelines for media representation were different from the way they are now. But, and it is a big but, this can only be done if we first acquaint ourselves thoroughly with what is regarded today as 'good practice' in the medium or media of our choice. If we are going to critique or break rules, it is first essential that we know what those rules are. A belief that the medium is the neutral carrier of the message, and that what we need to know is how to play by the rules of production, is often referred to as technicism. Media studies challenges such a belief.

The study of the media has to recognize that, while there are matters that are empirically verifiable (the Gulf War *did* take place), the representations and readings of empirically verifiable events must always be treated as problematic. In the case of the Gulf War, we need to ask, for instance, whether it could ever have been comprehended more than superficially through representations of electronic viewfinders, puffs of grey smoke and short-haired brawny males, canes in hands, as they stood near their flip charts. At the level of understanding, we have to ask whether the explanation of a war can be reduced to the 'evil' of one man, or whether economic interests, which would not be susceptible to such dramatic representation, might have had something to do with it. Some of these issues can be studied directly from the medium in question. Others have to be explored through the study of history, economics, politics and current affairs. The study of the media is also about these and other intellectual disciplines. They may be combined in a variety of ways in relation to specific study or research projects.

Other approaches to the study of the media have developed around specific conceptual fields, which have strong social, political and aesthetic ties. These include the representations of issues concerning 'race', gender, age, class, national and personal identity and sexual orientation. There are more, but this list is enough to demonstrate that studying the media is also about studying culture and societies. It requires a close engagement with specific media texts, but it is also, as indicated previously, about more general study. Opponents of media studies often suggest that it would be better first to study history or sociology or aesthetics, etc. This is an option, but for the media studies student it is not the most appropriate. Media studies requires a willingness to study constantly and on a broad front. There is a dialectic or tension in the fluctuating interrelationships of more established academic disciplines and the development of media study. Let me say again, it is this tension which is the driving force of media studies. It involves us all in an intellectual and educative process which, once entered upon, cannot end with (and does not depend upon) the award of a specific qualification. Studying the media also requires the constant development and/or acquisition of skills of analysis. There is also another centrally important issue in the study of the media: that of pleasure.

Pleasure

A great deal of public discussion about the media is morally superior, indignant, protective, elitist, condemnatory, and bemoans the implied or alleged stupidity and gullibility of the media audience. One medium is also likely to adopt a negative attitude towards another. We may find, for instance, television attacking the values and performance of the tabloid press. Occasionally, a particular medium takes a 'critical' look at itself, though this is more likely to happen on radio and television than elsewhere. All this negativity, much of it entirely misplaced, tends to ignore the enormous amounts of pleasure (or is it mind-numbing ideological subjugation?) which the media offer their audiences. The study of the media, especially in the period after the Second World War, tended to ignore pleasure in favour of blanket condemnation of everything that did not align with a narrow and often blinkered set of cultural and aesthetic criteria. These criteria were based around concepts of culture, which paid scant attention to the popular and tended towards elitism in music, theatre, film and literature. Where pleasure from the mass media was recognized as possible, it was often treated with disdain. The most sophisticated and intellectually troubling manifestation of this tendency can be found in the critique mounted by Adorno and Horkheimer (1978). They were particularly incensed about the cinema audience who, they argued, went into the cinema ready for a laugh at the expense of anyone and everyone else. This audience, they said, was made up of individuals who were only brought together in a caricature of solidarity (a condition which Adorno and Horkheimer respected) when they had a good laugh at someone's misfortune up on the silver screen. The audience had better laugh, they argued, because once the film was over they had to return to their alienated existence and go their separate ways in silence. This was and is a bleak analysis and it is not one with which it is easy to agree. There is, however, a nagging doubt that perhaps, on some occasions and in some circumstances, their analysis may have contained more than a grain of truth. What Adorno and Horkheimer did do was to focus attention on a very necessary debate about the nature of the pleasures which the media offer. Their value has been to highlight the tension between visions of the social world as a potential site for solidarity of purpose and creative well-being, and as a place of fragmentation and alienation. It is clear that both these positions have informed media studies and media research in specific ways in specific periods.

Problematizing pleasure is one of the key functions of media studies. This does not mean, however, that pleasure should be denied to the student or researcher! Before we rush to judgement about whether and how one form of pleasure from the media (such as watching football or baseball on television) is more worthy than another (such as listening to Radio 4 in the United Kingdom or watching *Jerry Springer* on television), we need to remember the importance of learning to describe the object of our study. We need to develop a language of description which allows us to recognize those moments of signification which offer identifiable pleasure, along with the social or individual patterns of consumption which add to or detract from such pleasure. This language of description may have to deal with aspects of media representations as diverse as dialogue, colour printing, type size, composition, narrative structure or star image. It means that such a language has to be developed carefully and patiently in relation to specific analytical skills or research methodologies. These, in turn, will be related to a possible range of conceptual and theoretical positions.

The psychoanalytic theorist, for instance, might argue that media study involves a consideration of the ways in which cinema-goers derive pleasure from sitting, voyeuristically, in the dark while they watch intimate moments of drama unfold before them. The pleasure taken in seeing the representation of the intimate moment would then need to be studied in relation to the pleasure which is derived by some from watching representations of unspeakable violence with only the vaguest link to narrative necessity. (See Berger, 1995: 103, for an accessible opening engagement with psychoanalytic theory.)

The social theorist might also study the pleasures associated with the regular viewing of specific television programmes or series. Research has been undertaken in recent years about the audiences for certain soap operas, but there are many other types of popular pleasure in need of investigation. Many viewers now take great pleasure in watching programmes on cooking, house redecoration or archaeology, all undertaken at breakneck speed. As I write this text, a programme has been running for some years on British television (with variations around the world) called *Changing Rooms*. Each week, two couples, by agreement, work with interior designers to transform one room in the house of the other couple. The couples are, at least when the programme begins, friends. The pleasures offered by such a programme include the possibility of agreeing or disagreeing with the type of redecorating undertaken, the colour schemes chosen and the soft drapes or bedspreads purchased for the occasion. There is then the pleasure to be gained from watching the couples being led back into their rooms, eyes closed. The moment of revelation as they see their transformed dwellings provides a weekly catharsis and it clearly brings pleasure to several million viewers. For the media studies student or researcher, it is the *nature* of that pleasure and its precise modes and patterns of signification which are of interest, along with their potential social significance. It is important to note that the pleasures offered by the media may vary from the everyday (reading the sports page or the 'stars' column in the paper) to the more occasional and demanding (such as watching drama like *Prime Suspect* on television). This tiny selection of examples is designed to illustrate the fact that pleasure is central to media consumption. It is also a phenomenon which manifests itself in many ways and with many potential consequences for individuals and their social existence. Media study requires a serious engagement with pleasures of all kinds, allowing for the certainty that there will be (and should be) disagreement about which pleasures are the most defensible or desirable. Pleasure, then, has to be made problematic at the point of production and the point of consumption.

It must also be recognized that the pleasure we gain from the media is usually of ideological significance, and for this reason it is not a fixed and inherent property of a text, though it may depend upon a relatively stable relationship between audience and text. That which is beautiful in terms of shape, weight and size, may change from one historical period to another. That which is amusing is also dependent upon a shared set of values, or a shared willingness to challenge values. Media studies is concerned with the ways in which pleasures are either innate and universal or historically specific and occasionally manufactured for consumption. The question of whether the media merely reflect the already existing preferences and pleasures of their audiences or provide the audiences with constructed pleasures which they then 'freely' choose is another core issue for media studies.

A matter of identity

This book has attempted to argue that a key factor in media studies is the importance of studying the media and questions of identity. This operates at the personal, local, national and global level, in ways that would have been inconceivable just 50 years ago. The literature concerned with the media and identity is growing at an impressive (or alarming) rate. There are several possible ways of studying such a development. It may be that the question of identity has become important to the massive media audiences because they sense that we have entered the new millennium and wish to establish for themselves a sense of worth and psychic equilibrium. It may also be that the question of identity is a phenomenon which sits happily alongside, and may have been invented or nurtured by, late capitalism and the consumer society. There is little doubt, as we have seen, that identity is on sale or on offer in a multitude of ways. Fashion (described by one theorist as 'change without change') is a key factor here. It seems that you can either buy or construct your identity with the direct or indirect help of the media. The issue of advertising takes on considerable significance here. Some would argue that advertising has become one of the most sophisticated of late twentieth-century art forms and should be studied as such. Others would suggest that the sophistication of advertising lies in its capacity to sell us an identity while convincing us that we are evolving as free agents in a free society. All the above understandings of identity and its representation and construction are based upon economic factors. If we don't have the money, the range of identities on offer to us are strictly limited. If we construct a new kind identity from affordable cast-offs, it is likely that the media will take that identity, repackage it and sell it back to us.

There is another dimension to the study of identity in which the media are heavily implicated. This is the identity of 'others'. These others may be represented at the personal, regional, national or global levels. Otherness is a complex concept and it needs careful study, but it is also something which is susceptible to analysis using the basic skills of media studies. The third field for media study is that which is concerned with the positive (some would argue 'empowering') potential of identity representation. The arguments among media analysts and media producers over the years have often centred on the value of what have been called 'positive images'. Those who believe that the positive image of a group, nation or gender can have positive effects on an audience are also likely to argue that negative representations will have a negative effect.

187

The very use of the word effect, as we have noted throughout this book, opens the door to another debate, which has been at the heart of a great deal of media study, much of which is highly questionable. The possible or alleged effects of the media have had billions of dollars (much of the research has been from the USA) spent upon their identification. The problem with all this research is that, used selectively, it can prove just about anything about the influence and impact of the media. The most prominent campaigns have usually been linked to research about the effects of violence, or sex and violence, upon usually 'innocent' audiences. While this book has also been concerned with the ways in which the media may impact upon our understandings of the world we inhabit, this should not be confused with arguments or research which purport to demonstrate that a given media message is likely to generate a given response. The process is almost never that mechanical. Nor should media effects be construed as something relevant only to deviants, malcontents and misfits. Rather than examining deviance as a focal point for media study, this book has argued that the media are much more significant as the means by which concepts of normality are kept in circulation. In a world where polycentric multiculturalism has become recognized as a distinctive trend, media representations of 'normality' are constantly extending and diversifying (Shoat and Stam, 1994: 13–54).

A question of democracy and power

I want to end the book by arguing that media study is essential to any healthy democracy. This means that critical thinking and sometimes oppositional thinking need to be manifest in both media study and the production of media texts. In relation to the latter, the question of the future of public service broadcasting is central. John Keane (1993) argues for a public service model which recognizes the humorous but desperately serious suggestion that we have to struggle against the stupidity of those who exercise power. It is a vain struggle, he suggests, but it should never be abandoned. Keane has noted that modern theorists of democracy spend very little time considering the media. It is also the case that too few media scholars see their work as centrally related to the sustenance and development of democracy.

Media study is not, however, solely about making calls for better broadcasting and a more responsible press. It is also about studying already existing media provision and asking questions about how that provision impacts upon the processes of democracy. The media studies student or questioner does not look for conflict-free communication. On the contrary, we see that controversy and the tensions thrown up by the analysis of media messages are essential. The advantages which media studies can offer are similar to those offered by the advantages of democracy:

> For the chief and unsurpassed advantage of democracy [and media studies in a democracy] is not that it guarantees peace and quiet and good decisions, but that it offers citizens the right to judge (and to reconsider their judgements about) the quality of those decisions. Democracy is rule by publics who make and remake decisions in public.
>
> (Keane, 1993: 251)

For media studies to be more than a mere inventory of media provision, it must be socially, aesthetically and politically involved. The idea that we can or could be dispassionate observers of society's foibles is neither productive nor responsible. Media questioners, students and researchers, like any other intellectuals, are implicated in the societies of which we are a part. Hence we are and should be involved with the political, though this does not mean that media studies has to be party political. What it does mean is that the media student is likely to seek a range of conceptual and theoretical bases from which to work. These may not all be the same – indeed it is better that they should not be – but they are all identifiable and will have an impact upon the kinds of analyses undertaken, and the choice of material or texts for analysis. That such research raises contradictions contributes to the effervescence which media studies can generate. One of the aims of this book has been to highlight some of these contradictions in relation to specific theoretical and analytical examples.

The issue of power is, of course, intimately linked with questions of democracy. One of the core powers of the media, as we have seen, is the power to define. The media may not always influence their audiences in any simple way, but they are able to define the subject of their interest and it is very difficult to challenge such definitions. This power to define is sometimes vividly illustrated when the media seem perplexed with themselves, as when a television commentator, reporting on a festival of popular music stated, 'the expected trouble did not occur'. Power is also exerted through the kinds of programmes which are deemed to be amusing or 'serious', or the choice of headlines and cartoonists in the press. The French philosopher Michel Foucault has noted that power permeates the operations of societies from the macro- to the micro-levels. It is absurd, however, to consider that all manifestations of power are on a par and somehow 'equal'. The complexities of representations of power have to be studied alongside the complexities of the powers of representation. This is the challenge for those of us involved in media studies. It is a rich, rewarding, frustrating and importantly productive field. It is also likely to offer what may be a last-ditch stand for those who believe in the values and aspirations of liberal democratic societies.

FURTHER READING

I have not offered comments about individual texts here. They are all first-rate introductions, each with a slightly different emphasis and direction. Take your pick.

Branston, G. and Stafford, R., 2002, *The Media Students' Book.*

O'Sullivan, T., 1998, *Studying the Media: an introduction.*

Price, S., 1993, *Media Studies.*

Van Zoonen, L., 1994, *Feminist Media Studies.*

Bibliography

Abelove, H., Blackmar, B., Dimock, P. and Schneer, J., 1983, *Visions of History*, Manchester: Manchester University Press.

Adorno,T. and Horkheimer, M., 1978, *Dialectic of Enlightenment*, London: Verso.

Allen, R. C. (ed.), 1992, *Channels of Discourse, Reassembled*, London: Routledge.

Althusser, L., 1971, Ideology and ideological state apparatuses: notes towards an investigation, in *Lenin and Philosophy and Other Essays*, London: New Left Books, 121–73.

Anderson, P., 1998, *The Origins of Postmodernity*, London: Verso.

Ang, I., 1996, *Living Room Wars: rethinking media audiences for a postmodern world*, London: Routledge.

Bach, S., 1985, *Final Cut: dreams and disaster in the making of* Heaven's Gate, New York: William Morrow & Company.

Bakhtin, M., 1984, *Rabelais and his World*, trans. Hélène Iswolsky, Bloomington: Indiana University Press.

Bakhtin, M., 1984a, *Problems of Dostoievsky's Poetics*, Minnesota: University of Minnesota Press.

Barker, M. and Petley, J., 1997, *Ill Effects*, London: Routledge.

Barthes, R., 1972, *Mythologies*, London: Jonathan Cape.

Barthes, R., 1977, 'The photographic message', in *Image, Music, Text*, London: Fontana.

Bauman, Z., 1989, *Modernity and the Holocaust*, Cambridge: Polity Press.

Bauman, Z., 1992, *Intimations of Postmodernity*, London: Routledge.

Bauman, Z., 1995, *Life in Fragments*, Oxford: Blackwell.

Bauman, Z., 2000, *Liquid Modernity*, Cambridge: Polity Press.

Bazin, A., 1951, *What is Cinema?* California: University of California Press.

Benjamin, W., 1970, *Illuminations*, London: Jonathan Cape.

Berger, A., 1995, *Cultural Criticism*, London: Sage.

Berger, J., 1972, *Ways of Seeing*, Harmondsworth: Penguin.

Berlo, D. K., 1960, *The Process of Communication*, New York: Holt, Rinehart & Winston.

Berman, M., 1992, 'Why modernism still matters', in Lash, S. and Friedman, J. (eds), *Modernity and Identity*, Oxford: Blackwell.

Berman, M., 1993, *All that Is Solid Melts into Air: the experience of modernity*, London: Verso.

Best, S. and Kellner, D., 2001, *The Postmodern Adventure*, London: Routledge.

Billig, M. *et al.*, 1988, *Ideological Dilemmas*, London: Sage.

Blackburn, S., 1994, *Dictionary of Philosophy*, Oxford: Oxford University Press.

Blumler, J. G. and Katz, E., 1974, *The Uses of Mass Communication*, Newbury Park, CA: Sage.

Bocock, R., 1986, *Hegemony*, London: Tavistock Publications.

Bolter, J. D. and Grusin, R., 2000, *Remediation: understanding new media*, Cambridge, MA: MIT Press.

Bondanella, P., 2001, *Italian Cinema from Neorealism to the Present*, New York: The Continuum International Publishing Group.

Bordwell, D., Staiger, J. and Thompson, K., 1985, *The Classical Hollywood Cinema*, London: Routledge and Kegan Paul.

Bordwell, D. and Thompson, K., 2003, *Film Art*, London: McGraw-Hill Education.

Branston, G. and Stafford, R., 2002, *The Media Students' Book*, London: Routledge.

Brunsdon, C. and Morley, D., 1978, *Everyday Television*, London: British Film Institute.

Buckingham, D., 1996, *Moving Images*, Manchester: Manchester University Press.

Burbach, R., Nuñez, O. and Kagarlitsky, B., 1997, *Globalization and its Discontents*, London: Pluto.

Butler, J., 1990, *Gender Trouble*, London: Routledge.

Callinicos, A., 1989, *Against Postmodernism*, Cambridge: Polity Press.

Callinicos, A., 1995, *Theories and Narratives: reflections on the philosophy of history*, London: Routledge.

Cameron, D., 2000, *Good to Talk?* London: Sage.

Campbell, C., 1995, *Race, Myth and the News*, London: Sage.

Camus, A., 1955, *The Myth of Sisyphus*, London: Hamish Hamilton.

Carey, J., 1992, *The Intellectuals and the Masses*, London: Faber and Faber.

Carnes, M., 1995, *Past Imperfect: history according to the movies*, New York: Henry Holt and Company.

Carr, E. H., 1978, *What is History?* London: Pelican.

Carter, C., Branston, G. and Allan, S., 1998, *News, Gender and Power*, London: Routledge.

Chandler, D., 'Personal home pages and the construction of identities on the Web', http://www.aber.ac.uk/media/Documents/short/webident.html#A

Chandler, D., 2001, *Semiotics: the basics*, London: Routledge.

Cohan, S. and Hark, I. (eds), 1993, *Screening the Male*, London: Routledge.

Cook, P. and Bernink, M., 1999, *The Cinema Book*, London: BFI Publishing.

Corner, J., 1996, *The Art of the Record: a critical introduction to documentary*, Manchester: Manchester University Press.

Corner, J., 2001, '"Ideology": a note on conceptual salvage', *Media, Culture and Society* 23(4), 525.

Cumberbatch, G. and Howitt, D., 1989, *A Measure of Uncertainty: the effects of the mass media*, London: John Libbey.

Daveson, M., 1990, *Desert Interlude*, Richmond: Mills & Boon.

Deacon, D., Pickering, M., Golding, P. and Murdoch, G., 1999, *Researching Communications*, London: Arnold.

De Certeau, M., 1988, *The Practice of Everyday Life*, London: University of California Press.

Denzin, N., 1991, *Images of Postmodern Society*, London: Sage.

Dobson, R. B., 1984, *The Peasants Revolt of 1381*, London and Basingstoke: Macmillan.

Douglas, S., 1994, *Where the Girls Are*, London: Penguin.

Du Gay, P., Evans, J. and Redmand, P. (eds), *Identity: a reader*, London: Sage.

Dyson, K. and Homolka, W., 1996, *Culture First!* London: Cassell.

Eagleton, T., 1991, *Ideology: an introduction*, London: Verso.

Eagleton, T., 1996, *The Illusions of Postmodernism*, Oxford: Blackwell.

Eagleton, T., 2003, *After Theory*, London: Allen Lane.

Ebert, R., 1997, 'An Officer and a Gentleman', *Cinemania*, Microsoft.

Eco, U., 1990, *The Limits of Interpretation*, Bloomington: Indiana University Press.

Eco, U., 1992, *Interpretation and Overinterpretation*, Cambridge: Cambridge University Press.

Ellis, J., 1982, *Visible Fictions*, London: Routledge.

Evans, R. J., 1997, *In Defence of History*, London: Granta.

Fairclough, N., 1995, *Media Discourse*, London: Edward Arnold.

Ferguson, R., 1985, *Television on History*, London: Institute of Education.

Ferguson, R., 1998, *Representing 'Race': ideology, identity and the media*, London: Arnold.

Ferro, M., 1984, *The Use and Abuse of History*, London: Routledge and Kegan Paul.

Fiske, J., 1989, *Reading the Popular*, London: Unwin Hyman.

Fiske, J., 1989a, *Understanding Popular Culture*, London: Unwin Hyman.

Fowler, R., 1986, *Linguistic Criticism*, Oxford: Oxford University Press.

Fowler, R., 1990, *Language in the News: discourse and ideology in the press*, London: Routledge.

Frow, J., 1995, *Cultural Studies & Cultural Value*, Oxford: Clarendon Press.

Frow, J., 1997, *Time and Commodity Culture*, Oxford: Clarendon Press.

Galtung, J. and Ruge, M., 1965, 'The structure of foreign news', *Journal of International Peace Research* 1, 64–90.

Gandy, O., 1998, *Communication and Race*, London: Arnold.

Gauntlett, D., 1995, *Moving Experiences*, London: John Libbey Media.

Gauntlett, D., 1995a, http://www.leeds.ac.uk/ics/arts-dg2.htm

Gauntlett, D., 2000, *web.studies*, London: Arnold.

Gauntlett, D., 2003, 'Ten things wrong with the effects model', http://www.theory.org.uk/effects.htm

Gauntlett, D. and Horsley, R., 2004, *Web.Studies*, Second Edition, London: Arnold.

Gillespie, M., 1994, *Television, Ethnicity and Cultural Change*, London: Routledge.

Gordon, C. (ed.), 1980, *Power/knowledge*, London: Harvester.

Gross, L. and Ward, L., 2004, *Digital Moviemaking*, London: Thompson Learning.

Grossberg, L., 1996, 'Identity and cultural studies: is that all there is?' in Hall, S. and du Gay, P. (eds), *Cultural Identity*, London: Sage.

Hahn, H., 1996, *The Internet Golden Directory*, New York: Osborne McGraw-Hill.

Hall, S., 1977, 'Culture, the media and the "ideological effect"', in Curran, J. *et al.* (eds), *Mass Communication and Society*, London: Edward Arnold.

Hall, S., 1980, 'Encoding/decoding', in Hall, S., Hobson, D., Lowe, A. and Willis, P. (eds), *Culture, Media, Language*, London: Hutchinson, 128–38.

Hall, S., 1996, 'Who needs identity?' in Hall, S. and du Gay, P. (eds), *Questions of Cultural Identity*, London: Sage.

Hall, S. (ed.), 1997, *Representation: cultural representations and signifying practices*, London: Sage.

Hall, S. and du Gay, P. (eds), 1996, *Questions of Cultural Identity*, London: Sage.

Hansen, A., Cottle, S., Negrine, R. and Newbold, C., 1998, *Mass Communication Research Methods*, London: Macmillan.

Hartley, J., 1999, *The Uses of Television*, London: Routledge.

Harvey, D., 1989, *The Condition of Postmodernity*, Oxford: Basil Blackwell.

Hayward, S., 1996, *Key Concepts in Cinema Studies*, London: Routledge.

Hewison, R., 1987, *The Heritage Industry*, London: Methuen.

Hill, J., 1986, *Sex, Class and Realism*, London: BFI Publishing.

Hobsbawm, E., 1997, *On History*, London: Weidenfeld and Nicolson.

Hobsbawm, E. and Ranger, T. (eds), 1983, *The Invention of Tradition*, Cambridge: Canto.

Hodge, R. and Kress, G., 1988, *Social Semiotics*, Cambridge: Polity Press.

Hodge, R. and Kress, G., 1993, *Language as Ideology*, London: Routledge.

Horne, D., 1984, *The Great Museum*, London: Pluto.

Jameson, F., 1991, *Postmodernism or the Cultural Logic of Late Capitalism*, London: Verso.

Jakubowicz, A., 1994, *Racism, Ethnicity and the Media*, London: Allen and Unwin.

Jencks, C., 1986, *What Is Postmodernism?* London: St Martin's Press Academy Editions.

Jenkins, K. (ed.), 1997, *The Postmodern History Reader*, London: Routledge.

Jenkins, K., 1999, *Why History?* London: Routledge.

Kael, P., 1987, *Taking it all in*, London: Arrow Books.

Keane, J., 1993, 'Democracy and the media – without foundations', in Held, D. (ed.), *Prospects for Democracy*, Cambridge: Polity Press.

Kellner, D., 1995, *Media Culture*, London: Routledge.

Klein, N., 2000, *No Logo*, Toronto: Alfred Knopf.

Koestler, A. *et al.*, 1950, *The God that Failed*, London: Hamish Hamilton.

Kovel, J., 1988, *White Racism: a psychohistory*, London: Free Association Books.

Kress, G., 1989, *Linguistic Processes in Sociocultural Practice*, Oxford: Oxford University Press.

Kress, G. and Van Leeuwen, T., 1990, *Reading Images*, Deakin, Victoria: Deakin University Press.

Kress, G. and Van Leeuwen, T., 2001, *Multimodal Discourse*, London: Arnold.

Krueger, H., 1991, *Artificial Reality II*, Reading, MA: Addison-Wesley.

Kundnani, A., 2000, '"Stumbling on"': race and class in England', in *Race and Class* 41(4), 1–18.

Lacqueur, W., 2003, *No End to War*, London: The Continuum International Publishing Group.

Lanham, R., 1993, *The Electronic Word*, Chicago: University of Chicago Press.

Laplanche, J. and Pontalis, J., 1988, *The Language of Psychoanalysis*, London: Karnac Books.

Lapsley, R. and Westlake, M., 1988, *Film Theory: an introduction*, Manchester: Manchester University Press.

Lasswell, H. D., 1947, *The Analysis of Political Behaviour*, London: Routledge and Kegan Paul.

Lerner, G., 1997, *Why History Matters*, New York: Oxford University Press.

Lévy, P., 2001, *Cyberculture*, Minneapolis: University of Minnesota Press.

Lodziak, K., 1986, *The Power of Television*, London: Frances Pinter.

Lodziak, K., 1995, *Manipulating Needs*, London: Pluto.

Lowery, S. and de Fleur, M., 1994, *Milestones in Mass Communication Research*, Reading, MA: Addison-Wesley.

Lyotard, J.-F., 1984, *The Postmodern Condition: a report on knowledge*, Manchester: Manchester University Press.

McDonald, M., 1995, *Representing Women: myths of femininity in the popular media*, London: Arnold.

McGraw, P., 1999, *Life Strategies*, London: Hyperion.

McGraw, P., 2000, *Relationship Rescue*, London: Hyperion.

McLuhan, M., 1964, *Understanding Media*, London: Routledge and Kegan Paul.

McQuail, D., 1983, *Mass Communication Theory*, London: Sage.

McQuail, D. (ed.), 2002, *Reader in Mass Communication Theory*, London: Sage.

McRobbie, A., 1991, *Zoot Suits and Second-Hand Dresses*, London: Macmillan.

McRobbie, A. (ed.), 1997, *Back to Reality?* Manchester: Manchester University Press.

Maccabe. C., 1974, 'Realism and the cinema: notes on some Brechtian theses', *Screen* 15(2), 8.

Mackenzie, J., 1995, *Orientalism: history, theory and the arts*, Manchester: Manchester University Press.

Malik, K., 1996, *The Meaning of Race*, Basingstoke: Macmillan.

Marcuse, H., 1972, *One-Dimensional Man*, London: Abacus.

Marris, P. and Thornham, S. (eds), 1996, *Media Studies: a reader*, Edinburgh: Edinburgh University Press.

Miller, J., 1993, *The Passion of Michel Foucault*, London: Flamingo.

Moores, S., 1993, *Interpreting Audiences*, London: Sage.

Morawski, S., 1996, *The Troubles with Postmodernism*, London: Routledge.

Moyers, B., 2002, http://www.pbs.org/now/commentary/moyers7.html

Nichols, B., 1991, *Representing Reality*, Bloomington: Indiana University Press.

Nightingale, V., 1996, *Studying Audiences: the shock of the real*, London: Routledge.

Nochlin, L., 1978, *Realism*, Harmondsworth: Penguin.

Oakley, A. and Mitchell, J., 1997, *Who's Afraid of Feminism?* London: Hamish Hamilton.

O'Sullivan, T., 1998, *Studying the Media: an introduction*, London: Arnold.

Parkin, F., 1971, *Class Inequality and Political Order*, London: MacGibbon and Kee.

Patai, R., 1973, *Golden River to Golden Road: society, culture, and change in the Middle East*, Philadelphia: University of Pennsylvania Press.

Perkins, V., 1972, *Film as Film*, Harmondsworth: Penguin.

Philo, G. and Miller, D. (eds), 2001, *Market Killing*, Harlow: Pearson Education.

Pieterse, J. N., 1992, *White on Black: images of Africa and blacks in western popular culture*, London: Yale University Press.

Price, M., 1980, *The Peasants' Revolt*, London: Longman.

Price, S., 1993, *Media Studies*, London: Thompson Learning.

Price, S., 1997, *The Complete A–Z Media and Communication Handbook*, London: Hodder and Stoughton.

Rabelais, F., 1955, *The Histories of Gargantua and Panatagruel*, trans. J. M. Cohen, London: Penguin Classics.

Rheingold, H., 1994, *The Virtual Community*, London: Secker and Warburg.

Roberts, D., 1994, *The Myth of Aunt Jemima*, London: Routledge.

Robins, K., 1998, 'Cyberspace and the world we live in', in Featherstone, M. and Burrows, R. (eds), *Cyberspace, Cyberpunk, Cyberbodies*, London: Sage.

Rosenblum, R. and Karen, R., 1979, *When the Shooting Stops . . . the Cutting Begins*, Harmondsworth: Penguin.

Said, E., 1978, *Orientalism*, London: Routledge and Kegan Paul.

Saint-Exupéry, A. de, 2003, *The Little Prince*, London: Harcourt Children's Books.

Schiller, H., 1996, *Information Inequality*, London: Routledge.

Seiter, E., 1999, *Television and New Media Audiences*, London: Routledge.

Selby, S., 1984, *Dark City: the film noir*, London: St James Press.

Shannon, C. and Weaver, W., 1949, *The Mathematical Theory of Communication*, Urbana: University of Illinois Press.

Shoat, E. and Stam, R., 1994, *Unthinking Eurocentrism*, London: Routledge.

Silverstone, R., 1999, *Why Study the Media?* London: Sage.

Slevin, J., 2000, *The Internet and Society*, Cambridge: Polity Press.

Sobchak, V., 1996, *The Persistence of History*, London: Routledge.

Sokal, A. and Bricmont, J., 1997, *Intellectual Impostures*, London: Profile Books.

Spice Girls, 1997, *Girl Power*, London: Zone/Chameleon Books.

Stead, P., 1989, *Film and the Working Class*, London: Routledge.

Thompson, J., 1990, *Ideology and Modern Culture*, Cambridge: Polity Press.

Todorov, T., 1993, *On Human Diversity*, Cambridge, MA: Harvard University Press.

Tudor, A., 1999, *Decoding Culture*, London: Sage.

Turkle, S., 1996, 'Virtuality and its discontents: searching for community in cyberspace', *The American Prospect* 24 (winter), 50–7 (http://www.prospect.org/print/V7/24/turkle-s.html).

Turkle, S., 1996a, *Life on the Screen: identity in the age of the Internet*, London: Weidenfeld and Nicolson.

Van Dijk, T., 1998, *Ideology*, London: Sage.

Van Zoonen, L., 1994, *Feminist Media Studies*, London: Sage.

Vidal, G., 1991, *Screening History*, Cambridge, MA: Harvard University Press.

Walkerdine, V., 1986, 'Video replay: families, films and fantasy', in Burgin, V., Donald, J. and Kaplan, C. (eds), *Formations of Fantasy*, London: Methuen.

Wayne, M., 1997, *Theorising Video Practice*, London: Lawrence and Wishart.

Webber, H., 1980, *The Peasants' Revolt*, Lavenham: Terence Dalton.

Wenger, K., 1997, 'The tele-vision of history', in *History and Its Interpretations*, Jeleff, S. (ed.), Strasbourg: Council of Europe Publishing.

White, H., 1980, 'The value of narrativity in the representation of reality', in Mitchell, W. T. (ed.), *On Narrative*, Chicago: Chicago University Press.

Whitehouse, M., 1967, *Cleaning up TV*, London: Blandford Press.

Wilde, O., 1996, *De Profundis*, New York: Dover Publications.

Williams, C., 1980, *Realism and the Cinema*, London: Routledge and Kegan Paul/BFI.

Williams, R., 1980, 'Base and superstructure in Marxist cultural theory', in *Problems in Materialism and Culture*, London: Verso.

Winston, B., 2000, *Media Technology and Society*, London: Routledge.

Wollen, P., 1972, *Signs and Meaning in the Cinema*, London: Secker and Warburg.

Woodward, K. (ed.), 1997, *Identity and Difference*, London: Sage.

Filmography

All About my Mother, 1998, Sony Pictures Classics, Pedro Almodóvar.
Barton Fink, 1991, Twentieth Century Fox, Coen brothers.
Batman, 1989, Warner Brothers, Tim Burton.
The Blair Witch Project, 1999, Blair Witch Film Partners/Haxan Entertainment, Daniel Myrick and Eduardo Sánchez.
Boyz N the Hood, 1991, Colombia Pictures, John Singleton.
Carousel, 1956, Twentieth Century Fox, Henry King.
Crimes and Misdemeanors, 1989, Orion Pictures, Woody Allen.
Les Enfants du Paradis, 1945, Pathé Cinema, Michel Carné.
Four Weddings and a Funeral, 1994, Channel 4 Films, Mike Newell.
From Here to Eternity, 1953, Columbia Pictures, Fred Zinnemann.
The Full Monty, 1987, Channel 4 Films, Peter Cattaneo.
The Godfather, 1972, Paramount Pictures, Francis Ford Coppola.
Heaven's Gate, 1980, United Artists, Michael Cimino.
A History of Britain, 2002, BBC, Simon Schama.
Ireland: A Television History, 1980, BBC Television, Robert Kee.
Mississippi Burning, 1988, Columbia Pictures, Alan Parker.
An Officer and a Gentleman, 1982, Lorimar Films, Taylor Hackford.
On the Waterfront, 1954, Columbia Pictures, Elia Kazan.
Poor Cow, 1967, Anglo Amalgamated Productions, Ken Loach.
The Searchers, 1956, Warner Brothers, John Ford.
The Seven Year Itch, 1955, Twentieth Century Fox, Bill Wilder.
Shane, 1953, Paramount Pictures, George Stevens.
Shoah, 1985, Historia, Claude Lanzmann.
Titanic, 1997, Paramount Pictures, James Cameron.
The Troubles, 1980, Thames Television, Richard Broad.
True Lies, 1994, Twentieth Century Fox, James Cameron.
War of the Century, 1999, BBC, Laurence Rees.

Index